The Illustrated Directory of

CLASSIC
AMERICAN
MOTORCYCLES

The Illustrated Directory of
CLASSIC AMERICAN MOTORCYCLES

Tod Rafferty

MBI Publishing Company

A Salamander Book

This edition first published in 2001 by
MBI Publishing Company,
729 Prospect Avenue, PO Box 1,
Osceola, WI 54020-0001 USA

The information in this book is true
and complete to the best of our
knowledge. All recommendations are
made without any guarantee on the
part of the author or publisher, who
also disclaim any liability incurred in
connection with the use of this data
or specific details.

We recognize that some words,
model names and designations, for
example, mentioned herein are the
property of the trademark holder. We
use them for identification purposes
only. This is not an official
publication.

MBI Publishing Company books are
also available at discounts in bulk
quantity for industrial or sales-
promotional use. For details write to
Special Sales Manager at
Motorbooks International
Wholesalers & Distributors,
729 Prospect Avenue, PO Box 1,
Osceola, WI 54020-0001 USA.

Library of Congress Cataloging-in-
Publication Data Available

ISBN 0-7603-1050-5

Credits

Project Manager: Ray Bonds
Designed by: Interprep Ltd.
Motorcycle photographs: Neil Sutherland
(unless where stated)
Color reproduction by: Studio Technology
Printed in: Hong Kong

The Author

Tod Rafferty has been riding and racing motorcycles for more than 35 years, and is the proprietor of the American Garage, purveyor of vintage cars, motorcycles, and related artifacts. The garage is also headquarters for his motorsports media production team, which is developing a feature film titled "Sunday Kind'a Love," a motorcycle racing adventure. Rafferty also manages Team Geezer, an unorganized racing group, and directs the activities of the Motor Jones Society, an association for recovering velocity addicts. He has written several books on aspects of motorcycles, including what have now become standard works on Harley-Davidson machines.

Contents

Introduction

For most of us, the term American motorcycle means either Indian or Harley-Davidson. And since the Indian was last produced in Massachusetts in 1953, Harley virtually owns the sole distinction as the twenty-first century unfolds.

But in the early years, during those three decades preceding the Great Depression of the 1930s, more than 300 American motorcycle manufacturers were represented in the market. Names such as Henderson, Thor, Merkel, Excelsior, Ace, Cleveland, Iver-Johnson, Sears, Pope, Waverly, Reading-Standard, Dayton, Yale, New Era, Pierce, Deluxe, Emblem, and Minneapolis were familiar to American riders.

Some of these machines had only brief lifespans. But that fertile period of experiment and innovation prior to World War I was the pioneer era for motorcycles, automobiles and aircraft. New concepts in design, engineering, style and manufacturing regularly brought new models to the roads in growing numbers. And while the automobile industry went on to new heights following the war, motorcycles were shifted to the margins of motorized transportation in the United States.

Largely because of the manufacturing and marketing acumen of Henry Ford, only a handful of motorcycle builders remained in the 1930s.

So this illustrated history of American motorcycles naturally draws heavily from those early years, when the industrial revolution was in full stride. We have included the fundamental technical data and specifications for these machines, and capsule histories of the companies that produced them. Our compilation is brought up to date with the significant models from the 52-year lifetime of Indian, and the continuing genealogy of Harley-Davidson. We have also included the American machines currently in production, such as the Rokon, Polaris Victory and the Harley-powered Buell hybrid.

The Illustrated Directory of Classic American Motorcycles is a testament and tribute to all the pioneers of the American motorcycle industry and sport. Although most of their work disappeared from public view over 70 years ago, their craft survives in these images of motorcycling's inaugural era.

Ace (1920–1927)

XP4
Engine: Air-cooled inline four
Displacement: 1262cc
Horsepower: 45 @ 5400rpm
Wheelbase: 59in (150cm)
Weight: 295lb (134kg).
Top speed: 129mph (208kph)
Price: Not sold

Ace had a brief but mighty run in the four-cylinder campaigns of the teens and twenties of the last century. But they stand in history as the final products of William Henderson's design and engin-eering, which first appeared under his own name in 1912.

Many collectors reckon the Ace was the best inline four ever built, which creates some vocal spec-ulation among owners of Indian, Henderson, Pierce and Cleveland fours. (All owe fealty to the FN marque of Belgian origin.) But Ace enthusiasts can boast of top speed honors, given its designation of "Fastest Motorcycle in the World." The record was established by the XP4 special built by Arthur Lemon and Everett De Long. In 1923, with Red Wolverton aboard, the Ace ran just a few ticks shy of 130mph (209kph), and the XP3 hauled a sidecar and ▶

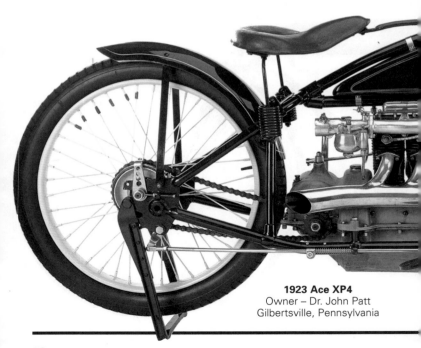

1923 Ace XP4
Owner – Dr. John Patt
Gilbertsville, Pennsylvania

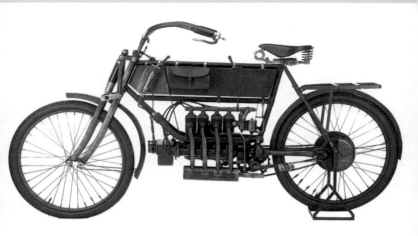

Above: The FN Four, designed by Paul Kelecom of Belgium, sparked a generation of American four-cylinder machines. Pierce would be the first.

Below: The XP4 was a one-off Ace built specifically for top speed, and regardless of expense. The machine reached nearly 130mph (209kph).

passenger up to 106mph (171kph). Big bragging rights accrued, but the company's financial foundation had crumbled by then and the company dissolved in 1924.

William Henderson, the foremost four-cylinder engineer in the country, had been killed by an automobile while test riding his latest model in December of 1922. He had begun building motorcycles in Detroit in 1911, sold the company to Ignaz Schwinn of Excelsior in 1917, and stayed on as chief engineer. Henderson left the Chicago firm in 1919, and set up manufacturing facilities for the Ace in Philidelphia.

Financing came from Max Sladkin of the Haverford Cycle Company.

Upon Henderson's death, his former protege Arthur Lemon left Excelsior to take up his mentor's work in Philadelphia, and test rider Red Wolverton came along as well. Lemon was charged with the creation of an exceptionally fast motorcycle, and provided a generous budget and a $7,500 dynamometer. The XP engine, its rods and pistons drilled for lightness, made 45 horsepower at 5400rpm. The aluminum Schebler carburetor was built for the engine, and the motorcycle weighed under 300 pounds (136kg). And the thing ▶

Below: The Ace four first appeared as a production model in 1920. The distinctive blue paint, cream-colored wheels and low profile attracted a number of buyers.

Right: Since it had to carry a sidehack, the XP3 was rather more stout than its top-speed sibling. Passenger Everett DeLong was nearly prone in a special Flxi sidecar with 110psi in the tire.

1920 Ace
Owner – Otis Chandler
Ojai, California

Road model
Engine: Air-cooled inline four
Displacement: 1262cc
Horsepower: 35
Wheelbase: 59in (150cm)
Weight: 380lb (172kg).
Top speed: 85mph (137kph)
Price: $335

Above: In 1923 Ace dropped the price of the road model to $335. Unfortunately, the motorcycles cost more than that to build.

Below: The XP3 was the not-quite-so expensive companion to the XP4. With a sidecar and passenger attached, the rig was good for 106mph (170kph).

1923 Ace XP3
Owner – Dr. John Patt
Gibertsville, Pennsylvania

1923 Ace Four
Owner – Dr. John Patt
Gilbertsville, Pennsylvania

just hauled ass. As the ads proclaimed, the Ace was the world's fastest motorcycle.

The mighty fours went on to extablish numerous records, following Cannon-ball Baker's cross-country mark of just under seven days in 1922. Ace riders captured the headlines in hillclimbs and endurance runs in the U.S. and Australia, and established the marque as the crowning achievement in speed and handling.

But by 1924 the auditors noted that Ace motorcycles were being sold below the costs of producing them. The owners saw little future in this sort of charity, and the company fell into bankruptcy and went to liquidation the following year. Efforts to revive production failed, and the Ace tooling and inventory went to the Michigan Motors Corporation. In 1927 the complete assets were purchased by the Indian Motocycle Company, which restored the fours to production in Springfield, Massachussetts.

With the demise of Ace, Excelsior (Henderson), Cleveland and Indian became the only manufacturers of American four-cylinder machines. Everett DeLong, former engineering assistant to Arthur Lemon, developed the Cleveland fours to higher standards. (DeLong was also the sidecar passenger in the XP3 106mph record run.) Indian gradually shifted the Ace four into their own chassis, but left the engine largely unchanged. In 1929 the Springfield engineers adopted a five-main bearing crankshaft to replace the three-main Ace arrangement.

Indian would extend the legacy of William Henderson's engineering by 15 years, and confirm his enduring status as a pioneer among the builders of American four-cylinder motorcycles.

Above right and below: By 1924 the price was back up to $375 for the standard model and $395 for the sport solo, but Ace was quickly slipping to history.

1925 Ace Four
Courtesy of Mike Terry
New Jersey

American IronHorse (1995-)

Engine: Ohv 45° V-twin
Displacement: 1573cc
Horsepower: 88
Wheelbase: 66.65in (169.3cm)
Weight: 615lb (279kg)
Top speed: 120mph (193kph)
Price: $25,500

Below: All American IronHorse models carry the 96-inch (1573cc) S&S engine with 10.2:1 compression and dual fire ignition system. The five-speed close ratio transmission carries the power to the final belt drive.

American IronHorse of Texas produces five Harley-pattern customs built around the 96-inch (1573cc) S&S engine. These power-plants run 10.2:1 compression, roller rocker arms and lifters and Mikuni carburetor. One of the five models, the Stalker, employs a rubber-mount engine. American IronHorse offers a 36-month or 36,000-mile warranty. Prices run from $23,500-29,500.

Apache (1907-1911)

Engine: IOE single
Displacement: 213cc
Horsepower: 2.25
Wheelbase: 51in (129.5cm)
Weight: 135lb (61kg)
Top speed: 25mph (40kph)
Price: $210

The Apache was the product of the Denver, Colorado, company of Brown & Beck. The motorcycle was one of several makes employing the Thor engine, made by the Aurora Automatic Machine Company of Illinois. The 2.25-horsepower engine also powered Indian motorcycles up until 1908.

The second generation Apaches gained an inch (2.54cm) in wheelbase and three-quarters of a horsepower in urge. The Thor spring fork was offered as an additional cost option. At $225, the Apache was more expensive than most of its single-cylinder competitors, which probably accounts for its relatively brief lifespan.

1999 Outlaw
Courtesy of American IronHorse
Fort Worth, Texas

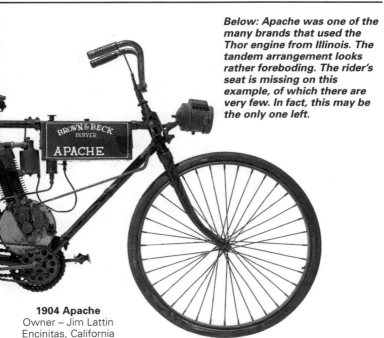

Below: Apache was one of the many brands that used the Thor engine from Illinois. The tandem arrangement looks rather foreboding. The rider's seat is missing on this example, of which there are very few. In fact, this may be the only one left.

1904 Apache
Owner – Jim Lattin
Encinitas, California

Armac (1902-1913)

Engine: IOE single
Displacement: 376cc
Horsepower: 3
Wheelbase: 53in (135cm)
Weight: 150lb (68kg)
Top speed: 35mph (56kph)
Price: $200

The first generation of Armac motorcycles were built in St. Paul, Minnesota in 1902, and shifted to Chicago a few years later. The three-horsepower single, designed by A.J. McCollum, sat very low in a loop frame. Armac offered inter-changeable belt or chain drive systems, with three ratios available for belt and six for chain.

The Armac was advertised as a "Perfectly Balanced" machine, and note was made that the engine was "placed in an upright position and is NOT a part of frame construction." The fuel and oil were carried in the frame. The Armac was also distinguished by the absence of any levers to adjust belt tension. A single twistgrip controlled both the spark and throttle.

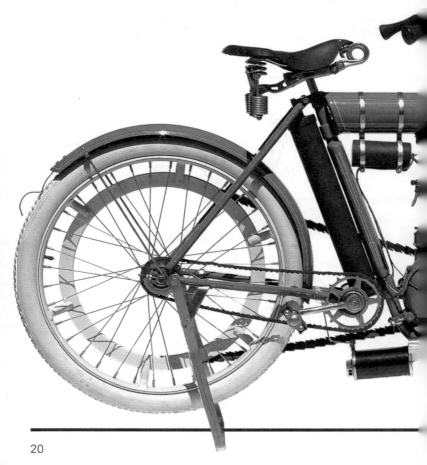

Right: After 1910 the Armac was offered only with belt drive. The company also provided machines to other marketing entities such as Montgomery Ward (Hawthorne) and Allied Motors (A.M.C.).

Below: The Armac was distinguished from most other brands in offering customers a choice between belt and chain drive.

1910 Armac
Owner – Jim Lattin
Encinitas, California

Arrow (1909-1916)

Engine: IOE single
Displacement: 499cc
Horsepower: 4
Wheelbase: 53in (135cm)
Weight: 175lb (79kg)
Top speed: 45mph (72kph)
Price: $225

The Arrow, produced by the Arrow Motor Company of Chicago, was a re-labeled version of the Marsh-Metz. The Marsh brothers and Charles Metz joined forces in 1906 to become the American Motor Company. Metz had been chief engineer at the Waltham Manufacturing Company of Massachussetts, which produced Orient motorcycles. The Marsh, also on the market since 1900, was built by the Motor Cycle Manufacturing Company of Brockton, Massachusetts.

When the companies merged the market was crowding with new brand names, many of which were bicycle and automobile manufacturers eager to join the motorized festivities. Some companies simply bought existing motorcycles under license, and attached their own logotypes. The Arrow was one such, and other purveyors of Marsh-Metz products were Peerless, National and Haverford.

Few of the trade marketing outfits made any substantive changes to the motorcycles. Paint and nameplates were the standard revisions, and sometimes a wider selection of accessories from the growing after-market industries. But this sort of badge engineering faded quickly, as the motorcycle marketplace grew more crowded with retailers without a corresponding increase in the number of buyers.

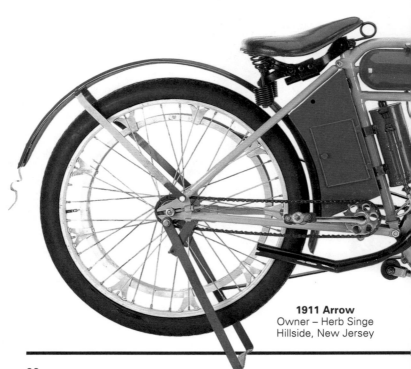

1911 Arrow
Owner – Herb Singe
Hillside, New Jersey

Right: The Aviation Type Motor was a slogan created by Arrow copywriters. "The motor that has made this machine 25 percent faster with 50 percent less strain and gasoline consumption." In 1912 an Arrow single could be purchased for $100 down payment and $12.50 per month for 12 months.

Below: Both the Arrow single and twin engines were built by the American Motor Company of Brockton, Massachusetts, whose own bikes were the Marsh-Metz brand.

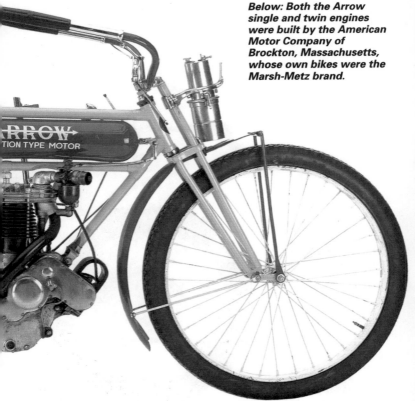

ATK (1987-)

ATK was founded in 1983 by Austrian transplant Horst Leitner in southern California. His first design was a chain-tensioning device for dirt bikes, which in English-German was called the Anti-Tension Kettenantrieb, and abbreviated was ATK.

Leitner began building motorcycles in 1987, using Honda engines and selling frame kits to home builders. The next generation ATK employed the Austrian-built Rotax engines, which remain the powerplants today. The company was among the first to offer specialized four-stroke machines for off-road recreational and competition use. In 1993 ATK was purchased by investors, and operations moved to Centerville, Utah near Salt Lake City.

ATK also builds a 50cc mini-motocrosser, 250cc enduro, 350 and 490cc four-stroke cross-country and enduro models, and 500/600cc dirt-track machines.

1998 ATK 260E
Courtesy of ATK
Centerville, Utah

(605E)
Engine: Four-stroke single
Displacement: 598cc
Horsepower: 38
Wheelbase: 59in (150cm)
Weight: 305lb (138kg)
Top speed: 110mph (177kph)
Price: $6500

Right: Rotax four-stroke engines have had wide application in custom dirt bikes worldwide. The 605 has a Paioli 46mm fork, Ohlins shock, and Brembo brakes.

(260E)
Engine: Liquid-cooled two-stroke single
Displacement: 251cc
Horsepower: 28
Wheelbase: 58.5in (149cm)
Weight: 245lb (111kg)
Top speed: 95mph (153kph)
Price: $5500

Left: The 260E is the two-stroke enduro model. The machine features a six-speed transmission, Paioli 46mm fork and Ohlins rear shock.

1998 ATK 605E
Courtesy of ATK
Centerville, Utah

Auto-Bi (1900-1912)

Engine: IOE single
Displacement: 442cc
Horsepower: 2.5
Wheelbase: 53.5in (136cm)
Weight: 130lb (59kg)
Top speed: 35mph (56kph)
Price: $175

The Auto-Bi is generally considered the first production motorcycle made in America. When bicycle chassis configuration became more or less uniform by the turn of the 20th century, the primary

question for the motor-minded was where to put the engine. This consideration led to all manner of experimentation.

E. R. Thomas was a pioneer in early motorcycle engine design and engineering, and sold engines to many of the other fledgling manufacturers. By 1901 Thomas had his second generation model on the market; and the engine was fitted high on the front downtube, the cylinder head adjacent to the the upper tube and steering head. The long drive belt passed over a tensioner attached to the center post.

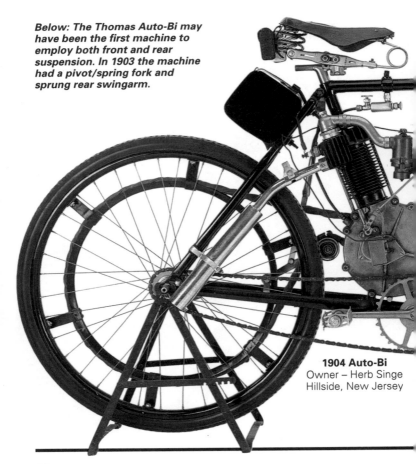

Below: The Thomas Auto-Bi may have been the first machine to employ both front and rear suspension. In 1903 the machine had a pivot/spring fork and sprung rear swingarm.

1904 Auto-Bi
Owner – Herb Singe
Hillside, New Jersey

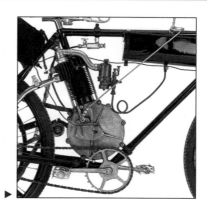

Right: The second generation Auto-Bi used the Indian-style integration of the engine and seatpost. Designer E.R. Thomas was one of America's first motorcycle manufacturers.

Other marques of the period using this configuration were Mitchell, Stratton, Michigan, Driver and Morgan. Thomas also offered a tandem version of the machine, with the front half of a lady's bicycle grafted on to the steering head and fork of the ▶

standard motorcycle.

By this time the Buffalo, New York, company was the country's largest producer of single-cylinder, air-cooled engines. In 1903, following the lead of other early builders like Marsh and Holley, Thomas repositioned the motor at the lower frame junction. Earlier concerns about distancing the rider from engine heat gave way to considerations of efficient drivetrains and ease of handling. Some manufacturers stayed with the high forward engine scheme, but consensus was arriving that for all practical purposes the motor was best situated near the middle of the motorcycle.

In 1905 the Thomas Auto-Bi, ridden by W.C. Chadeayne, established a new cross-country record of 48 days. The Thomas models, which included the three-wheeled Auto-Tri and two-place Auto-Two three-wheeler had established themselves as early leaders in the burgeoning motorcycle market. But by the early teens, the number of manufacturers had eclipsed the potential for profit. By then Thomas was a leading car builder, and left the two-wheeled marketplace to other contenders.

Below: As one of the first mass-produced motorcycles in America, the Auto-Bi introduced thousands of riders to the new form of transportation.

Right: The earliest Auto-Bi carried the engine high in a modified bicycle frame. Thomas experimented with numerous frame configurations and engine positions in the first few years.

1900 Auto-Bi
Rosedale, New York
Photograph by David Heald
Guggenheim Museum

1901 Auto-Bi
Owner – Herb Singe
Hillside, New Jersey

Autoped (1915-1921)

Engine: Side-valve single
Displacement: 155cc
Horsepower: 1.5
Wheelbase: 36.5in (93cm)
Weight: 60lb (27kg)
Top speed: 15mph (24kph)
Price: $110

The Autoped, classified as a motor scooter, was built in New York city by the Autoped Company of America. The folding control bar included acceleration and brake controls, and folded flat for stowage in the trunk or sidecar. The vertical riding position limited high-speed handling, but such velocities were not easily obtained.

The 155cc four-stroke single could, however, be modified for more urge, and this was done. The Autoped was spiffy transport in the burgeoning metropolis of New York City, and some fun to fly through traffic upon. Groups of rowdy youth were soon terrorizing the boroughs of Brooklyn, Queens and even Manhattan. One such was the Long Island Bogtrotters, led by the eventually legendary Fat Burns himself, who conducted the first and last Yonkers Gran Prix and the storied Peekskill Scramble. These hooligans were held responsible for the term scooter trash.

Below: The Autoped was one of the first practical combinations of motor and scooter. New York City was the country's primary immigration funnel in the early 1900s, and dealing with the congestion of trolleys, automobiles and horses called for creative solutions.

1917 Autoped
Owner – Dale Walksler
Mt. Vernon, Illinois

31

Big Dog (1996-)

(Pro Sport)
Engine: Ohv 45° V-twin
Displacement: 1750cc
Horsepower: 116
Wheelbase: 66.5in (169cm)
Weight: 600lb (272kg)
Top speed: 125mph (201kph)
Price: $24,900

*Below: The Big Dog is one of a
dozen Harley-style custom
cruisers manufactured by
independent companies, without
using any Harley-Davidson parts.*

Big Dog offers three rubber-mount and two solid-mount versions of the Harley-style V-twin custom. The engine runs 9.6:1 compression and is fitted with an S&S Super G carburetor. Performance Machine 4-piston caliper brakes are used on both wheels, and the rear suspension carries Paioli gas shocks. Big Dogs come with a three-year, unlimited-mileage warranty. Prices run from $19,000-27,000.

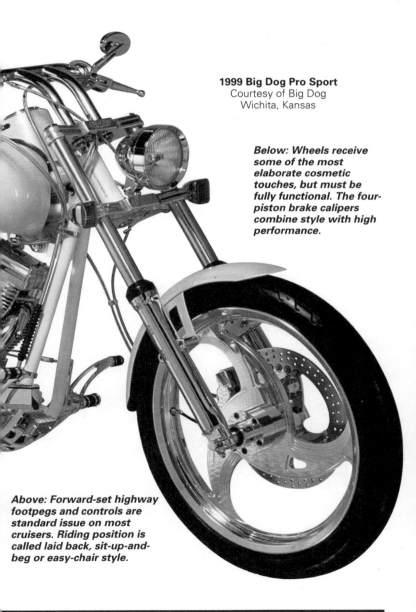

1999 Big Dog Pro Sport
Courtesy of Big Dog
Wichita, Kansas

Below: Wheels receive some of the most elaborate cosmetic touches, but must be fully functional. The four-piston brake calipers combine style with high performance.

Above: Forward-set highway footpegs and controls are standard issue on most cruisers. Riding position is called laid back, sit-up-and-beg or easy-chair style.

Buell (1988-)

Erik Buell was a roadracer, an apprentice engineer at Harley-Davidson, and a fellow who wanted to build his own motorcycles. As a senior project engineer he worked on Milwaukee's heavyweight cruisers and touring bikes, all the while hankering to put together a sport bike. Buell left Harley and scraped together the funds to build a prototype roadracer.

For six years Buell built and sold Sportster-powered sport bikes in his birdcage chassis. In 1993 Harley-Davidson bought half-interest in Buell Motorcycle Company, and became majority owner five years later. Erik Buell remains as chairman and chief engineer, and given Harley's financial horsepower and production resources, the motorcycles got both better and less expensive.

Buell has undertaken to contest experienced builders like Ducati, BMW and a growing number of specialized V-twins from Europe and Japan. Anyone who can produce a high performance motorcycle that gets faster, handles better, doesn't gain weight and costs less has recorded an achievement.

Below: This S2 has been fitted with optional saddlebags. The S2T came equipped with higher handlebars, fairing lowers and higher footpegs, as well as the bags.

Right: The RR 1200 was fitted with the Evolution engine, hidden behind the full bodywork.

1990 Buell RR 1200
Owner – Otis Chandler
Ojai, California

1995 Buell S2
Owner – Ray Earls
Foster City, California

(S1 Lightning)
Engine: Ohv 45° V-twin
Displacement: 1203cc
Horsepower: 91 @ 6000rpm
Wheelbase: 55in (140cm)
Weight: 440lb (200kg)
Top speed: 130mph (209kph)
Price: $9,995

Below: In 1996 the Lightning signaled the part-ownership of Buell by Harley-Davidson. The machine was more powerful than its predecessor, lighter and less expensive.

(X1 Lightning)
Engine: Ohv 45° V-twin
Displacement: 1203cc
Horsepower: 101 @ 6000rpm
Wheelbase: 55in (140cm)
Weight: 460lb (209kg)
Top speed: 140mph (225kph)
Price: $10,599

Right: The new Lightning boasts digital fuel injection, a streamlined airbox and a tidier exhaust system. The frame is also new, including the cast-aluminum tail section.

1996 Buell S1 Lightning
Courtesy of Buell Motorcycle
Company
East Troy, Wisconsin

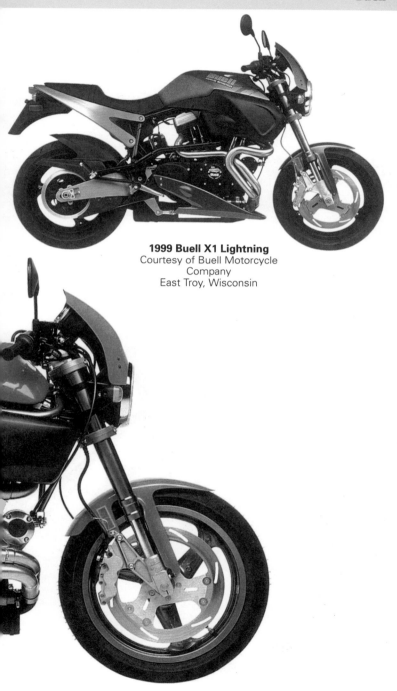

1999 Buell X1 Lightning
Courtesy of Buell Motorcycle
Company
East Troy, Wisconsin

California (1901-1903)

Engine: IOE four-stroke single
Displacement: 200cc
Horsepower: 1.25
Wheelbase: 46in (117cm)
Weight: 100lb (45kg)
Top speed: 25mph (40kph)
Price: $150

Roy C. Marks was one of the first California engineers to offer gasoline engine kits for bicycles, selling his first units in 1898. J.W. Leavitt and J.F. Bill owned bicycle shops in San Francisco, Oakland and San Jose, and in 1901 they formed the California Motor Company. Marks hired on as chief engineer, and created the California Motor Bicycle.

In 1903 the California became the first motor vehicle to cross the continent. Rider George Wyman left San Francisco on May 16 and arrived in New York July 6 with stories to tell. In 1903 the California Motor Company

was sold to the Consolidated Manufacturing Company of Toledo, Ohio. These purveyors of Yale and Snell bicycles sought to expand into motorcycles, as so many other velocipede builders were doing. If people were buying engines for their bicycles, why not sell them the whole package.

Thus the California became the Yale-California, and with later designs appearing in 1909, simply the Yale. In this configuration the flywheel moved indoors and the larger bore and stroke had horsepower up to 3.5. The motorcycle was larger overall than its progenitor, and weighed some 60 pounds (27kg) more. (See also Yale.)

Right: The California was the first motor vehicle to cross the United States in 1903. Rider George Wyman made the journey in 50 days.

1902 California
Owner – Mark Michel
Sterling Heights, Michigan

California (CMC) (1995-)

Engine: 45° V-twin
Displacement: 1442/1639cc
Horsepower: 70/80
Wheelbase: 63.75/67in (162/170cm)
Weight: 630lb (288kg)
Top speed: 110/120mph
(177/193kph)
Price: $15,000-30,000

The CMC (California Motorcycle Company) evolved from a shop specializing in customized Harley-Davidsons. Among the first of a dozen Harley replicators, CMC became one of the largest, with 24 models and production of about 1,000 per year.

The CMC is powered by a 1442 or 1640cc S&S engine in one of five frames, most patterned on the Harley Softail. The standard engine is rated at 70 rear-wheel horsepower, and the price range runs from $15,000-30,000. CMC recently announced a limited edition model to be signed by Evel Knievel.

Below: CMC offers standard and stretched frames with solid- or rubber-mount engines in two sizes. The front fork is made by Showa. The CMC Stingrey is one of two dozen custom V-twins produced by the California company. This model has a solid-mount engine and 18-inch wheels.

1999 CMC Flash Widerider
Courtesy of CMC
Gilroy, California

Above: The Flash Widerider carries a wide 18-inch rear wheel and a 21-inch in front, with Avon tires. Two other Widerider models feature the rubber-mount engine and spoked wheels.

1999 CMC Stingrey
Courtesy of CMC
Gilroy, California

Cleveland (1902-1905) (1915-1929)

The first Clevelands were built by the American Cycle Manufacturing Company of Hartford, Connecticut. They shared with the American, and several other bicycle marque labels, configuration nearly identical to the first Indian motorcycles. Which actually came first remains a matter of dispute.

Below: Ease of handling, and its practical nature, made the Cleveland A2 a popular choice with students, women and business enterprises employing couriers and light delivery riders. And the relatively low price was an added incentive.

The more recognizable and distinct Clevelands were made by the Cleveland Motorcycle Manufacturing Company in Ohio. The 220cc two-stroke engine was mounted transverse to the frame, with a worm drive to power the countershaft sprocket for final chain drive. The shaft exited the two-speed gearbox and extended ▶

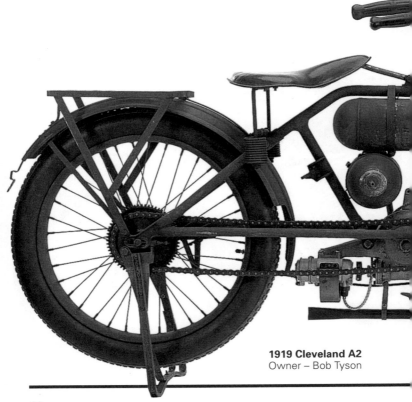

1919 Cleveland A2
Owner – Bob Tyson

1902 Cleveland
Owner – Jim Lattin
Encinitas, California

Above: The Connecticut Clevelands shared the same configuration with the Columbia, Imperial, Crescent, Monarch, Tribune and Rambler marques.

past the rear downtube to drive the magneto, hung just forward of the rear wheel.

In 1920 the machine grew larger, adding footboards, incorporated fuel/oil tank and wider fenders. The weight went up again the following year with a larger fuel/oil tank and seat and a battery. To offset the additional load, the engine displacement was enlarged to 270cc. For 1923 the company offered a sport solo Model E, with battery and electric lights.

Although the Cleveland two-strokes appeared a little flimsy compared to some motorcycles of the period, their light weight and moderate power combined for easy riding. When heavy weather and nasty terrain slowed heavier machines, the Cleveland was more apt to plug on regardless. The two-strokes set several lightweight endurance records and routinely won their division in 100- and 200-mile races.

So there was a market for a $150, 150-pound (68kg) motorcycle of moderate power and few pretensions. The Cleveland Light served a wide market of working stiffs who couldn't afford a Flying Merkel ($275), and women riders who appreciated

(1917 Light)
Engine: Two-stroke single
Displacement: 220cc
Horsepower: 3.5
Wheelbase: 53in (135cm)
Weight: 150lb (68kg)
Top speed: 30mph (48kph)
Price: $150

Below: Despite the relatively small engine, the Cleveland was successful in many endurance contests, owing largely to its absence of weight and mechanical compexity.

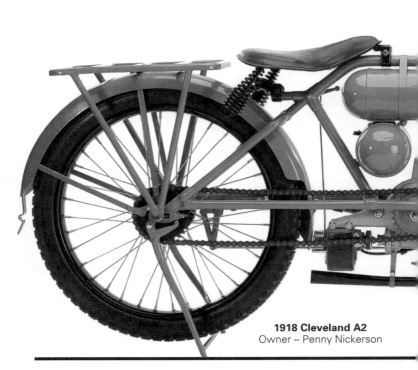

1918 Cleveland A2
Owner – Penny Nickerson

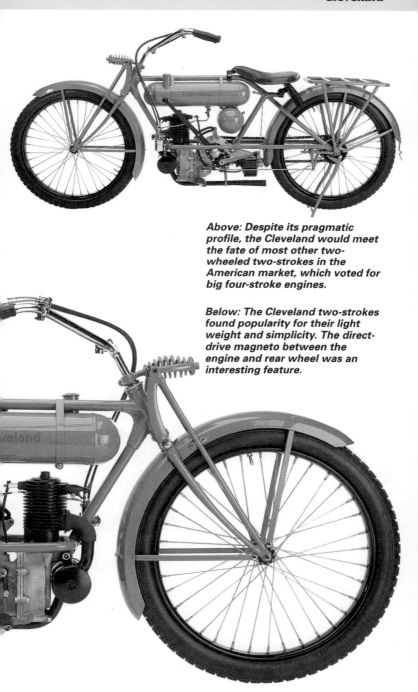

Above: Despite its pragmatic profile, the Cleveland would meet the fate of most other two-wheeled two-strokes in the American market, which voted for big four-stroke engines.

Below: The Cleveland two-strokes found popularity for their light weight and simplicity. The direct-drive magneto between the engine and rear wheel was an interesting feature.

the light weight and handling ease. Indian also offered a two-stroke single at the same price, but their K model was a heavier and taller machine.

The two-stroke was in production until 1925, when it was superseded by a 350cc four-stroke single designated the F-25. Also a two-speed, the F model was heavier, slower and destined for a brief production run. Then, in a lavish burst of Lake Erie optimism, Cleveland hired automobile engineer L.E. Fowler and built a four-cylinder motorcycle.

Below: In 1920 the fuel and oil tanks had a common housing and the footpegs were replaced by footboards. Clevelands finished first and second lightweights in the 1919 Marion, Indiana race.

The 600cc T-head four was a side-valve, with the intake cam on the left and exhaust cam on the right. Cleveland retained the perimeter cradle frame design with the four-cylinder engine hung in the middle. Additional tubing connected the frame's mid-section to the rear axle, and a leading link spring fork graced the front end. The engine, patterned on the Pierce four, had a three-speed transmission. But the 600cc four was well off the performance pace set by Henderson and Ace, and the next engine was a 750cc F-head four

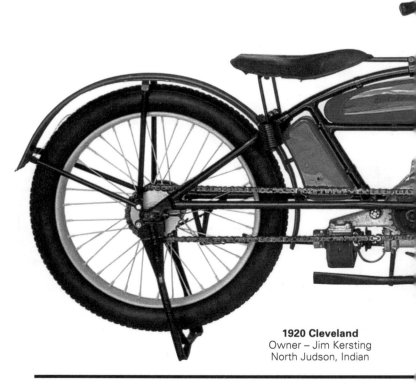

1920 Cleveland
Owner – Jim Kersting
North Judson, Indian

designed by former Henderson engineer Everett DeLong. The engine was a four-pot monobloc casting, with the cylinder head and intake manifold in a single casting. The three-speed transmission could be removed without removing the engine. The new chassis featured a traditional split-downtube cradle frame and no rear suspension.

In 1927 the displacement went to 1000cc, and the Cleveland was no longer sucking wind behind the Henderson and Ace fours. The engine was rubber-mounted and the motorcycle was the first on the market with a front drum brake. The four's finale came with the Tornado in 1929. A new frame dropped the seat by 2.5 inches (6.3cm), and light alloy pistons and more compression increased power. For 1930 Cleveland announced the Century model guaranteed good for at least 100mph (161kph), with a brass plaque to certify it had been pre-tested at that speed.

But as the Century entered production, the Wall Street stock market collapsed and the Cleveland Motorcycle Manufacturing Company soon followed suit.

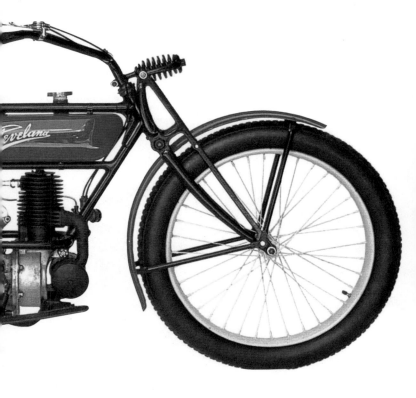

(1926 Four)
Engine: Inline side-valve four
Displacement: 750cc
Horsepower: 18
Wheelbase: 59in (150cm)
Weight: 395lb (179kg)
Top speed: 75mph (121kph)
Price: $375

1926 Cleveland Four
Owner – Otis Chandler
Ojai, California

Right: The first Cleveland Four was housed in a frame based on the two-stroke model. The 600cc T-head engine was designed by Detroit engineer L.E. Fowler. The Fowler four featured a three-speed transmission with the magneto mounted above it. Originally designed for shaft drive, the projected costs forced a switch to chain drive.

Below: Development of the Cleveland four reached its peak with the Tornado model in 1929. The new frame lowered seat height by 2.5 inches (6.35cm), and the fuel tank reflected the streamlining trend.

The Tornado marked Cleveland's move from a 750 to a 1000cc engine, in the quest for higher performance. The company claimed a top speed of 100mph (161kph).

Below: In 1929, racer Arthur Fournier rode a stripped version of the Tornado to a speed of 108mph (174kph) at Playa Del Rey, California. This was the final year of Cleveland production.

1929 Cleveland Tornado
Owner – Otis Chandler
Ojai, California

49

Columbia (1902-1905)

Engine: IOE single
Displacement: 220cc
Horsepower: 2.25
Wheelbase: 53in (135cm)
Weight: 125lb (57kg)
Top speed: 35mph (56kph)
Price: $175

Right: The Pope Manufacturing Company built bicycles under various brand names, and did likewise with motorcycles. The Columbia was one among them.

The Columbia was another multiple-brand motorcycle built by Chicago's American Cycle Manufacturing Company. The single had 8:1 compression, and could be spun to 2600rpm. The triangulated fuel tank held 1.5 gallons (5.7lit), reportedly good for at least 100 miles (161km). The Columbia and its brethren (American, Crescent, Imperial, Rambler) featured a rear coster brake and front tire-scrubber hand brake.

Confederate (1996-)

(Hellcat)
Engine: Ohv 45° V-twin
Displacement: 1852cc
Horsepower: 120
Wheelbase: 65in (165cm)
Weight: 530lb (240kg)
Top speed: 125mph (201kph)
Price: $25,960

Confederate Motorcycles was formed in 1991, and spent three years researching design and fabrication sources. The first prototype was built in 1994 in Baton Rouge, Louisiana. The company produced four more machines in 1995 and conducted more testing. Confederate builds two models, the Hellcat Roadster and America GT, both powered by the Harley-style S&S V-twin.

Both models have three-inch (7.6cm) diameter steel backbone frame, 1.5-inch (3.8cm) single downtube and 1 x 2-inch (2.5 x 5cm) box-section steel swingarm. The Works Performance twin shocks attach to the frame below the seat; the inverted front fork is from Paioli. A second disc brake and tachometer are optional.

1902 Columbia
Owner – Herb Singe
Hillside, New Jersey

*Below: The 1852cc
Confederate (S&S) V-twin is
blueprinted and balanced. The
close ratio five-speed gearset
is provided by Andrews.*

1999 Confederate Hellcat
Courtesy of Confederate
Motorcycles
Abita Springs, Louisiana

51

Crocker (1934~1941)

(Speedway)
Engine: Ohv single
Displacement: 500cc
Horsepower: 40
Wheelbase: 51in (130cm)
Weight: 240lb (109kg)
Top speed: 65mph (105kph)
Price: $350

Al Crocker started as a rider/designer with Thor in the teens, and later became an Indian dealer in Denver, Colorado. His next position was the Kansas City representative for Indian, where he served with distinction for many years. In 1928 he acquired the Indian franchise for Los Angeles, California, and hired a brilliant young engineer/designer named Paul Bigsby. Together they set about building some racing machines.

The first efforts were speedway racers with Indian Scout 750cc V-twin engines. But the short-circuits were better suited to lighter, single-cylinder machines, and Crocker began building 500cc overhead-valve singles. A gear-driven magneto sat in front of the cylinder and a twin-float Amal carburetor provided the mixture, good for about 40 horsepower in a 240-pound (109kg) package. These racing bikes did quite well in the hands of speedway stars Jack and Cordy Milne, who would later be world champions. But Crocker was losing the horsepower race to the British JAP engine, and his attention turned to a sporting twin for the road.

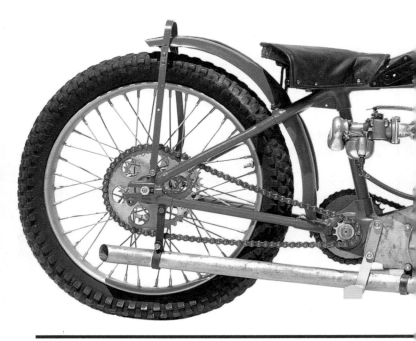

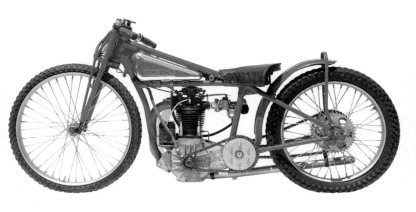

Above and below: Probably fewer than 50 of the Crocker Speedway bikes were built between 1933 and 1934. The pushrods shared a common tube and the magneto was gear-driven.

1934 Crocker Speedway
Owner – Carl Fronk
Langhorne, Pennsylvania

The first batch of 1000cc V-twins were hemi-head engines with exposed valve springs, arranged at 90 degrees as the speedway engine had been. Likewise, the pushrods shared a common tube. Compression was 7.5:1 and the engine made 50 horsepower at 5800rpm. And the motorcycle weighed just 480 pounds (218kg). Crocker made liberal use of aluminum throughout; engine cases, fuel tank, generator case, footboards, instrument panel and tail light were alloy items.

The running gear was heavy duty. The gearbox was cast as an integral part of the frame, and the gears in the three-speed constant-mesh unit were oversized to deal with heaps of horsepower. Steel plates on either side of the case kept everything in alignment.

But another overhead-valve hot rod appeared at the same time. Harley-Davidson debuted the 1000cc Knucklehead in 1936, and it was widely heralded in the press and on

Right:The racing brothers Jack and Cordy Milne helped develop the Crocker cinder-track machines. A few years later, aboard JAP racers, they came first and third in the world championship.

Below: Crocker was commited to the enthusiast's credo of adding horsepower and lightness. The fuel tanks, footboards, instrument panel and taillight were aluminum.

1936 Crocker
Owner – Chuck Vernon
La Mirada, California

Left: Minor detail changes were made to the Crocker during its brief run. Some engines were built to certain dimensions specified by the buyers.

Below: The last batch of Crockers were built in 1940. Opinions on total production figures run between 70 and 100 machines.

1940 Crocker
Owner – Dale Walksler
Mt. Vernon, Illinois

the road. The Harley may have been some 80 pounds (36kg) heavier than the Crocker, and down by about 10 horsepower, but it was a production line machine built by a veteran manufacturer. And it cost about $150 less than the custom-built California twin.

So the Crocker was no threat to Indian or Harley in the marketplace, and fewer than 100 of the V-twins were built. But it stood as sterling testament to the spirit and skill of independent builders, willing to invest their own time and talents to create a superior piece of equipment. Crocker didn't make any money on the sporting V-twins, but he showed what could be done. Between 1939 and 1943 he also built a stylish motor scooter called the Scootabout, but it was not destined for long-term

(Twin)
Engine: 45° ohv V-twin
Displacement: 1000cc
Horsepower: 40
Wheelbase: 60.5in (154cm)
Weight: 480lb (218kg)
Top speed: 110mph (177kph)
Price: $500-550

*Below: As a hand-crafted motorcycle, the Crocker was simply too expensive to build in limited numbers. The advent of World War II effectively ended their production.
Both pushrods in the Crocker engine shared a common tube. The transmission was designed as an integral part of the frame.*

production either.

None of which diminishes Albert Crocker's contribution to the American motorcycle sport, or his lifelong career as a rider, engineer, dealer, entrepreneur and designer. He had hoped that Indian would buy the manufacturing rights to the ohv twin, but the advent of World War II intervened. Crocker retired after the war and died in 1961 at the age of 79.

1938 Crocker
Owner – Otis Chandler
Ojai, California

Crosley (1939-1952)

Engine: Opposed side-valve twin
Displacement: 580cc
Horsepower: 13
Wheelbase: 60in (152cm)
Weight: 630lb (286kg)
Top speed: 70mph (113kph)
Price: unknown

Powell Crosley was a major force in the radio and refrigerator industries, but he always hankered to build cars. After a few false starts, he undertook production of a small car powered by a 580cc opposed twin. The first Crosley automobile appeared in 1939, in the hope that Americans were ready for a small transportation device.

Nearly two years earlier, as the clouds of war descended on Europe, the U.S. government had begun looking for military hardware. Prototype motorcycles were commissioned from Indian, Harley-Davidson and Crosley. The opposed twin was adapted to two- and three-wheeled vehicles, but neither went beyond the preliminary testing stage.

Crosley resumed car production after the war. In 1949 the Hotshot appeared, arguably the first American sports car, with a 750cc four-cylinder engine. The lightweight had 27 horsepower and was good for 90mph (145kph).

Above: The three-wheeled Crosley prototype employed the same Waukesha engine and most of the same running gear as its two-wheeled sibling. Neither model ever reached production. Powell Crosley would go on to achieve some fame in the automobile business.

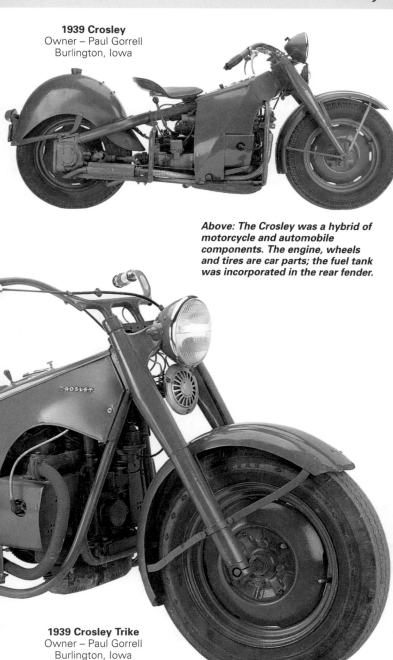

1939 Crosley
Owner – Paul Gorrell
Burlington, Iowa

Above: The Crosley was a hybrid of motorcycle and automobile components. The engine, wheels and tires are car parts; the fuel tank was incorporated in the rear fender.

1939 Crosley Trike
Owner – Paul Gorrell
Burlington, Iowa

Crouch (1905-1908)

Engine: IOE single
Displacement: 380cc
Horsepower: 3
Wheelbase: 53in (135cm)
Weight: 145lb (66kg)
Top speed: 35mph (56kph)
Price: $175

The Crouch Motor Company didn't stay long in the motorcycle business, but the belt-drive single earned a good reputation for economy and performance. The engine featured common bore and stroke dimensions (3³/₃₂in, 79mm) and was rated at three horsepower. The Massachussets firm made its own carburetor, though a Schebler was offered as an option, and the large fuel tank had a capacity of two gallons (7.6lit), warranted to be good for 100 miles (161km). The only tank carried only one pint (0.5lit).

Crouch stayed with the forward-mounted engine and wooden rims for the duration. The 1.5-inch (3.8cm) belt was controlled by an idler wheel. The Crouch, with battery and coil ignition, was competitively priced at $175.

Below: The Crouch featured an interesting frame design, with the engine straddled by a yoke. Frame dimensions were also rather unorthodox.

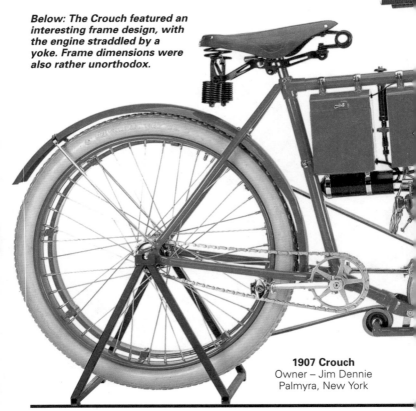

1907 Crouch
Owner – Jim Dennie
Palmyra, New York

Above: Belt drive remained popular for its predictable performance characteristics. The belt tensioner was attached to the engine case.

Left: The folks in Stoneham had their own ideas about how a motorcyle should be assembled, and so far as we know it worked out okay.

Curtiss (1901~1913)

(Single)
Engine: IOE single
Displacement: 500cc
Horsepower: 2.5/3.0
Wheelbase: 58in (147cm)
Weight: 130lb (59kg)
Top speed: 45mph (72kph)
Price: $200

Glenn Curtiss achieved his greatest fame as an aviation pioneer, but before that he was a brilliant rider, engineer and designer. And promoter. General surveys of American motorcycle history often register Curtiss as a footnote to the accomplishments of Oscar Hedstrom, Cannonball Baker, Bill Harley and Walter Davidson. But in the first decade of motorcycling, the young man from Hammondsport, New York was the brightest flame in the industry.

Glenn Hammond Curtiss was born in 1878, and showed early abilities in mathematics and tinkering. As a young man he found employment with Western Union as a bicycle

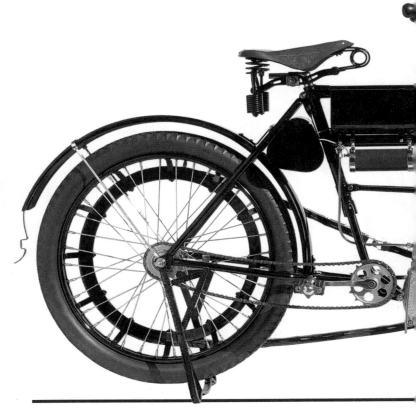

Below: Glenn Curtiss was convinced that belt drive outweighed the disadvantages of chains. He developed a 28-degree V-belt that performed without the slippage of flat belts.

The standard Curtiss single made 2.5 horsepower at 1500rpm. The muffler cut-out, for country running, was operated by lever on the tank.

1908 Curtiss Single
Owner – Wes Allen
Yuba City, California

messenger, and discovered his lust for speed. From sprints with his fellow couriers he moved to organized bicycle racing, and got in the habit of winning. And in 1901, when E.R. Thomas began selling engine kits, Curtiss bought one for his bicycle. The creation became known as the Happy Hooligan, and inspired Curtiss's enthusiasm to build a better engine.

The good people of Hammondsport hoped it would be quieter as well, but young Glenn had settled on

the engineering thesis for his entire career; more horsepower and less weight. He had his own castings made and built his first single in 1901. His bicycle and sporting goods business now included motorcycles, and by the spring of 1902 he had shops in Bath and Corning as well as Hammondsport. Both his bicycles and motorcycles wore the trade name Hercules (see p.122). The next objective was to build a V-twin and go racing.

On the horse track at the

Below: Charles Darling, restorer and student of Curtiss history, points out that this 500cc model is not fitted with the correct front wheel, controls or pedals.

Right: The Curtiss ads claimed a top speed of 45-50mph (72-80kph) for the single. The standard gear ratio was 5:1, and 3.5:1 for racing.

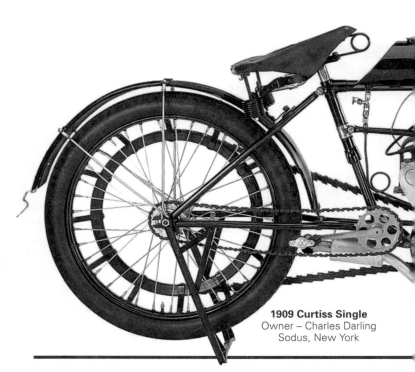

1909 Curtiss Single
Owner – Charles Darling
Sodus, New York

Syracuse, New York fairgrounds in 1905, Curtiss set three new records and went unchallenged in the 5-mile open race. He went on to win major dirt-track events and broke two speed records at Ormond Beach, Florida. The Curtiss single had bore and stroke squared at 3.0 inches (76mm); the crankshaft rode roller bearings in the polished aluminum cases, and the cast-iron cylinder and head had the valve pocket in front. Horsepower was rated at 2.5 at 2000rpm, and the machine weighed 130 pounds (59kg). The second generation saw bore and stroke enlarged to 3.25 inches (82.5mm) and horsepower rise to three.

A California company then claimed legal right to the name Hercules, so Curtiss affixed his own name to the machines. The 5-horsepower V-twin got the same displacement increase as the single and was rated at six horsepower. The motorcycle weighed 160 pounds

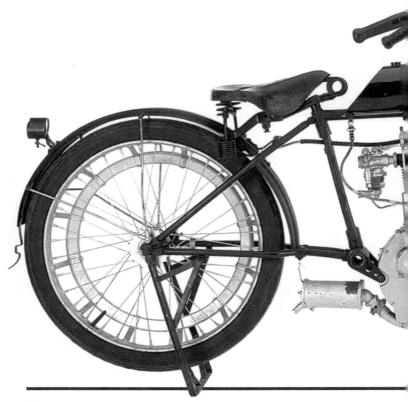

Below: There was considerable mix and match in the days of pioneer motorcycling. This example combines an early Wehmann frame (after the designer) with a later model engine and components.

1909–13 Curtiss Single
Courtesy of Curtiss Musuem
Hammondsport, New York

(73kg) and was good for 60mph (97kph) in stock trim. The original Hercules Double Cylinder sold for $310 in 1904, putting it in the high end of the market. By 1909 the price had dropped to $275. Curtiss remained unconvinced of the need for chain drive, and stayed with flat leather belts. A leather covering on the drive pulley minimized slippage. He later developed a 28 degree V-belt with improved grip.

If, by 1907, there were any doubters on the benefits of light weight, high horsepower and long wheelbase, Glenn Curtiss diasabused

(Twin)
Engine: IOE 50° V-twin
Displacement: 1000cc
Horsepower: 5.0/6.0
Wheelbase: 58in (147cm)
Weight: 160lb (73kg)
Top speed: 60mph (97kph)
Price: $275

Below: Curtiss had built the first V-twin on the American market in 1903. The engine was rated at 5 horsepower at 1500rpm, but "can be speeded to 2000." Cylinders were cast iron, the crankcase of aluminum.

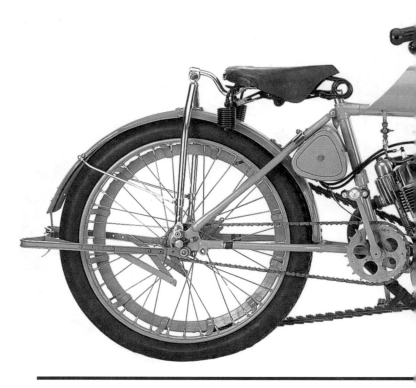

Above: The Curtiss V-twin was unique in the single cam operating both exhaust valves. The engine carried racers to many wins in hillclimb, dirt-track and endurance events.

1909 Curtiss V-Twin
Owner – Charles Darling
Sodus, New York

their notions at Ormond Beach, Florida. On the V-twin, the New Yorker set a new world record for the mile at 76mph (122kph). When the scheduled events were over, Curtiss and two friends rolled out a seven-foot (2.1m) long motorcycle with a V-8 engine. The engine made nearly 40 horsepower at 1800rpm, with direct shaft drive to the rear wheel. The machine weighed 275 pounds (125kg). Moments later, after a two-mile run to get up to speed, Glen Curtiss flashed by the line at 136.36mph (219.4kph) and became the fastest man on earth. "It satisfied my speed craving," he allowed.

Shortly thereafter Curtiss shifted his attention to aviation projects, for which the V-8 was originally intended. His two-wheeled creations remained in production for another six years, and came under the direction of Curtiss's old racing pal Tank Waters. Later models were sold under the Marvel name.

(V-8)
Engine: IOE 90° V-8
Displacement: 4000cc
Horsepower: 40
Wheelbase: 64in (163cm)
Weight: 275lb (125kg)
Top speed: 136mph (219kph)
Price: Not sold

Below: The one-quart oil tank was fitted below the seat; the fuel tank had a capacity of 2.5 gallons (9.5lit). The rudimentary rear V-brake required about a mile to slow the machine from 136mph (219kph).

1907 Curtiss V-8
Courtesy of Curtiss Museum
Hammondsport, New York

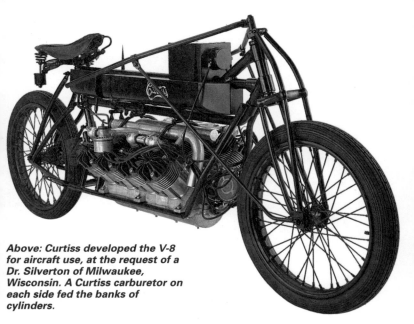

Above: Curtiss developed the V-8 for aircraft use, at the request of a Dr. Silverton of Milwaukee, Wisconsin. A Curtiss carburetor on each side fed the banks of cylinders.

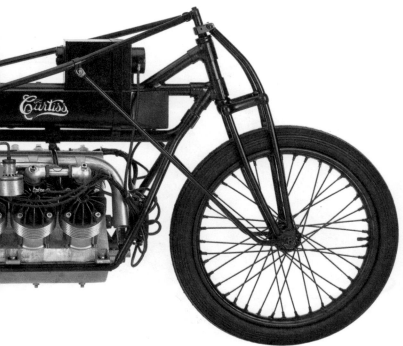

Cushman (1936-1965)

(1947 Cushman)
Engine: Side-valve single
Displacement: 221cc
Horsepower: 4
Wheelbase: 54in (137cm)
Weight: 260lb (118kg)
Top speed: 40mph (64kph)
Price: $220-365

Cushman had been building small motors for decades when the motor scooter notion came along. It came from California's E. Foster Salsbury, who introduced a scooter designed by Austin Elmore. The Moto-Glide, from which the Cushman Auto-Glide was copied, appeared in 1935. The Cushman engine was their venerable single-horse Husky flathead, sold mostly as a water-pump motor.

By 1940 the horsepower had doubled and a two-speed trans-mission was available. Then Cush-man introduced its Floating Drive Clutch, in respose to Salsbury's Self-Shifting Transmission. The latter's centrifugal clutch featured a spring-loaded, two-piece drive pulling that varied the drive ratio according to engine speed. This fundamental torque converter came to be called

Below: The basic Cushman profile was unchanged since 1936. The knee action front suspension and automatic clutch meant easy riding.

1947 Cushman Model 52
Owner – Hal O'Connor
Phelps, New York

the Salsbury Clutch, and was a widely used form of power transmission in all manner of engines from then on.

During World War II, Cushman built several military models for non-combat use. Since scooters were considered energy savers for civilian transport, the company was permitted to continue domestic prod-uction during the war. After the war the scooter boom blossomed worldwide, and Cushman introduced the 50 Series model, nicknamed the Turtleback, with a four-horsepower Husky engine. The 60 Series, which began in 1949, saw horsepower go up to options of 4.8 or 7.3, and the tail section grew larger.

(1958 Cushman)
Engine: Side-valve single
Displacement: 318cc
Horsepower: 8
Wheelbase: 54in (137cm)
Weight: 22lb (10kg)
Top speed: 55mph (89kph)
Price: $375

Below: The Cushman Eagle appeared in 1949, when scooter styling began to emulate that of full-scale motorcycles. The Eagle stayed in production for 17 years.

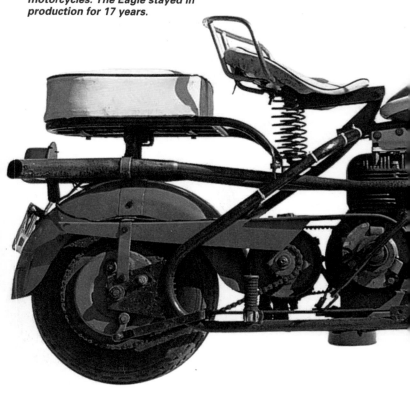

1958 Cushman Eagle
Owner – Randy Youngs
Grand Rapids, Ohio

Cushman released the Eagle the same year, which signaled the return to unenclosed engines and the move to motorcycle styling. The concept, proposed by one of the salesman, proved to be the best-selling Cushman ever built. Prompted by the Mustang, built in 1947 in California, the Eagle was designed as a miniature Harley-Davidson. Cushman produced several other enclosed models until 1961, and the Eagle remained in production through 1965 when the company dropped scooters.

Right: By 1965 the Cushman had been eclipsed by imports from Europe and Japan. This example has been painted, chromed and dressed up for parade duty.

Below: The Eagle was favored by fraternal organizations such as the Shriners, who could order them in fleets with special paint, plenty of chrome, saddlebags and flag poles.

**1965 Cushman
Super Silver Eagle**
Owner – Sam Simmons

Cyclone (1913-1916)

Engine: 45° ohc V-twin
Displacement: 1000cc
Horsepower: 45
Wheelbase: 53in (135cm)
Weight: 260lb (118kg)
Top speed: 110mph (177kph)
Price: $350

The Cyclone was built by the Joerns Motor Manufacturing Company, which grew from the Thiem Manufacturing Company, an engine builder from 1903–1911. Professional motorcycle racing was a high-stakes game at this point; Indian ruled the roost and Harley-Davidson was playing catch-up. Cyclone added some spice to festivities with a 1000cc overhead-cam V-twin, ridden by a skilled racer named Don Johns. In 1914, development engineer J.A. McNeil posted a speed of 111mph (179kph) on a boardtrack.

These bevel-drive ohc twins were designed by Andrew Strand, and were the most powerful factory hot

Above right: The short-coupled, stripped stock model was one of the first cafe racers. The Model 7 was fitted with clutch, rear brake and footboards.

Right: In 1914, the Cyclone Model 7, R-15 was the fastest motorcycle on the road.

rods of their day. The crankshaft ran in four-row caged roller bearings on the drive side and self-aligning ball bearings on the other end. Lightweight connecting rods rode on three-row roller bearings, and the magneto was also driven by shaft and bevel gears. But while Johns

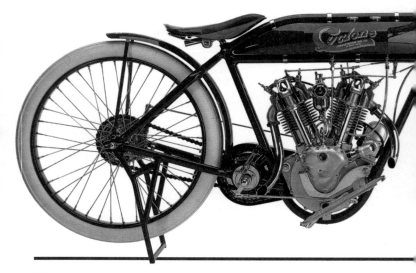

1914 Cyclone
Owner – Daniel Statnekov
Tesuque, New Mexico

Left: Both the single overhead cams and the magneto were powered by bevel drive shafts. Swedish SKF bearings were used throughout.

routinely put the Cyclone in front of the Indian and Harley factory machines, reliability was another matter.

By 1915 most of the mechanical problems were sorted out, but the Cyclone was plagued by minor difficulties. In the 300-mile national championship at Dodge City in 1915, Johns was retired by a leaking fuel tank. Fellow Cyclone rider Dave Kinnie was out with a broken frame.

Sales of road models were insufficient to support the Minnesotans' underdog effort, and the Joerns company expired in 1916.

Right: The final Cyclones were manufactured in 1915. Tooling and parts passed through several hands, but production never resumed.

Below: For a few years, the Cyclones were the fastest machines on two wheels. But reliability problems and the lack of development funding put them into the history books early.

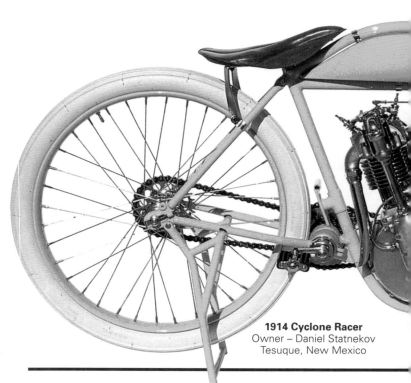

1914 Cyclone Racer
Owner – Daniel Statnekov
Tesuque, New Mexico

1915 Cyclone
Owner – Otis Chandler
Ojai, California

Dayton (1911-1917)

Engine: Ohv 45° V-twin
Displacement: 1573cc
Horsepower: 88
Wheelbase: 66.65in (169.3cm)
Weight: 615lb (279kg)
Top speed: 120mph (193kph)
Price: $250/500

Dayton motorcycles, motor bicycles and bicycles were made by the Davis Sewing Machine Company of Dayton, Ohio. They offered two V-twins (not shown), one with their own 1000cc engine and another with the 1190cc DeLuxe powerplant built in Chicago.

The Dayton Motor Bicycle incorporated the engine, drive system and footboards on the front wheel of a modified bicycle. The engine was supported by two hollow aluminum beams, bolted at each end to the leaf spring/front fender. A reduction gear drove the disc front wheel. In 1917 the machine was offered in men's and ladies' models, with or without clutch.

Right: The Dayton Motor Bicycle was offered as a complete machine, with 1.5-horsepower engine for $100. Another $10 was charged for the clutch model.

Doodle Bug (1946-1950)

Engine: Side-valve single
Displacement: 98cc
Horsepower: 1.5
Wheelbase: 37in (94cm)
Weight: 120lb (54kg)
Top speed: 25mph (40kph)
Price: $160

When the scooter bug arrived after World War II, the Gamble Hardware Company commissioned the Doodle Bug from Beam Manufacturing Company of Iowa. Powered by the venerable horse-and-a-half Briggs & Stratton engine, the mini-scooter was marketed by mail order catalog. The small size and weight of the Doodle Bug put it in the youngster category, although racers found it handy as a pit bike. A California company recently announced plans to market a contemporary version called the Ladybug.

Right: The Doodle Bug was the first mini-scooter, and offered the exclusive "flexi-matic clutch." Some 40,000 were produced from 1946 to 1950. Most Doodle Bugs were powered by the standard 1.5-horsepower Briggs & Stratton engine. When B&S ran short for a spell in 1946, Beam switched to the Clinton engine temporarily.

1917 Dayton Motor Bicycle
Owner – William Owens
Millington, Michigan

1946 Doodle Bug
Owners – Jeff & Patricia Brink
Ottawa, Illinois

Eagle (1909-1915)

Engine: 45° IOE V-twin
Displacement: 1000cc
Horsepower: 7
Wheelbase: 60in (152cm)
Weight: 365lb (166kg)
Top speed: 55mph (89kph)
Price: $275

The Eagle was produced by the Sterling Motor Company of Massachussets, using the proprietary Spacke engine from Indianapolis, Indiana. The same engine was offered under the Dayton, DeLuxe Crawford and Sears imprints. Nine horsepower was the big figure for V-twins on the cusp of the national professional racing era. The power figures, already conservative ratings, would escalate on road models as well in the next few years. But, come 1915, Eagle would be unable to stay in the game.

Right: In its original state the Eagle was painted French gray, with black tank panels and gold outlines. The Eagle Twin was offered in both seven- and nine-horsepower renditions. The single was available in either four- or five-horse trim. The aluminum footboards were adjustable. The Spacke engine featured roller-bearing connecting rods, and Eclipse multiple disc clutch.

Emblem (1907-1925)

The Emblem originated in western New York state in 1907. The early singles were offered with options of direct drive or clutch, and flat or V-belt motivation. When the company introduced a twin in 1913, it was a robust 1255cc engine rated at ten horsepower. In 1916, customers could choose a 12- or 14-horsepower powerplant. The less power-hungry were offered the 800cc twin, or the venerable 600cc, seven-horse single. Emblem had a brief period of professional racing effort, but soon retired to less costly enterprises.

Right: Emblem offered the options of flat or V-belt drive, and direct drive or clutch engine.

By 1917 the competition for motorcycle sales had narrowed the field, owing largely to the motoring economics introduced a few years earlier by Henry Ford. Emblem came to market with a roster of one model that year, a V-twin of moderate displacement (530cc) and performance. The lightweight twin was good for 50mph (80mph) and sold for $175, the same price their single brought the year before. ▶

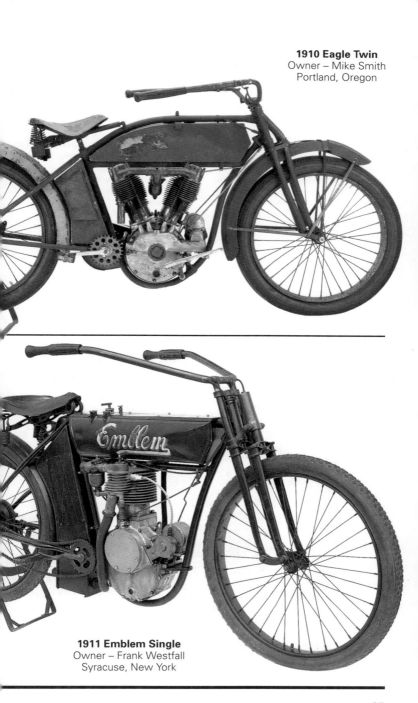

1910 Eagle Twin
Owner – Mike Smith
Portland, Oregon

1911 Emblem Single
Owner – Frank Westfall
Syracuse, New York

The basic model was a one-speed with an Eclipse clutch, and a three-speed version was available. The mechanical oil pump was optional. The front fork featured a triple crown cartridge spring design, which allowed 2.5 inches (6.35cm) of wheel travel. With its low seat height, center of gravity and short wheelbase (52 inches/132cm) the

Emblem was a nimble machine. But American riders had cast their dollar votes for big twins, and fours, with more heaps of horsepower. The lightweight Emblem was virtually lost in the shuffle. Although it remained in production for another eight years, the Emblem was sold almost exclusively as an export model.

Below: The Emblem single was a stout machine, with the engine mounted quite low in the loop frame. The muffler was tucked in nicely below the rear frame section. A luggage rack was a popular accessory item. Emblem machines were widely used by police and postal services in the northeast.

Right: The big-bore trend began in 1913, when Emblem introduced a 1255cc twin rated at ten horsepower. The factory allowed as how it had even more grunt, and guaranteed a top speed of 70mph (113kph).

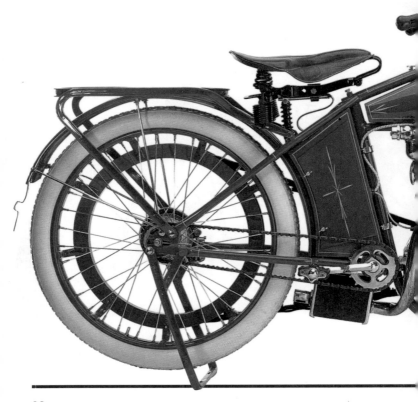

1913 Emblem Twin
Owner – Bud Ekins
North Hollywood, California

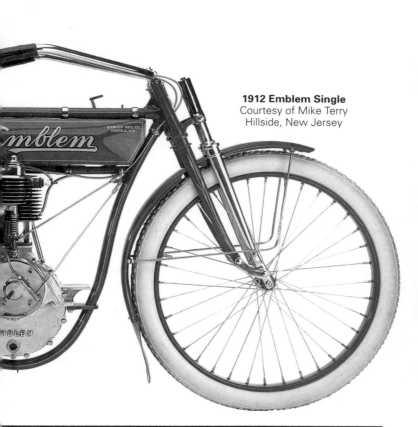

1912 Emblem Single
Courtesy of Mike Terry
Hillside, New Jersey

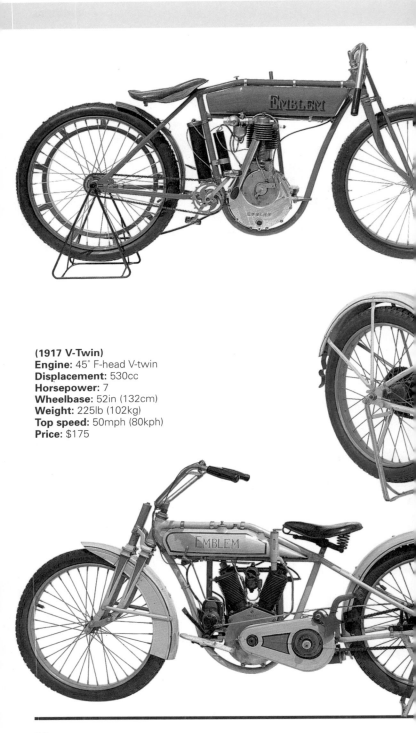

(1917 V-Twin)
Engine: 45° F-head V-twin
Displacement: 530cc
Horsepower: 7
Wheelbase: 52in (132cm)
Weight: 225lb (102kg)
Top speed: 50mph (80kph)
Price: $175

1914 Emblem Single
Owner – Jim Lattin
Encinitas, California

Left: A few Emblems were set up for racing in 1912–13, but there was never a large-scale factory effort. Belt drive was a disadvantage in the increasingly fast sport.

1917 Emblem Twin
Owner – Frank Westfall
Syracuse, New York

Left and above: In 1917 the standard Emblem twin was available with either direct drive or, for $35 more, a three-speed transmission. The triple crown cartridge spring fork offered 2.5 inches (6.35cm) of travel, "ample to absorb all road shocks."

Evans (1916-1924)

Engine: Two-stroke single
Displacement: 120cc
Horsepower: 1.5
Wheelbase: 50in (127cm)
Weight: 75lb (34kg)
Top speed: 40mph (64kph)
Price: $135

The Cyclemotor Corporation began with an engine kit in 1916, and expanded to complete motorcycles two years later. The 120cc two-stroke single was rated at 1.5 horsepower and drove the V-belt countershaft pulley by chain. The Evans was a genuine lightweight at 75 pounds (34kg).

The Evans found favor on the twisty mountain roads of the northeastern United States of America, and elsewhere, for its nimble handling and ease of operation. But these qualities were insufficient to sustain the company in the steadily constricting market.

Excelsior (1908-1931)

(Single)
Engine: IOE single
Displacement: 500cc
Horsepower: 4
Wheelbase: 56in (142cm)
Weight: 170lb (77kg)
Top speed: 45mph (72kph)
Price: $185

Excelsior was third of the big three in the teens and twenties. Indian and Harley-Davidson were the other two major players, and would become the only survivors of the Great Depression. But until its demise in 1931, Excelsior and its offspring the Super-X, insured a dynamic three-way tussle for domination of the American motorcycle market. On and off the racetrack, it was a genuine contest.

The original Excelsior Supply Company began building motorcycles in 1906. They came to market in 1908 with a well-tested belt-drive 500cc ▶

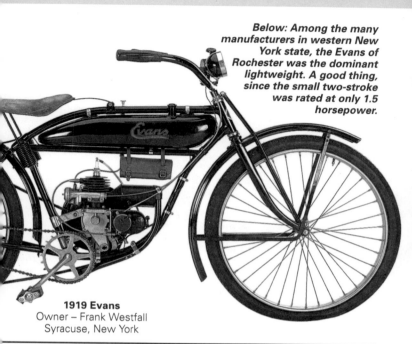

Below: Among the many manufacturers in western New York state, the Evans of Rochester was the dominant lightweight. A good thing, since the small two-stroke was rated at only 1.5 horsepower.

1919 Evans
Owner – Frank Westfall
Syracuse, New York

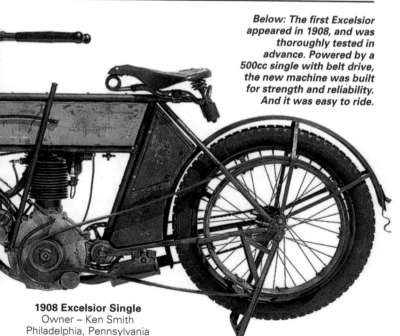

Below: The first Excelsior appeared in 1908, and was thoroughly tested in advance. Powered by a 500cc single with belt drive, the new machine was built for strength and reliability. And it was easy to ride.

1908 Excelsior Single
Owner – Ken Smith
Philadelphia, Pennsylvania

93

single, with the crankcase cast integral with the frame. The machine carried a leading-link dual-spring front fork and two gallons (7.6lit) of gas. Three Excelsior singles entered the Chicago-Kokomo Reliability Run, and all finished with perfect scores. Motorcycles had thus moved beyond the framework of the motorized bicycle, and become integrated entities, purpose-built machines informed by design and engineering rather than assemblies of miscellaneous components.

Harley-Davidson had by this time built itself a reputation for reliability, and Indian had come to dominate the sporting side of motorcycle spectrum. Excelsior determined to cover both considerations, and also address the issues of easy starting, handling and overall operational ease. And as the sport of professional motorcycle racing gained popularity, the prospect of higher speeds imposed new standards for design, engineering and materials.

Excelsior produced their own version of the popular Sager-cushion front fork, and a stout frame with

Below: The 500cc Excelsior single was raced with success for many years. But it would be the "Big X" twins that pushed Indian and Harley to higher standards of performance. The single-cylinder magneto model, priced at $250 in 1911, fell to $225 in 1912. The single remained in production for only four years.

Above right: In 1911, its first year, the 1000cc Excelsior Twin sold for $310. The following year the price was dropped to $250 as inexpensive cars intensified the motorcycle market.

1911 Excelsior Twin
Owner – Otis Chandler
Ojai, California

1911 Excelsior Single
Owner – Jim Lattin
Encinitas, California

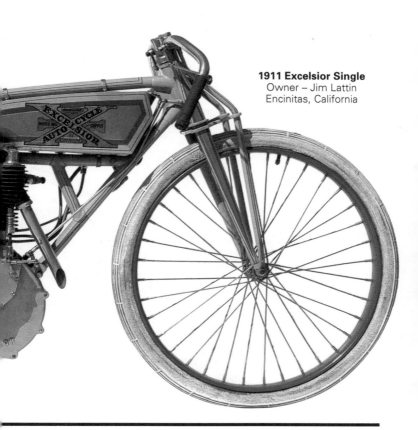

(V-Twins)
Engine: IOE V-twin
Displacement: 820/1000cc
Horsepower: 8/10/15
Wheelbase: 58in (147cm)
Weight: 250/290lb (113/132kg)
Top speed: 45/60/75mph
(72/97/121kph)
Price: $185-295

Below: The 1000cc V-twin began winning races from the get-go. Factory riders Joe Wolters and Jake DeRosier were making life hard for the Indian factory team. The heated rivalries and close racing drew huge crowds to the spectacle of boardtrack racing.

1914 Excelsior Twin
Courtesy of Mike Terry
Hillside, New Jersey

1913 Excelsior Twin
Owner – Jim Lattin
Encinitas, California

1915 Excelsior Twin
Owner – Otis Chandler
Ojai, California

Left: In 1914 factory riders Joe Wolters, Bob Perry and Carl Goudy turned in winning rides against the mighty teams from Indian and Harley-Davidson. Perry won at Sacramento and Chicago, and Wolters claimed victory in the Birmingham, Alabama national meet.

Below: The Excelsior production racer sold for $250. In addition to numerous professional wins, Excelsior claimed the national amateur championship in 1914 with rider Bill Leuders.

Left: The acquisition of Excelsior by Schwinn in 1911 led to expanded development in terms of engineering, performance and styling. Head to head with Indian and Harley-Davidson, Excelsior was one of the big three. The streamlining trend reached Excelsior with the 1915 model, which had new frame, fenders, tank and seat. Motorcycles were being given rounder shapes. This was also the first year for a three-speed transmission.
In addition to contemporary styling themes, improved suspension components were making motorcycles more comfortable to ride. And extending both their range and durability.

drop-forged fittings. Forged control levers were also standard; "there are no brass castings used at any point." The Excelsior featured a positive oiling system that forced oil through the crankshaft to the crankpin bearing, and by grooved mainshaft to the main bearings. The company claimed "one of the most thorough and efficient oiling systems ever used in connection with a gas engine."

The Chicago bunch also gave some attention to the problems of belt drive, the issue of linear engagement in particular. Excelsior crafted a pulley and idler wheel that delivered progressive power take-up, and allowed the engine to idle freely with

the idler released.

In 1910 Excelsior introduced its V-twin to the market, an 820cc engine with mechanical intake valves. A 1000cc model appeared the following year, followed by a significant change in the Excelsior corporate structure. The company was acquired by the Arnold-Schwinn and Company of Chicago, a leading manufacturer of bicycles. No model changes were instituted for 1912, but a year later the company was called Excelsior Motor Manufacturing and Supply, and the single was gone from the roster.

In 1911, racer Joe Wolters was blistering the tracks on his Excelsior twin, pushing the record to nearly

Below: With the end of World War I, the motorcycle manufacturers returned to civilian production. Few styling changes had been made, and the supply of green paint lasted several years.

Above right: In the late twenties, Excelsior had two racing heros in Joe Petrali and Gene Rhyne. The factory built several overhead-valve engines to win the national hillclimb championship, which they did in 1929 and 1930.

1919 Excelsior Twin
Owner – Bob McClean
Davenport, Iowa

1928 Excelsior Hillclimber
Owner – Dale Walksler
Mt. Vernon, Illinois

Above: Excelsior developed a Big Valve version of this engine for racing, and set several distance records.

90mph (145kph). Former Indian racer and international star Jake DeRosier had jumped to Excelsior and was immediately setting records. And in 1913 rider Lee Humiston put the Chicago marque indelibly in the record books with the first 100mph (161kph) average in sanctioned competition, at a boardtrack race in Los Angeles. Indian engineer Oscar Hedstrom had designed an 8-valve ohv engine to challenge the Excelsior, and in Milwaukee the Harley-Davidson founders began reconsidering a factory racing team. The game was afoot.

Ignaz Schwinn brought to the motorcycle business a wealth of production and marketing experience, and sufficient funding to upgrade the motorcycle and increase production. A two-stroke Lightweight model was

(Super-X)
Engine: IOE V-twin
Displacement: 750cc
Horsepower: 20
Wheelbase: 61in (155cm)
Weight: 450lb (204kg) est.
Top speed: 65mph (105kph)
Price: $325

Below: The Super-X made its debut in 1925. Though still a traditional F-head design, the engine carried its transmission within the crankcases and had helical-gear primary drive.

The Super-X exhaust valves were enclosed in 1927, a front brake was added in 1928. The effects of the Great Depression put Excelsior out of business in 1931.

introduced in 1914, and factory racers Carl Goudy and Bob Perry were were posting good results with the big twin. Perry won three 100-mile events in 1915, and Goudy won the Chicago 300-miler on the Excelsior Big Valve twin at an average of 86mph (138kph). Harley-Davidson now had a fully staffed racing department with four of the best riders in the country.

The next rider to grab headlines for Excelsior was Wells Bennet, who specialized in cross-country endurance events. But the big news in 1917 was posted by Alan Bedell, who rode a Henderson Four from Los Angeles to New York in 7 days, 16 hours to beat Cannonball Baker's Indian mark by nearly four hours. In October of the same year, Ignaz Schwinn bought the Henderson Motorcycle Company.

1930 Super-X
Owner – Otis Chandler
Ojai, California

Excelsior-Henderson (1998-)

Engine: 50° dohc V-twin
Displacement: 1386cc
Horsepower: 82
Wheelbase: 65in (165cm)
Weight: 670lb (304kg)
Top speed: 120mph (193kph)
Price: $19,000

The contemporary revival of Excelsior-Henderson is the brainchild of the Hanlon brothers of Minnesota. Encouraged by Harley's apparent inability to keep up with the worldwide demand for cruisers in 1993, Dave and Dan Hanlon set themselves the task of building a new motorcycle with an old name. They were able to raise $100 million dollars from investors and build a motorcycle plant.

The new Super-X hit the market in 1999. The retro-cruiser runs a 1386cc V-twin with dual overhead cams and four valves per cylinder. The fuel-injected motor motivates a five-speed transmission with final drive via belt. The chassis combines the rigid-look rear frame section on a single shock with the leading-link vintage-style front fork, each end getting four inches (10.2cm) of travel.

Will Excelsior-Henderson be able to compete directly with Harley-Davidson in the American cruiser market? The crystal ball remains clouded, but it's early yet.

Right: Original Super-X styling cues are relected by the fork springs, leading-link suspension and front fender. The rubber mounted (Torsion Activated Vibration Absorbing System) 50° V-twin has fuel injection and dual overhead cams. Power is delivered by geared primary to a five-speed transmission, and by belt to the rear wheel. The wheelbase is 65 inches (165cm).

1999 Super-X
Courtesy of Excelsior-Henderson
Belle Plain, Minnesota

Feilbach (1912-1915)

(V-Twin)
Engine: 45° IOE V-twin
Displacement: 1100cc
Horsepower: 10
Wheelbase: 60in (152cm)
Weight: 350lb (159kg)
Top speed: 60mph (97kph)
Price: $290/Twin shaft $310

The name Limited was borrowed from the railroad business, where the term denoted "Speed, Comfort and Quality." The first Feilbach Limited was a belt-drive single, which faced a tough market at $250. The price dropped with the introduction of the V-twin.

The V-twin was offered with either chain or shaft drive, the latter a $20 option. Feilbach advertised the Limited as "The Vibrationless Motorcycle." In addition to a smooth engine, the Limited boasted the comfort afforded by the horizontally sprung seat; the second frame tube carried a full-length spring. "There is nothing directly beneath the saddle. The rider actually rests on air."

Feilbach floated into history in 1915.

Below: The Limited, in both single and twin models, was equipped with front and rear (seat) suspension. The company also offered another version with shaft drive.

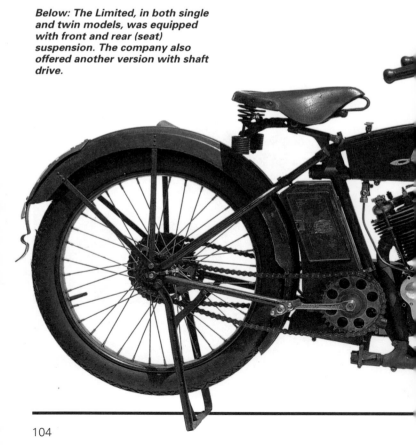

Above: The big Limited twin had its valve train outboard on both cylinders. The rear-exit exhaust port was claimed to provide improved engine cooling. Cams and magnetos were gear-driven.

1914 Feilbach Limited
Owner – Todd Bertrang
Sylmar, California

Flanders (1911-1914)

(Single)
Engine: IOE single
Displacement: 485cc
Horsepower: 4
Wheelbase: 57in (145cm)
Weight: 270lb (122kg)
Top speed: 45mph (72kph)
Price: $165

The Motor Products Company of Detroit attempted, as others had, to build a comfortable and reliable machine and offer it at a reasonable price. The Flanders 4 (as in horsepower) had a 485cc single and belt drive, with a compression and rebound spring on the front fork. The single sold for $165.

The 1914 twin, with enclosed chain drive, was advertised as "The Packard of Motorcycle Value." Rated at seven to nine horsepower, the side-valve twin claimed the only direct chain drive with the "smoothness and flexibility of a belt." Flanders took some pride in offering good value at low cost, which was $210 for the twin; significantly less than the relatively rudimentary Harley-Davidson at $285. But in three years Flanders had faded into the archives.

1911 Flanders 4
Owner – Otis Chandler
Ojai, California

Right: The Flanders fork offered a dual spring system; one worked on compression, the other on rebound.

Below: The Flanders seemed to offer sound construction and good performance at a low price, but the company only lasted four years.

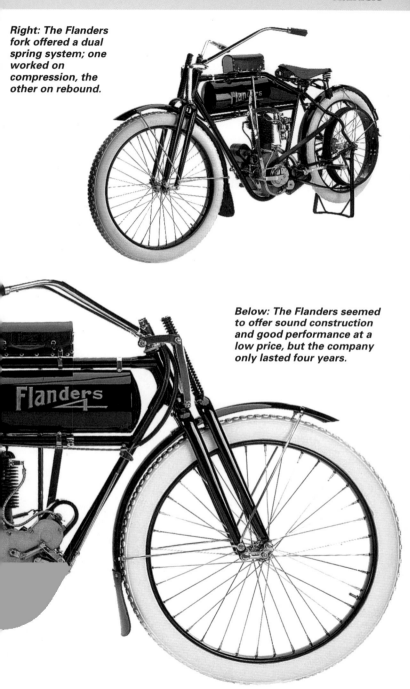

Geer (1905-1909)

(Green Egg)
Engine: 60° V-twin (not shown)
Displacement: 350cc
Horsepower: 2.5
Wheelbase: 55in (140cm)
Weight: 130lb (59kg)
Top speed: 35mph (56kph)
Price: $160

The Harry R. Geer Company built complete motorcycles and also sold complete engines and components to individuals and the trade. The Geer Bluebird carried a forward-mount single in a loop frame; The belt-drive, four-horsepower rig apparently only weighed 150 pounds (68kg), and sold for $200 in 1907, including the tool bag and tools. Bore and stroke were 3.5 x 4 inches (89 x 102mm). A smaller 2.5-horsepower version sold for $160.

The Green Egg, with claimed weigh-in at 165 pounds (75kg), featured a low-mount 350cc V-twin rated at 5 horsepower. Also a belt-drive model, the Egg was offered with either battery or magneto ignition. Fitted with a truss fork, 1.5-gallon (5.7lit) fuel tank, 1.5-quart (1.4lit) oil tank, on a 56-inch (142cm) wheelbase, the twin sold for $225. Few of either model remain extant.

Greyhound (1907-1914)

(Single)
Engine: IOE single
Displacement: 494cc
Horsepower: 4
Wheelbase: 54in (137cm)
Weight: 130lb (59kg)
Top speed: 50mph (80kph)
Price: $180

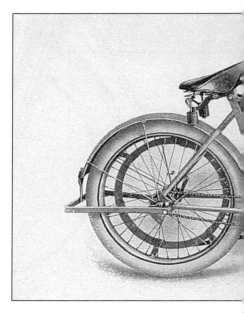

Right: The 1910 Greyhound catalog shows the vertical engine configuration, and re-designed frame and fork. Weight was obviously gained in the process.

1906 Geer Green Egg
Owner – Jim Lattin
Encinitas, California

Above: The Green Egg was offered with both single-cylinder and twin engines. The four-horsepower twin, in a different frame, sold for $225

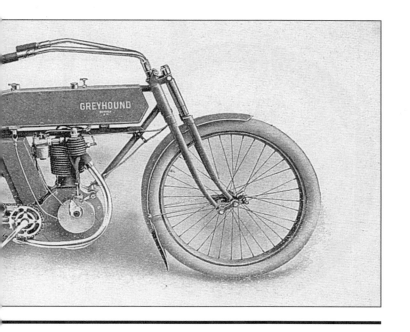

The Greyhound was united hand-in-glove with the Aurora Auto-matic Machine Company near Chicago, Illinois. Aurora manufactured the engines for Indian motorcycles, and marketed the same engines under their Thor label. The Greyhound was fitted with the Thor engine until 1910, when Aurora was struggling to meet its own brand requirements.

The marque then switched to motors from E.R. Thomas of Buffalo, New York and the Auto-Bi brand. The Greyhound was offered with a 494cc single or a V-twin, but by this time the market was ruled by the big three of Indian, Harley and Excelsior. Few examples of the Greyhound have survived the century.

Below: The single-spring girder fork was used by several motorcycle manufacturers. Torpedo-style tanks had reached their stylistic terminus.

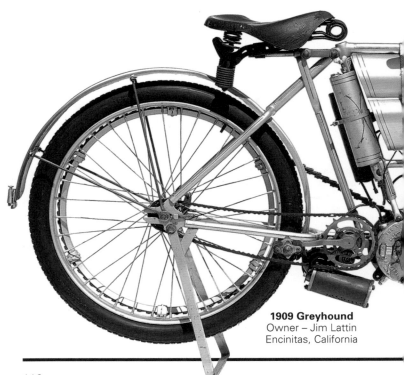

1909 Greyhound
Owner – Jim Lattin
Encinitas, California

1910 Greyhound Single
Owner – Frank Westfall
Syracuse, New York

111

Harley-Davidson (1903-)

(1903 Single)
Engine: IOE single
Displacement: 405cc
Horsepower: Approx. 3
Wheelbase: 51in (130cm)
Weight: 178lb (81kg)
Top speed: Approx. 35mph (56kph)
Price: $200

Harley-Davidson didn't exactly get a headstart in the motorcycle business. None of the founding foursome were trained engineers, designers or inventors. And at least 70 American companies were in the marketplace by 1903, with more on the way. But William Harley and the Davidson brothers, Arthur, Walter and William, figured they had as good a chance as anyone. Bill Harley had some design ideas, Walter Davidson was a machinist, Arthur had some marketing savvy and Bill could run a factory.

Their first motorcycle in 1903 was little different from a half-dozen other brands on the market. The IOE single

(1907 Single)
Engine: IOE single
Displacement: 440cc
Horsepower: Approx. 4
Wheelbase: 51in (130cm)
Weight: 185lb (84kg)
Top speed: Approx. 40mph (64kph)
Price: $210

Below: The lever at the rear of the tank controlled the hinged cutout on the muffler. Subdued tones in town, out in the country let 'er bark.

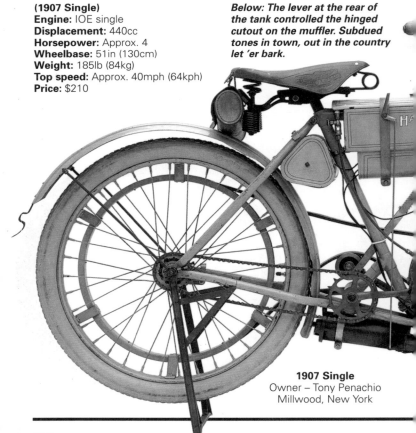

1907 Single
Owner – Tony Penachio
Millwood, New York

1903 Single
Owner – Harley-Davidson
Milwaukee, Wisconsin
Artwork by Rod Ferring

Above: The first Harley-Davidson was a simple but stout construction, the engine fitted low in a loop frame and fuel, oil and battery containers strapped topside.

Below: The wooden twistgrip connected by chain, rod, lever and pinion to the carburetor. This connection was infinitely adjustable.

was bolted low in a loop-style bicycle frame, with pedal start and belt drive. Their first engine was marginal for horsepower, so they went up on the bore and stroke and flywheel size. Then it would go up most hills without pedaling.

By 1906 the Harley single grew to 27 cubic inches (440cc) and acquired a dual-spring, leading link front fork. Production went up to

154 machines the following year, and the Harley-Davidson Motor Company became a corporation with the sale of $35,000 in stock to the 18 employees. William Harley was chief engineer and treasurer, Arthur Davidson was appointed sales manager and secretary, Walter Davidson as president and brother William became vice pres-ident and factory manager.

Right: Clutch action was provided by a spring-loaded tensioning wheel. Both the hand lever and wheel arm were fastened to the engine.

Far right: In 1907 the 440cc single was rated at four horsepower, and with belt drive could be coaxed upwards of 40mph (64kph), conditions permitting.

Below: The leading-link, dual-spring fork helped soften the impacts of rugged roads, and added assurance at breathtaking speeds.

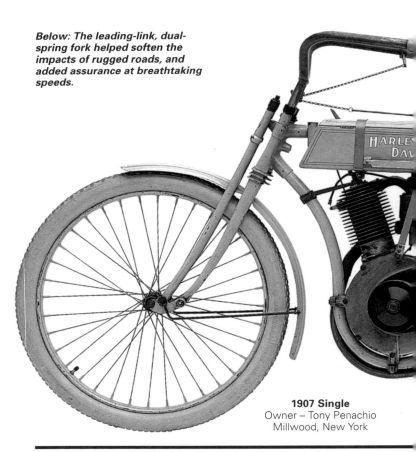

1907 Single
Owner – Tony Penachio
Millwood, New York

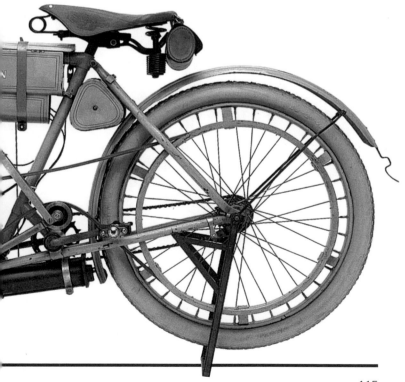

Harley-Davidson did not participate officially in racing events, but good results by privateers were not likely to go unpublicized. The founders had established durability as the top priority in the construction of motorcyles, and chose endurance contests as the best showcases for the equipment. Of the founding four, only Walter Davidson developed as an accomplished motorcylist and proved himself quite adept at it. In 1908 he recorded a perfect score in the Catskill-New York national endurance meet, and was awarded the special diamond medal for consistency.

Six years would pass before Milwaukee was forced by Indian to enter the professional speed contests, but the results of privateer entries were posted in company advertisements and racing models were offered for sale to the public.

(1910 6A)
Engine: IOE single
Displacement: 440cc
Horsepower: Approx. 4
Wheelbase: 51in (130cm)
Weight: 185lb (84kg)
Top speed: Approx. 40mph (64kph)
Price: $210

Above: The motorcycles were becoming more integrated, less like motorized bicycles. Throttle and spark controls were wires inside the handlebar.

1910 6A
Owner – Joy Baker
Vallejo, California

1909 5D Twin
Owner – Harley-Davidson
Milwaukee, Wisconsin
Photograph by Ron Hussey

*Above: The first Harley-Davidson
V-twin fell short of expectations.
Absent from the roster in 1910,
the twin was back a year later
with new stuff.*

Harley's production nearly tripled between 1909 and 1910, rising to more than 3,000 machines. The first Harley-Davidson V-twin appeared in 1909, but its performance failed to meet contemporary standards. Only 27 of the first twins were built.

(1911 7D)
Engine: IOE 45° V-twin
Displacement: 811cc
Horsepower: 6.5
Wheelbase: 56.5in (143.5cm)
Weight: 295lb (134kg)
Top speed: 60mph (97kph)
Price: $300

Below: With the addition of cylinders and displacement came horsepower and speed. Production V-twins could pass 60mph (97kph). The magneto had moved from the front to the rear of the V-twin. The new frame was stronger with the straight front downtube.

But the twin was back in 1911, with mechanical intake valves and and a belt tensioner. The new engine was housed in a redesigned and reinforced frame with a straight front downtube. But at $300 the new twin faced a tough market. ▶

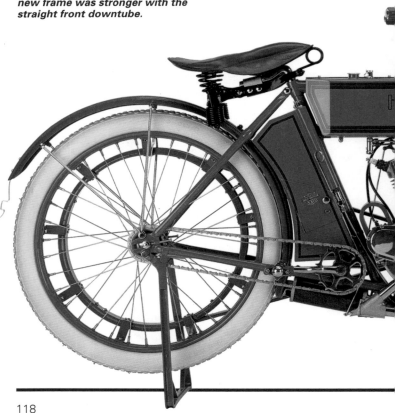

1910 6A
Owner – Joy Baker
Vallejo, California

Above: Cylinder finning was extended over the exhaust port. The gear-driven magneto sits directly behind the cylinder.

1911 7D
Owner – Dave Bettencourt
Gilroy, California

119

(1912 X8E)
Engine: IOE 45° V-twin
Displacement: 989cc
Horsepower: 8
Wheelbase: 56.5in (143.5cm)
Weight: 312lb (142kg)
Top speed: 65mph (105kph)
Price: $285

Right: Harley-Davidson's first clutch, located in the rear hub, was operated by the lever at the left rear of the tank.

Below: The new V-twin got roller bearings on the big ends of the connecting rods. The seat post spring brought the Ful-Floteing (sic) seat. The twin was also available with either chain or belt drive. The engine was fitted with self-aligning ball bearings for a happy crankshaft.

1912 X8E
Owner – Jeff Gilbert
Los Angeles, California

Above: Glass insulators made spark plug function visible from the outside.

In 1912 Harley modified the twin further, with a new frame that lowered the seat height. The lower saddle was mounted on a sprung seatpost, and labeled the Ful-Floteing seat. And the V-twin was now available in a 989cc version, with a healthy eight horsepower. Plus, the new models featured the option of a clutch, mounted in the rear wheel hub, and the choice of either chain or belt drive.

The fuel tank now fitted flush with the frame tubes. The big twin also featured self-aligning ball bearings to support the crankshaft, and the connecting rods rode on roller bearings. The crankcase breather incorporated an oiling device for the primary chain.

The single for 1913 was called the 5-35 motor (5 horsepower, 35 cubic inches). At 565cc, the one-lunger also had both valves operated mechanically, had the rear hub clutch and sold for $290. The big twin had risen in price to $350. Production had jumped to just shy of 13,000 machines from Milwaukee. In 1914 came more technological jumps, with a two-speed transmission, kickstarter (no pedals) and enclosed valve springs.

(1914 10F)
Engine: IOE 45° V-twin
Displacement: 811cc
Horsepower: 6.5
Wheelbase: 56.5in (143.5cm)
Weight: 310lb (141kg)
Top speed: 65mph (105kph)
Price: $285

Below: Footboards appeared in 1914. The internal rear brake was operated by either the brake pedal or back pressure on the bicycle pedals.

1913 9A
Owner – Armando Magri
Sacramento, California

Above: The "5-35" (horsepower and cubic inches) appeared in 1913. The single, with belt or chain drive, was $60 less than the twin.

1914 10F
Owner – Bud Ekins
North Hollywood, California

123

Harley-Davidson had yet to match Indian's production numbers, but they were growing fast. Now the time had come to contest the Springfield factory's long domination on the racetracks. Milwaukee had hired William Ottaway, fomerly a development engineer for Thor, and put him in charge of the new professional racing department. Ottaway assembled a strong group of racers who would soon come to be known as the Harley Wrecking Crew.

Team riders Otto Walker and Red Parkhurst finished 1-2 in the 300-mile race in Venice, California. And in the prestigious Dodge City 300, Harley team riders logged six of the first seven positions. The 8-valve V-twin, built in response to Indian's similar

Left: Racing motor numbers were prefaced by the letter M. The tube between the cylinders delivered oil to the primary chain.

1915 11K
Owner – Daniel Statnekov
Tesuque, New Mexico

124

model, was released in 1917. The Federation of American Motorcyclists stipulated that racing machines be offered for sale to the general public. To discourage privateers from buying the 8-valve, Milwaukee set the price at $1500. It worked.

In 1917, with preparations for war well underway, Harley-Davidson's standard color shifted from gray to olive drab. Milwaukee would somehow manage to stretch their supply of green paint over a period of 15 years. The V-twin was awarded the four-lobe cam designed originally for the 8-valve racer, and the engine was rated at 16 horsepower at 3000rpm. Bosch magnetos were replaced by Dixie units.

In the 1910s, considerable inter- ▶

(1915 11K)
Engine: F-head 45° V-twin
Displacement: 1000cc
Horsepower: 12
Wheelbase: 53in (135cm)
Weight: 260lb (118kg)
Top speed: 100mph (161kph)
Price: $250

Below: Harley-Davidson decided, reluctantly, to join the professional racing game, largely because Indian and Excelsior were generating plenty of advertising.

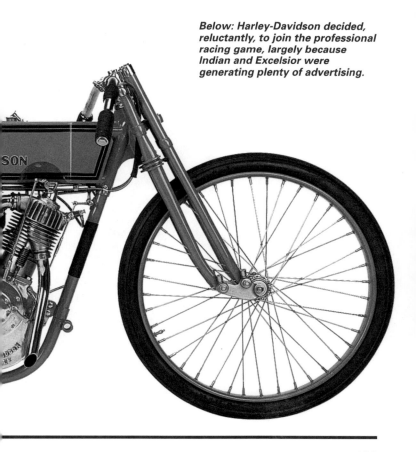

(1923 8-Valve Racer)
Engine: Ohv 45° V-twin
Displacement: 988cc
Horsepower: Approx. 14-16
Wheelbase: 51.5in (131cm)
Weight: 275lb (125kg)
Top speed: 105-115mph (170-185kph)
Price: $1500

Right: The 90-degree valve angle and hemispherical combustion chambers followed aircraft engine design principles developed in World War I.

Below: The 8-valve racer featured the least of everything except motor. Pedals were strapped to the frame and served only as footrests.

1923 8-Valve
Owner – Daniel Statnekov
Tesuque, New Mexico

change occured between American and European motorcyclists. Indian and Harley-Davidson machines were well known overseas, and Springfield's reputation was solidified by their 1-2-3 sweep of the Isle of Man TT in 1911. Americans weren't unfamiliar with FN, Peugeot, Minerva, Clement, Douglas and Sunbeam motorcycles. Developments on both sides of the Atlantic were well documented in enthusiast pub-lications in

the U.S., Britain, France, Belgium and Germany.

But much of this moto-melange was supported by the common interest in professional racing, among major manufacturers as well as racers and enthusiastic spectators. This healthy brew of shared interests was well served until World War I, and even then the Europeans were exposed to more American machines. After the war, when it was apparent

(1919 W Sport Twin)
Engine: F-head opposed twin
Displacement: 584cc
Horsepower: 6
Wheelbase: 57in (145cm)
Weight: 265lb (120kg)
Top speed: 50mph (80kph)
Price: $335

*Below: The luggage carrier was a
$6 option. Riders could choose
Firestone, Goodrich or Goodyear
tires.*

1919 W Sport Twin
Owner – Otis Chandler
Ojai, California

Above: The opposed twin, based on the British Douglas, was appreciated for its lack of vibration but was not widely sold in the U.S.

Below: The 1000cc J model was a popular machine with sporting riders of the 1920s. But motorcycle sales were well down in 1921.

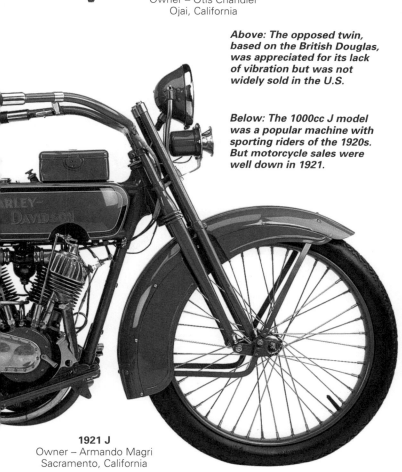

1921 J
Owner – Armando Magri
Sacramento, California

129

that American motorcycling would be primarily recreational, new lightweight machines appeared. The Harley Model W Sport Twin, modeled on the British Douglas, came to market in 1919. But in its five-year lifespan, more were sold in England and Europe than at home.

(1926 JD)
Engine: F-head 45° V-twin
Displacement: 1207cc
Horsepower: 24
Wheelbase: 59.5in (151cm)
Weight: 405lb (184kg)
Top speed: 60mph (97kph)
Price: $335

Harley's signature bike was the J model, a 1000 or 1200cc V-twin with good horsepower and without extraneous weight. The 1200cc JD of 1926 was a streamlined highway hauler, rated at 24 horsepower in a package of little more than 400 pounds (181kg).

Below: A 1200cc V-twin will propel a 400-pound (180kg) machine down the road in smart fashion. The seat post spring was lengthened for a softer ride. The styling trends of streamlining moved from cars to motorcycles in the mid-1920s. Tanks and fenders gained graceful lines.

Above: Hinged rear fenders made tire changing a less complicated chore. More rounded shapes gave the machines a sporty demeanor.

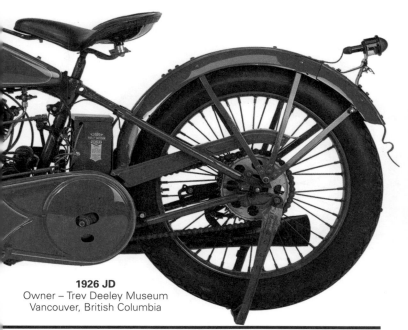

1926 JD
Owner – Trev Deeley Museum
Vancouver, British Columbia

Motorcyle racing resumed in earnest after the war, with Indian and Harley again the leading contenders. But large factory racing efforts were things of the past, and Harley-Davidson discontinued their team in 1921. By the mid-1920s the less expensive (and not so fast) singles were the focus of a new emphasis on sportsman competition. The side-valve singles were aimed at riders interested in low-cost transportation, while the overhead-valve versions appealed to sport riders and racers.

Harley designated the side-valves as A and B models (magneto and battery respectively), and the overheads as AA and BA. The overhead-valve racer was the model S. The 350cc class debuted in 1926, and this Harley-Davidson became known as the Peashooter for its staccato exhaust note.

In 1929 some of Milwaukee's

(1926 BA)
Engine: Ohv single
Displacement: 346cc
Horsepower: 12
Wheelbase: 56.5in (143.5cm)
Weight: 263lb (119kg)
Top speed: 60mph (97kph)
Price: $275

Right: The overhead-valve 350 was rated at 12 horsepower at 4000rpm. Export models sold well.

Below: Milwaukee continued looking for lightweight success. The 350cc single was developed in both side-valve and overhead-valve versions.

1926 BA
Owner – Trev Deeley Museum
Vancouver, British Columbia

racing expertise was put to work in the new JDH road model. Known as the Two-cam, the 1200cc JDH had dual intake valve springs, and tappets rather than roller arms. The com-pression went up with the use of domed alloy pistons. This was a factory hot-rod, built to run with the Indian Chief and the revived Ace Four.

But it was also the grand finale for the J series twins, which had been in production for nine years. Indian and Excelsior had estsblished the suitability of side-valve engines, in terms of both performance and production economy. Here ends the pocket-valve era.

(1929 JDH)
Engine: F-head 45° V-twin
Displacement: 1200cc
Horsepower: 29
Wheelbase: 59.5in (151cm)
Weight: 408lb (185kg)
Top speed: 85mph (137kph)
Price: $370

Right: The J series had a nine-year run, but the front brake arrived in 1928. The end of the F-head engine, and the advent of the side-valve, was at hand.

Below: Even the mufflers were given streamlined styling touches, and more tubes added quietness in response to public moodiness with noise.

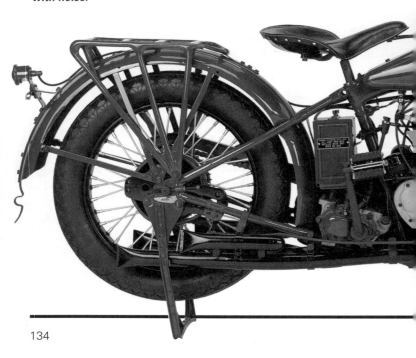

1929 JDH
Owner – Otis Chandler
Ojai, California

(1929 DL)
Engine: Flathead 45° V-twin
Displacement: 746cc
Horsepower: 18.5
Wheelbase: 57.5in (146cm)
Weight: 390lb (177kg)
Top speed: 70mph (113kph)
Price: $290

Right: The 750cc D model (and its high-compression brother the DL) appeared in 1929.

1929 D
Owner – Harold Mathews
Fresno, California

(1932 VL)
Engine: Flathead 45° V-twin
Displacement: 1208cc
Horsepower: 30
Wheelbase: 60in (152cm)
Weight: 529lb (240kg)
Top speed: 85mph (137kph)
Price: $320

Below: Indian won all the big races in 1928 and 1929 with side-valve engines. Milwaukee took up the call, and ohv versions were forthcoming.

1932 VL
Owner – Trev Deeley Museum
Vancouver, British Columbia

Left: The oval toolbox replaced the cylindrical version in 1931. The new horn was a disc-type unit with a chromed face.

Below: Styling made another shift in the 1930s as Art Deco reached the motorcycle design studios. Style gained force in the Depression.

1934 VLD
Owner – Mike Lady
Arroyo Grande, California

Absent any forecast of the impending doom on Wall Street, Milwaukee released two new models in 1929; the 500cc single (C model) and 750cc side-valve V-twin (D model). The single sold for $255 and the the V-twin was priced at $290. The new Forty-five twin (750cc equates to 45 cubic inches) was not built as a sport bike, but by the following season the model had an improved frame and the addition of a sportier version (DLD) with more horsepower. Harley engineers were also at work on on overhead-valve rendition for serious competition.

Early versions of the side-valve Seventy-four (1200cc) V model met with less success. The 1930 machines were plagued with clutch failures, lubrication problems, broken flywheels and other mechanical woes. The problems were corrected within the year, but the early performance of the side-valve big twins did little to capture the fancy of long-term fans of the J models.

The shift to flatheads was accompanied by more weight, probably the loudest complaint of the sporting riders, but the power was sufficent to move the bike and rider along at a reasonable rate. And the V had bigger brakes and tires, more ground clearance and lower seat height. By 1933, in addition to more streamlined tanks and fenders, the big twin had improved cylinders, better intake manifold, more efficient oil pump and aluminum alloy pistons. And a healthy output of 36 horsepower. ▶

Although the Depression had severely curtailed motorcycle sales, Harley-Davidson had demonstrated the power and strength of its side-valve engines in the early 1930s. But the founders had decided by 1932 to build an overhead-valve, 1000cc V-twin with recirculating oil system. Nearly five years in development, the E 61 appeared in 1936 and quickly picked up its nickname, the Knucklehead, an allusion to the bulbous rocker boxes atop the engine.

The bony rocker box covers and polished pushrod tubes announced the arrival of many a motorcyclist's fondest dream, more horsepower. The Knucklehead combined engine design and styling in the fashion of aircraft engines, and threw in 37

(1936 EL)
Engine: Ohv 45° V-twin
Displacement: 989cc
Horsepower: 40
Wheelbase: 59.5in (151cm)
Weight: 565lb (256kg)
Top speed: 100mph (161kph)
Price: $380

Below: One of the most enduring graphics ever produced, the Art Deco tank emblem was used from 1936 through 1939. Teak red and black was one of the most popular color schemes for the Knucklehead. The stylized fishtail exhaust tip was a handsome touch.

horsepower in the high-compression EL, with a double-loop cradle frame and four-speed transmission. The standard E would pull to about 90mph (145kph), and the more robust EL could touch 100 (161kph). Here began the musclebike movement, soon to be curtailed by the advent of World War II.

Right: Instrument panels had also fallen within the designer's domain. This was the first standard equipment Harley speedometer.

1936 EL
Owner – Otis Chandler
Ojai, California

To Milwaukee's good fortune, the Knucklehead came to market just as the Depression was on its way out. No other motorcycle had captured the attention of American riders in the way the E models had. And to certify their bragging rights in the top speed dialogues, Harley-Davidson sent racer Joe Petrali to Daytona, Florida in March of 1937. The San Francisco flash put the Knucklehead through the timing lights at 136mph (219kph). The new model, which would stay in production for 12 years, met with early success and gave Milwaukee another stride on Springfield.

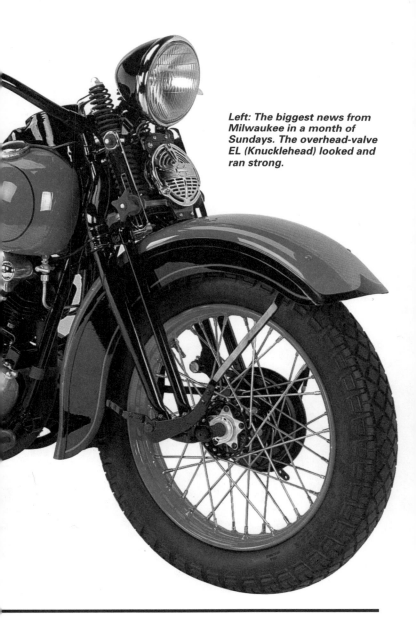

Left: The biggest news from Milwaukee in a month of Sundays. The overhead-valve EL (Knucklehead) looked and ran strong.

The appearance of the Knucklehead did not mean the end of the venerable side-valve twins. The 80-inch (1340cc) VLH also debuted in 1936, with new cylinder heads with modified combustion chambers. The big twin came in response to the similar model offered by Indian, and to cover all bets since the ohv engine was as yet unproven in the marketplace. The flatheads also offered the recirculating oil system.

(1936 VLH)
Engine: Flathead 45° V-twin
Displacement: 1340cc
Horsepower: 34
Wheelbase: 60in (152cm)
Weight: 545lb (247kg)
Top speed: 90mph (145kph)
Price: $340

In 1938 the V-series machines switched to the U designation, with the double-downtube frame and four-speed transmission as standard equipment. The 1000 and 1200cc engines shared a common bore, which allowed economy of production for pistons. The ammeter and oil gauge were replaced in 1938 by red and green warning lights, and new color options were added.

The side-valve Forty-five inherited

Right: Sherwood green and silver was an optional color scheme in 1936. The fork spring cover was one-year-only item on the big twins.

Below: Both the Seventy-four and Eighty were offered with an optional four-speed transmission for an additional fee of $15.

1936 VLH
Owner – Dave Royal
Arroyo Grande, California

Above: The high-performance option added $25 to the cost of a standard model. The roller-bearing engine was good for 27 horsepower.

most of the improvements made to the big twins. Harley-Davidson was pressed for a response to the popular Indian Sport Scout, and consideration was given to an overhead-valve 750. That project was shelved as too costly, and the engineers proceeded to upgrade the R models. The WLDR was built as the basis for a Class C racing motorcycle. Much of the credit for increasing the horsepower of the flathead Forty-fives went to San Jose dealer Tom Sifton. His work would make the Harleys more competitive with the Indian racers.

▶

(1938 WLDR)
Engine: Flathead 45° V-twin
Displacement: 746cc
Horsepower: 27
Wheelbase: 56.5in (143.5cm)
Weight: 390lb (177kg)
Top speed: 85mph (137kph)
Price: $380

Below: Class C dirt-track racing was picking up speed. The WLDR was introduced in 1937, with more hot rods on the way. Althought the Harley-Davidson 750 was not quite so agile as its Indian counterpart, nor as quick, the battle was heating up nicely.

1938 WLDR
Owner – Armando Magri
Sacramento, California

Harley's three-wheeled Servi-Car was first produced in 1932. Motive power came from the flathead Forty-five with a three-speed transmission (pluse reverse). The drivetrain was standard chain to the rear axle where a sprocket spun the auto-type differential. The trike found broad application in auto repair shops, small businesses, police forces and among moonshiners. In 1941 the Servi-Car had a stronger frame and brake drums, with the front stopper from the Seventy-four.

(1941 GA)
Engine: Flathead 45° V-twin
Displacement: 742cc
Horsepower: 22
Wheelbase: 61in (155cm)
Weight: 1,360lb (619kg)
Top speed: 50mph (80kph)
Price: $510

The most rigorous attention was now devoted to the war situation, and the increasing inevitability of American participation. Government contracts called for a prototype motorcycle that would get to at least 65mph (105kph) and perform at continuous low speeds without overheating. Both Indian and Harley-Davidson created military versions of their Forty-fives, and by 1940 Milwaukee was shipping the WLA to the U.S. Army and the British military. Soldiers in the Chinese and Soviet

Above and below: Although never produced in large quantities, the Servi-Car was serviceable and extended the life of the 750cc side-valve.

1941 GA Servi-Car
Owner – Trev Deeley Museum
Vancouver, British Columbia

armed forces would also be aboard Harleys during the war.

The XA was built on the notion that since BMWs had performed well in the African desert, the allied forces might need a boxer clone. The XA had shaft drive, four-speed foot-shift trans-mission and plunger rear suspension, and the front fork was borrowed from the WLA. Harley-Davidson built about 1,000 of the opposed twins, but the army then weighed the expense/performance ratio against the WLA and chose the latter. Plus, the arrival of the Jeep fullfilled the military requirements for a light, most-terrain vehicle.

Right: The BMW-style opposed twin was built at the request of the military, which had been impressed with the German bike's performance. Although the shaft-drive opposed twin never saw combat in World War II, it was an imposing presence with the fork-mounted Thompson submachine gun.

(1941 WLA)
Engine: Flathead 45° V-twin
Displacement: 740cc
Horsepower: 23.5
Wheelbase: 57.5in (146cm)
Weight: 540lb (245kg)
Top speed: 65mph (105kph)
Price: $380

Below: The standard front fork was lengthened nearly 2.5 inches (6.35cm) to provide added ground clearance. The WLA saw active service with most Allied forces.

1942 XA 750
Owner – Fred Lange
Santa Maria, California

1942 WLA
Owner – Trev Deeley Museum
Vancouver, British Columbia

(1941 FL)
Engine: Ohv 45° V-twin
Displacement: 1208cc
Horsepower: 48
Wheelbase: 59.5in (151cm)
Weight: 575lb (261kg)
Top speed: 95mph (153kph)
Price: $465

1941 FL
Owner – Armando Magri
Sacramento, California

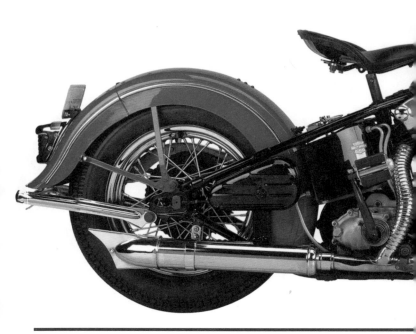

Left: The Knucklehead added a 1200cc version in 1941, with both bore and stroke increases. The rocket-fin muffler was another styling touch.

Below: Only the Deluxe model had touches like the chromed rims and instrument panel. Stainless steel trim was added to the tank. Two-tone paint was no longer available in 1941, and customers could choose from a menu of only four solid colors. Fatter 5.00 x 16in tires were standard on the big twins, for a claimed improvement in riding comfort. Low speed handling suffered.

Harley-Davidson began refining the Knucklehead from the beginning, first with an improved clutch in 1937. Two years later it tried a new transmission that combined constant-mesh and sliding gear systems, which put neutral between second and third gears. This proved not altogether satisfactory, and and a new transmission appeared the following year. The 74-inch (1200cc) model was first offered in 1941, and both big twins had new crankcases, stronger crankpins and an improved lubrication system.

Knucklehead styling was changed only slightly in 1941. Stainless steel strips adorned the sides of the fuel tank, and the

(1941 ULH)
Engine: Flathead 45° V-twin
Displacement: 1340cc
Horsepower: 34
Wheelbase: 60in (152cm)
Weight: 545lb (247kg)
Top speed: 90mph (145kph)
Price: $410

Below: The big-inch flathead made its final bow in 1941. Aluminum heads were standard on the Eighty and optional equipment on the Seventy-four.

speedometer face had larger silver numbers on a black background. Cruiser green replaced Squadron gray on the paint roster.

The war postponed any further development of the motorcycles, and Milwaukee was well occupied with the production of military machines. Improvements made before the shift to combat hardware, however, were now standard equipment; aluminum heads, cast iron brake drums and stronger forks. The eighty-inch flathead made its final appearance in 1941.

Harley-Davidson did take civilian casualties during the war, albeit from natural causes. Walter Davidson died in 1942 at age 64, and William Harley, 63, passed in 1943.

▶

1941 ULH
Owner – Harold Mathews
Fresno, California

By 1945 Milwaukee was looking ahead to the resumption of civilian production, and some of the art deco styling touches began fading away. The cat's-eye instrument panel and streamlined beehive taillight made their last appearance in 1946. Few Knuckleheads had been produced during the war, and by 1946 the numbers of Seventy-four and Sixty-one engines was on the rise again. The big-bore engine in the FL sold in much greater numbers.

Material shortages were still in effect, however. Some of the early models for 1946 lacked chrome tank badges and stainless steel trim pieces. The only color options were gray and red until the middle of the year, when blue and black were available once again.

With victory in Europe came manufacturing rights from DKW of Germany, and the appearance of the 125 S two-stroke single. The little three-horsepower transportation special would launch the motorcycling careers of thousands of youngsters in the 1940s and 1950s, many of whom naturally moved on to heavyweight Harleys when financial stability permitted. The 125, latter tagged the Hummer, eventually grew to 165cc and 175cc engines and expanded to dual-purpose models. The Teutonic two-stroke stayed on the Milwaukee menu for 20 years.

(1946 FL)
Engine: Ohv 45° V-twin
Displacement: 1208cc
Horsepower: 48
Wheelbase: 59.5in (151cm)
Weight: 575lb (261kg)
Top speed: 95mph (153kph)
Price: $465

Below: The hinged rear fender remained standard. Optional saddlebag styles with choices of trim began to appear after the war.

Right: The shock absorber between the fork springs first appeared in 1946. Only red and gray paint were available until half way through the year.

1946 F
Owner – Ken Lang
Oakville, Ontario, Canada

1948 125 Model S
Owner – Fred Lange
Santa Maria, California

(1948 125 Model S)
Engine: Two-stroke single
Displacement: 125cc
Horsepower: 3
Wheelbase: 50in (127cm)
Weight: 185lb (84kg)
Top speed: 50mph (80kph)
Price: $325

Left: After the war, Harley shared
with BSA the rights to the
German DKW 125cc two-stroke.
Later it would be rechristened the
Hummer.

Below: The lightweight was not
embraced by most Harley dealers,
but it did provide a start for novice
riders on a tight budget.

One engineering development that emerged from the war years was the adoption of a hydraulic shock absorber on the front fork. But the Knucklehead itself was headed for the background, and the final editions were built for 1947. The last E models wore the new speedball nameplate on the tanks, and the "tombstone" taillight. The instrument panel was also revised for 1947. The last Knuckleheads, nearly 12,000

machines, accounted for more than half of the year's total production.

Milwaukee's next large evolutionary step came with the Panhead in 1948. So named for its inverted pan valve covers, the new engine varied little from the Knucklehead in the bottom end. But the new cylinders carried oil lines on the inside, the heads were made of aluminum and the pushrods rode on hydraulic valve lifters. The new FL ran cooler than its

Below: The last of the Knuckleheads, officially known as the E and EL models, appeared in 1947.

Right: Skyway blue, Cruiser green, Flight red and Brilliant black were the color options. Milwaukee built nearly 12,000 Knuckleheads for 1947.

1947 FL
Owner – Trev Deeley Museum
Vancouver, British Columbia

predecessor, required less fine tuning and generally lasted longer.

The new engine was slightly larger, which necessitated a new frame, but the size and weight of the Panhead was on par with the Knuckle. The engine produced about two more horsepower than the earlier version. The 1948 model gained the double distinction of being the first Panhead and the last edition of the springer front fork. In 1949 Harley-Davidson took another hop in the contemporary modern world we live in today with the introduction of the telescopic Hydra-Glide fork.

(1948 FL)
Engine: Ohv 45° V-twin
Displacement: 1208cc
Horsepower: 50
Wheelbase: 59.5in (151cm)
Weight: 565lb (256kg)
Top speed: 100mph (161kph)
Price: $650

Below: The hinged fender remained a standard feature for easy access to the rear wheel. The oil tank and tool box were originally painted black. Mufflers were also still painted black, but many owners had them chromed to match the rest of the shiny bits.

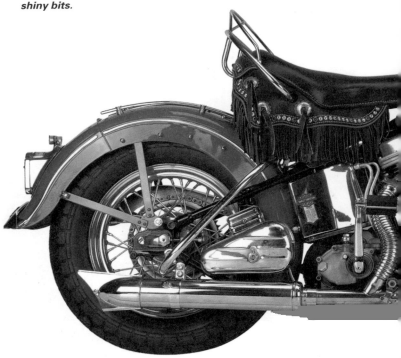

1947 FL
Owner – Mike Lady
Arroyo Grande, California

Above: The Deluxe Solo Group included chrome fender tips, exhaust pipe covers, wheels and other items, adding $92 to the price.

Harley dealers were provided with demonstation models for the first time in 1950, and encouraged to offer test rides to customers. The post-war rise in motorcycle sales, and foreign competition, were accompanied by greater efforts to promote the sport at the dealer level. And the prominent selling point was the new Hydra-Glide front fork, introduced in 1949. Two new colors, burgundy and

peacock blue, were also added to the roster. Metallic congo green was available for an additional $8.00.

Telescopic front suspension was just the first of several improvements from Milwaukee in the 1950s. The intake ports on the ohv twins were redesigned and enlarged for more power in 1950, and quieter mufflers were introduced to combat the growing problem created by in-

(1950 EL)
Engine: Ohv 45° V-twin
Displacement: 989cc
Horsepower: 40
Wheelbase: 59.5in (151cm)
Weight: 565lb (256kg)
Top speed: 95mph (153kph)
Price: $735

Right: The Panhead's next modern attribute was the telescopic front fork. And the options of foot shift and hand clutch were not far off.

Below: The Deluxe Solo Saddle was an alternative to the Buddy Seat. It was also included in the Standard Police Group for officers of the law. King Size saddlebags were a $34 option in 1950. Smaller Streamliner bags were $27.

Basic black was soon joined by other colors. The tank nameplate, designed by Brooks Stevens for 1947 models, was used for the last time in 1950.

1950 EL
Owner – Trev Deeley Museum
Vancouver, British Columbia

creasingly loud motorcycles. The year ended sadly when Arthur Davidson, last of the four founding members, died in an automobile accident.

The Hydra-Glide label became an official model name in 1952, and Harley twins would henceforth have names rather than just numbers. But the big news in '52 was the debut of foot shift and hand clutch as an option, although the hand shift would remain on the Milwaukee menu for another 20 years. Even quieter mufflers were introduced and the exhaust valves were designed to rotate when open, which equalized wear and maintained good compression.

(1952 FL)
Engine: Ohv 45° V-twin
Displacement: 1208cc
Horsepower: 55
Wheelbase: 59.5in (151cm)
Weight: 590lb (268kg)
Top speed: 100mph (161kph)
Price: $970

Below: The foot-shift mechanism was a bit awkward, and incorporated a booster system nicknamed the "mousetrap."

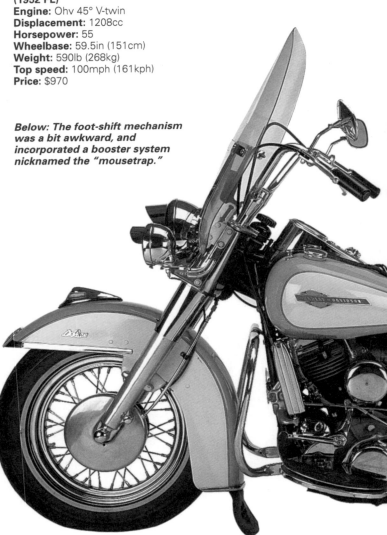

1952 FL
Owner –John Tosta
Hanford, California

Above: The Modern Age arrived in full with the adoption of foot shift and hand clutch controls in 1952. Hand shift remained an option.

The flathead Forty-five continued its evolutionary climb with the K model in 1952. The four-speed transmission, shifted by foot, was incorporated within the engine cases, the clutch operated by hand and both wheels were hydraulically suspended. The mildly-tuned 30-horsepower engine didn't set any performance records, but the K model indicated that Milwaukee had recognized the need for a sports machine to combat the growing number of British imports.

The racing version, designated KR, would replace the venerable WR in dirt-track and roadracing trim. Bill Miller won the 1952 Peoria TT on the new model, and in 1953 Paul Goldsmith broke the Norton string by winning the Daytona 200 and the Langhorne, Pennsylvania national. Joe Leonard won four national events in '53, and with eight wins in '54

(1952 K)
Engine: Flathead 45° V-twin
Displacement: 743cc
Horsepower: 30
Wheelbase: 56.5in (143.5cm)
Weight: 400lb (181kg)
Top speed: 80mph (129kph)
Price: $865

(1955 FL)
Engine: Ohv 45° V-twin
Displacement: 1208cc
Horsepower: 60
Wheelbase: 59.5in (151cm)
Weight: 598lb (271kg)
Top speed: 105mph (169kph)
Price: $1,083

Below: The K model offered swingarm rear suspension, unit construction transmission, foot shift and choice of buckhorn or low handlebars. Tire options included 3.25 x 18 or 19, and potential hot-rod riders could order up a 4.00 x 18 on the rear and 3.50 x 18 front.

1955 FLH
Owner – Paul Wheeler
Van Nuys, California

*Above: Speed King saddlebags,
Buddy seat with auxiliary springs
and Trumpet Jubilee horn adorn
the sylish FLH.*

1952 K
Owner – Fred Lange
Santa Maria, California

became the first national champion based on total points.

The 1000cc Panhead was deleted in 1953 in favor of the more popular 1200cc version. New intake manifolds with better sealing were adopted in 1954, and the more powerful FLH made its appearance the following year. The new Panhead was stronger throughout, with higher compression and a rating of 60 horsepower. In addition to five standard colors, Hollywood green was offered as an extra cost option at $10.

Right: For just $1000, the sporting rider could afford one of the flashiest Harley-Davidsons ever to roll on the highways.

Below: In 1955 the KHK included a speed kit composed of a roller-bearing bottom end, polished ports and hotter cams. High performance was coming.

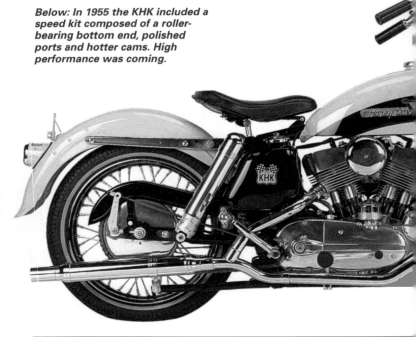

1955 KHK
Owner – Otis Chandler
Ojai, California

The KH Sports Twin was awarded a Speed Kit in 1955, and with the $68 option was designated the KHK. The H was added in 1953 when the Forty-five became a Fifty-four, and the displacement grew to 883cc. The racing model KR remained a 750. Brad Andres won the national title in 1955, and Joe Leonard was again champion in 1956 and '57. An overhead-valve version of the K

model had been in development for several years.

The XL, also known as the Sportster, arrived in 1957. The hot rod movement reached a high pitch in the mid-fifties; cars and motorcycles seemed suddenly faster, flashier and far more visible. Young men became more distracted from their studies, and young women from the cautions of their mothers. As the Korean War

(1957 XL)
Engine: Ohv 45° V-twin
Displacement: 883cc
Horsepower: 40
Wheelbase: 57in (145cm)
Weight: 495lb (225kg)
Top speed: 101mph (163kph)
Price: $1,103

Below: Pepper red and black and Skyline blue and white were popular color schemes. Metallic midnight blue and white was an option.

1957 XL
Owner – Otis Chandler
Ojai, California

Above: The subdued tank badge gave no hint of the Sportster's intentions as a street racer. And, at first, neither did the performance.

faded to history, Americans decided the time had come to rock 'n roll.

Like the K model, the Sportster did not set speed records tumbling in its first iteration. But ensuing editions quickly displayed the potential offered by unit construction, less weight and more horsepower. Milwaukee had

Below: The trumpet jubilee horn made the transition from the big twins. Gears were inside the cases and were shifted by the right foot.

once again introduced a new model in conservative trim, and waited to see how the motorcycling public would react. That reaction was over-whel- mingly positive, and the Sportster soon took its place as the premier American factory street racer among the two-wheeled hot-rodders. ▶

Form and function were both enhanced in 1958 with the arrival of the Duo-Glide, with rear suspension and whitewall tires. The successor to the Hydra-Glide also boasted a hydraulic rear brake, stronger clutch and transmission, better exhaust manifolds and a new oil tank. The least popular change was the plastic nameplate on the tank. (Though some old timers failed to see the need for rear shock absorbers.)

Although the Panhead was gaining weight and moving parts, the motorcycle generally ran better and longer than its predecessors and was relatively easy to ride. The rear suspension made two-up travel a more comfortable proposition, especially when long distances were involved. And Harley-Davidson offered still more complete lists of

(1958 FLH)
Engine: Ohv 45° V-twin
Displacement: 1208cc
Horsepower: 52
Wheelbase: 60in (152cm)
Weight: 648lb (294kg)
Top speed: 100mph (161kph)
Price: $1,320

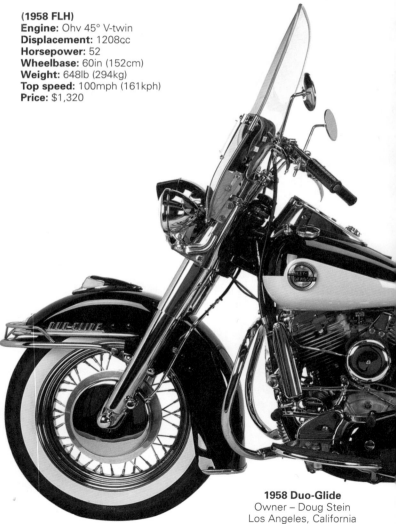

1958 Duo-Glide
Owner – Doug Stein
Los Angeles, California

*Above and below: What was
Hydra-Glide was now Duo-Glide,
with the addition of swingarm
suspension behind the seat. Thus
the Duo-.*

options; the King of the Higway group included saddlebags, chrome luggage rack, dual exhausts, fender tips and bumpers.

The Sportster lineup expanded in 1958 with the addition of the XLH and XLCH. The latter fulfilled the hot rodders' requests for a high-performance version for road and track. The CH was built originally as a scrambler, with a 19-inch front wheel and no battery, lights or muffler. The flathead K model remained the official racing rig, but the Sportster hearalded a new generation of Milwaukee roadsters. ▶

(1958 XLCH)
Engine: Ohv 45° V-twin
Displacement: 883cc
Horsepower: 45
Wheelbase: 57in (145cm)
Weight: 480lb (218kg)
Top speed: 115mph (185kph)
Price: $1,155

Below: The hot rod movement led directly to the 1968 XLCH Sportster, a lean and mean street-fighting machine from the beer capital of America.

Right: The KR replicates the motorcycle ridden by Texan factory rider Carroll Resweber, who won the national title four years running.

1960 KR
Owner – Ron Stratman
Sturgis, South Dakota

Below: The XLCH image had been pared down to the essentials in terms of both form and function. Big motor, small tank, wheels. Go. The leanest Sportster was still pushed hard against the Norton, BSA and Triumph on the open roads; but it pushed back.

1968 XLCH
Owner – Otis Chandler
Ojai, California

179

Facing the influx of imported British and European lightweights, Harley-Davidson purchased part ownership of Italy's Aeronautica Macchi in 1960. Aermacchi/Harley-Davidson brought in the 250cc Sprint, an overhead-valve single slung horizontally in a single-strut frame. The line was later expanded to include a 350cc version in road trim and off-road configurations.

(1961 Sprint)
Engine: Ohv horizontal single
Displacement: 246cc
Horsepower: 18
Wheelbase: 52in (132cm)
Weight: 275lb (125kg)
Top speed: 75mph (121kph)
Price: $690

Below: The persistent urge to offer a lightweight motorcycle was hanging on in Milwaukee. The Aermacchi filled some of the need.

The XLR became the competition edition of the Sportster, with ball-bearing crankshaft, hot cams, and racing pistons, valves and heads. The R model was built for TT scrambles racing, one component of the national championship series. With the aid of San Francisco tuner Jim Belland at Dud Perkins Harley-Davidson, factory riders Mert Lawwill and Mark Brelsford did well on the XLR.

Right: The XLR distilled the competition image even further, and backed it up with less weight and more horsepower. This engine was used in all forms of motorcycle racing equipment. The bracing below the steering head helped keep the frame in one piece.

1962 XLR
Owner – Sam Mathews
Fresno, California

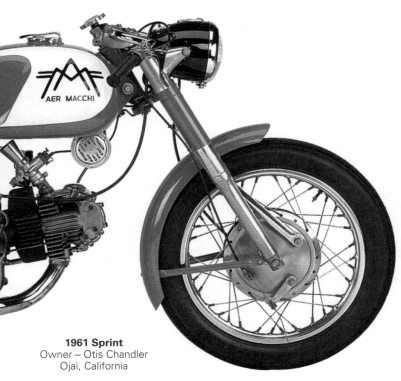

1961 Sprint
Owner – Otis Chandler
Ojai, California

The XLCH remained the street rod rendition of the Sportster, and by 1964 was just about the fastest machine on the road. With about 60 horsepower, the XLCH got to 60mph (97kph) in six seconds and was capable of 14-second quarter-mile times. Few stock motorcycles of the day could keep up with the lean Sportster. The full-width aluminum front brake hub was an Aermacchi product. The Sporty reached its high-performance pinnacle in the mid-sixties.

(1964 XLCH)
Engine: Ohv 45° V-twin
Displacement: 883cc
Horsepower: 60
Wheelbase: 57in (145cm)
Weight: 480lb (218kg)
Top speed: 115mph (185kph)
Price: $1,360

Below: The XLCH Sportster retained its profile as a purpose-built street scrambler for the urban jungle as well as the rural backroads.

1962 XLR
Owner – Sam Mathews
Fresno, California

*Above: The magneto had moved
from the side of the engine to the
front. Heads, cams, pistons and
valves were all performance items.*

1964 XLCH
Owner – Randy Janson
El Cajon, California

The Duo-Glide yielded in 1965 to the Electra Glide, the first big twin with an electric starter and the final Panhead. In steady production for 18 years, the trusty engine was a Harley for all purposes and deserved meritorious retirement. The final edition featured 12-volt electrics, new frame and of course more weight. The motorcycle sales boom had arrived, and Harley-Davidson saw its market share diminish. So it was time for New Products.

The Electra Glide carried its oil tank on the left, yielding space to the large battery on the right. The engine

(1965 FLH)
Engine: Ohv 45° V-twin
Displacement: 1208cc
Horsepower: 60
Wheelbase: 60in (152cm)
Weight: 783lb (355kg)
Top speed: 100mph (161kph)
Price: $1,595

Right: The addition of an electric starter insured collector status for the 1965 Electra Glide. Production of the Panhead reached almost 7,000 in 1965, the highest number since its introduction in 1948.

Below: Saddlebag styles evolved to integrate more readily with the motorcycles. The first fiberglass units came in 1963.

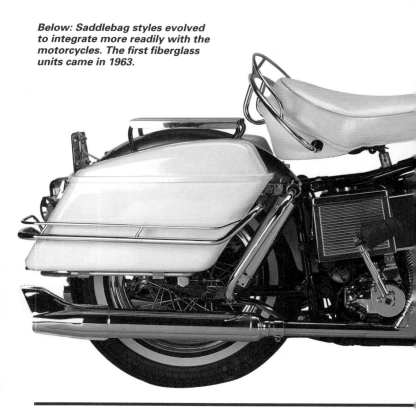

Above:

1965 FLH
Owner – Fred Lange
Santa Maria, California

cases were strengthened to accommodate the added stress of the electric starter, and the spark advance was now an automatic rather than manual affair. And the jubilee trumpet horn was gone, replaced by a disc type. Most importantly, the engine started with the push of a thumb.

The Electra Glide name carried on in 1966, but the engine designation became the Shovelhead, so named for its industrial rocker boxes. And, despite some internal struggles with new management (and subsequent quality control bothers), the Shovel endured for 18 years just as the Panhead had. The new heads were enlarged aluminum versions of the Sportster heads, with combustion chambers good for an increase of five horsepower.

(1966 FLH)
Engine: Ohv 45° V-twin
Displacement: 1208cc
Horsepower: 60
Wheelbase: 60in (152cm)
Weight: 783lb (355kg)
Top speed: 100mph (161kph)
Price: $1,610

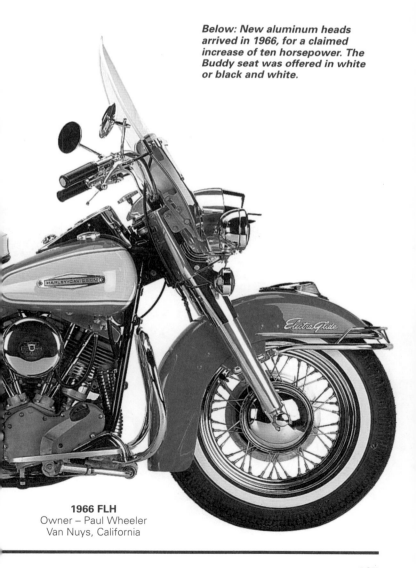

Below: New aluminum heads arrived in 1966, for a claimed increase of ten horsepower. The Buddy seat was offered in white or black and white.

1966 FLH
Owner – Paul Wheeler
Van Nuys, California

The Sportster for 1966 benefited from more radical cam and head work, for an engine rated at 60 horsepower. The "ham can" air cleaner also made its debut, the result of federal noise and emission standards, and was not well received in terms of style. The Tillotson carburetor was also a new item.

The Sprint lineup expanded in the mid-1960s to include an on/off-road model, scrambler and roadracer. Italian roadracing star Renzo Pasolini was third in the world championship in 1966 on a 350 version. In 1967 the engine had more bore and less stroke, and featured aluminum cylinders and heads. Factory riders Fred Nix and Bart Markel campaigned Sprints successfully in short-track dirt racing.

When the American Motorcycle Association discarded the 750cc

Below: The Italian single was a strong contender in the lightweight class, though it would soon be outgunned by the Japanese two-strokes.

1966 XLH
Owner – Trev Deeley Museum
Vancouver, British Columbia

Above: The XLH in standard trim as a sport-touring machine. Few Sportsters remained in this configuration.

1966 Sprint CRTT
Owner – Trev Deeley Museum
Vancouver, British Columbia

flathead/500cc ohv rule, Harley-Davidson was caught with an obsolete racing bike. The factory made do with a de-stroked XLR , with iron heads and cylinders, until the new alloy engine was available in 1972. Under the direction of racing chief Dick O'Brien, Harley engineers created a racing engine with good power over a broad range that would not blow up too often. The XR 750 went on to dominate American dirt-track racing for most of the next three decades.

(1980 XR 750)
Engine: Ohv 45° V-twin
Displacement: 750cc
Horsepower: 90
Wheelbase: 57in (145cm)
Weight: 320lb (145kg)
Top speed: 130mph (209kph)
Price: $4,000

Right: Exhaust systems were tuned for optimum power output at the high end of the engine's capability; and they were kept clear of the ground.

Below: The XR 750 changed little over the years. The engine proved especially well suited to the demands of dirt-track racing. Dirt-track tires offered the best combination of traction and predictable sideslip. Racers hand-cut treads to suit track conditions. Front brakes were deemed unneccesary for flat-track racing, and the possibility for accidents ruled them out.

1980 XR 750
Owner – Otis Chandler
Ojai, California

1971 FX Super Glide
Owner – Otis Chandler
Ojai, California

In 1969 Harley-Davidson, steadily losing customers to European and Japanese manufacturers, agreed to a buyout from American Machine and Foundry Company (AMF). The objectives were to build more motorcycles and improve their quality. The first objective was met.

William G. Davidson, grandson of the founding William A. and son of former president William H., joined the company as styling director in 1963. One of his design projects was a synthesis of contemporary motorcycle styles that culminated in the Super Glide for 1971. Designated the FX, the new model combined elements of the Electra Glide and the Sportster, a 1200cc sport/cruiser. Although not notably successful in ▶

Left: The Euro-style seat/tail-section was not met with approval by most American riders. It was discontinued in short order. The Super Glide was an experiment that achieved success in the long run, leading to several generations of factory customs.

(1971 FX)
Engine: Ohv 45° V-twin
Displacement: 1208cc
Horsepower: 65
Wheelbase: 62in (157.5cm)
Weight: 560lb (254kg)
Top speed: 110mph (177kph)
Price: $2,500

terms of design (the boat-tail seat/fender was shouted down), the Super Glide became the fundamental platform for generations of "factory customs." The FX was a kick start-only model for its first three years, and disc brakes also came along with the option of electric start. A smaller tank and seat were also on the menu.

With the high-performance push coming from Japan, Harley-Davidson pumped up the Sportster with more power in 1972. Milwaukee took the traditional approach of adding cubic inches, so the Sporty went from 883 to 1000cc. The big-bore Sportster accelerated quicker and had a top speed close to 120mph (193kph).

(1972 XLH)
Engine: Ohv 45° V-twin
Displacement: 1000cc
Horsepower: 61
Wheelbase: 58.5in (148.5cm)
Weight: 530lb (240kg)
Top speed: 116mph (187kph)
Price: $2,120

*Below: Most riders equipped the
Sportster with minimal seating
capabilities. A front disc brake
appeared a year later.*

1972 XLH
Owner – James Kirchner
San Diego, California

Below: Tinted windshields remained popular accessories. This is an early 1972 model, reflected by the drum rather than disc front brake.

The transition of family-owned Harley-Davidson to coporate-owned AMF H-D was not entirely smooth. Management disputes, labor difficulties and increasingly tight government regulations caused numerous problems. And it took most of the decade to sort them out.

In 1972 the Electra Glide received a front disc brake, though early models were delivered with drum brakes. Production under AMF had increased markedly, with total output for 1972 at almost 60,000 machines. But the rush to build more motorcycles created quality control ▶

(1972 FLH)
Engine: Ohv 45° V-twin
Displacement: 1208cc
Horsepower: 66
Wheelbase: 61.5in (156cm)
Weight: 783lb (355kg)
Top speed: 100mph (161kph)
Price: $2,500

Below: Spotlights were among the long list of optional equipment available for the Electra Glide. Chromed sidecovers were accessory items. The saddlebags and the tank nameplate are items from earlier eras.

1972 FLH
Owner – Bob Rocchio
San Francisco, California

problems, which would often have to be solved by the dealers, which made them unhappy. The moodiness extended to customers when the machines failed to perform as expected. In 1973 Harley-Davidson manufactured more than 70,000 motorcycles.

The Sprint had been abandoned in favor of two-stroke lightweights from Aermacchi. The growth of off-road riding and motocross had expanded considerable in ten years, and the field was crowded with European and Japanese two-strokes. Milwaukee's efforts in this market were too little too late, and in 1978 the Aermacchi interest was sold to the Italian Cagiva group. ▶

(1975 SX 250)
Engine: Two-stroke single
Displacement: 243cc
Horsepower: 18
Wheelbase: 54in (137cm)
Weight: 270lb (122kg)
Top speed: 73mph (117kph)
Price: $1,130

Right: The dual-purpose two-stroke was expanded from 175cc to 250cc, and replaced the four-strokes as Milwaukee's off-road lightweights.

(1975 MX 250)
Engine: Two-stroke single
Displacement: 243cc
Horsepower: 32
Wheelbase: 58in (147cm)
Weight: 247lb (112kg)
Top speed: 70mph (113kph)
Price: $1,695

1976 MX 250
Owner – Oliver Shokouh
Glendale, California

1975 SX 250
Owner – Trev Deeley Museum
Vancouver, British Columbia

*Below: Milwaukee's entry in the
growing motocross market was
hampered by lack of development.
The Aermacchi link was eventually
abandoned in 1978.*

199

Harley-Davidson's next editions in the hot rod and cruiser modes were considerably more focused than the original FX. The cruiser market had grown steadily during the first half of the 1970s, and the second generation Super Glide garnered higher sales each year. The sport bike movement, driven largely by racing enthusiasts in the motorcycle press, also showed potential for more numbers.

Willie G. attempted to capture some of the Euro-style cafe racer market with the XLCR, a modified Sporster with cast alloy wheels, small fairing and low handlebar. The black-on-black motif made an arresting image, and the performance was a few notches above the standard Sportster. But as a street-legal roadracer the XLCR was no match for better-handling mounts from Europe and the increasingly powerful four-cylinder machines from Japan. The Cafe Racer was discontinued after two years.

(1977 XLCR)
Engine: Ohv 45° V-twin
Displacement: 1000cc
Horsepower: 68
Wheelbase: 58.5in (148.5cm)
Weight: 515lb (234kg)
Top speed: 110mph (177kph)
Price: $3,623

Below: The Sportster engine was given a black paint job and siamesed exhaust system which bumped the horsepower by five over the standard. The bikini fairing, Morris cast wheels and Kelsey-Hayes brakes helped give the XLCR the appearance of a serious backroads scratcher.

1977 XLCR
Owner – Oliver Shokouh
Glendale, California

Above: The Cafe Racer was an attempt to capitalize on the Euro-style street rods of the 1970s, but it lasted for only two years.

1977 XLCR
Owner – Otis Chandler
Ojai, California

Much greater success was achieved by Willie's other design, the FXS Low Rider, patterned on the styles made popular by individual builders of customs and choppers. Cruiser styling became more popular each year, and soon the Japanese manufacturers were enticed to join the trend. None succeeded so well as the Low Rider, which set the standard for custom/cruiser looks and spawned several more generations in the FX series which remain in prod-uction today.

(1977 FXS)
Engine: Ohv 45° V-twin
Displacement: 1208cc
Horsepower: 65
Wheelbase: 63.5in (161cm)
Weight: 623lb (283kg)
Top speed: 100mph (161kph)
Price: $3,475

Below: In its debut year the FXS was offered only in gunmetal gray. The low handlebar and stepped seat mirrored the chopper style of the 1970s. The success of the Low Rider helped counteract the lack of response to the Cafe Racer. The FXS spawned a growing roster of factory customs.

Right: Traditional dual tanks held the speedometer and tachometer. The oil pressure and neutral indicator lights resided on the FXS headlight nacelle.

1977 FXS
Owner – Oliver Shokouh
Glendale, California

By 1978, Harley-Davidson's 75th anniversary, the popularity of cruisers was well established. Milwaukee celebrated the mark with anniversary editions of the Electra Glide and Sportster in black and gold livery. And the big twin got bigger, with an 80 cubic inch (1340cc) engine. The Eighty would see duty the following year in the FXEF, also known as the Fat Bob, an earlier appellation for a customized big twin. With capital letters it became a registered trademark owned by Harley-Davidson.

The FXEF carried the Low Rider look a step further, with larger fuel tanks, more deeply stepped seat and dual exhausts providing a more muscular image. Available with either the 1200 or 1340cc engine, the Fat Bob signaled Milwaukee's intention to keep pace with the evolving custom trends and offer customers more choices. That was more apparent the following year with the introduction of another Willie G. special, the Sturgis.

The next cruiser configuration carried the designation FXB, and the final letter was significant because it

(1979 FXEF)
Engine: Ohv 45° V-twin
Displacement: 1338cc
Horsepower: 66
Wheelbase: 63.5in (161cm)
Weight: 642lb (291kg)
Top speed: 105mph (169kph)
Price: $4,260

Below: The FXEF was available with either the 1200 or 1340cc engine, and cast or traditional spoked wheels.

1979 FXEF
Owner – Brad Richardson
Hemet, California

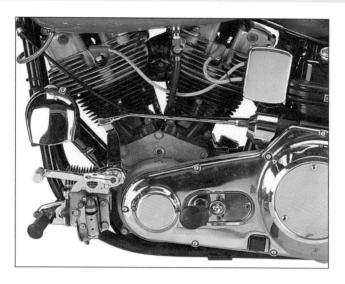

Above: Forward-mounted controls were essential for highway cruising; standard pegs were retained for city riding. The horn is mounted at the front of the engine.

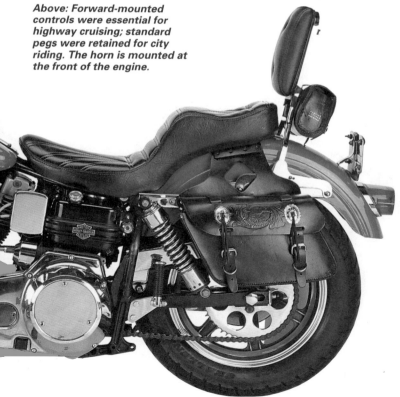

205

indicated belt drive. Since Harley-Davidson hadn't used belts since 1914, this came as something of a surprise and caused a bit of apprehension. But fears about breakage and reliabilty proved unfounded, and the drive belts performed better than even Milwaukee had expected. The Gates belts, reinforced with nylon fiber, were good for up to 40,000 miles (64,300km). The Sturgis (named after South Dakota's annual biker bacchanal), was black on black with orange trim. This was Willie G.'s factory road warrior.

(1980 FXB)
Engine: Ohv 45° V-twin
Displacement: 1338cc
Horsepower: 65
Wheelbase: 64.7in (164cm)
Weight: 610lb (277kg)
Top speed: 106mph (171kph)
Price: $5,687

Below: The Sturgis was chosen to showcase the re-introduction of belt drive to production motorcycles. The scooped seat with separate pillion pad continued the cruiser theme, and kept seat height a reasonable reach from the tarmac. The mighty 1340cc engine had electronic ignition and two-into-one exhaust plumbing. The oil cooler was standard equipment.

Above: The new drive belts were reinforced with nylon for added strength and endurance. The wear factor was better than expected.

1980 FXB
Owner – Otis Chandler
Ojai, California

207

(1980 FXWG)
Engine: Ohv 45° V-twin
Displacement: 1338cc
Horsepower: 65
Wheelbase: 63.8in (162cm)
Weight: 586lb (266kg)
Top speed: 102mph (164kph)
Price: $5,683

Below: The Wide Glide announced Milwaukee's intent to expand on the custom themes, with extended fork and flaming paint.

1980 FXWG
Owner – Otis Chandler
Ojai, California

Below: A five-gallon fuel tank provided plenty of geography between stops. The engine's three-point rubber-mount attachment reduced vibration.

Consistent with the continuing deployment of new models, Harley-Davidson released both the FLT Tour Glide and FXWG Wide Glide in 1980. The latter was another variation of the Super Glide, but the Tour Glide had little in common with its Electra brethren. The FLT carried a new frame, with the 1340cc engine situated by a three-point rubber-mount system. The swingarm was bolted to the transmission case, which contained a five-speed gearset.

The Tour Glide signaled ▶

(1980 FLT)
Engine: Ohv 45° V-twin
Displacement: 1338cc
Horsepower: 65
Wheelbase: 62.5in (159cm)
Weight: 781lb (354kg)
Top speed: 95mph (153kph)
Price: $6,961

Below: The Tour Glide incorporated a number of new approaches to the sport touring concept. The frame-mount fairing had dual headlights. Belt drive had yet to reach the FL series, but a new chassis, triple disc brakes and five-speed transmission denoted changes in the wind. Front dual disc brakes and revised frame geometry improved the handling character-istics of the big twin. Seat height was 29 inches (74cm).

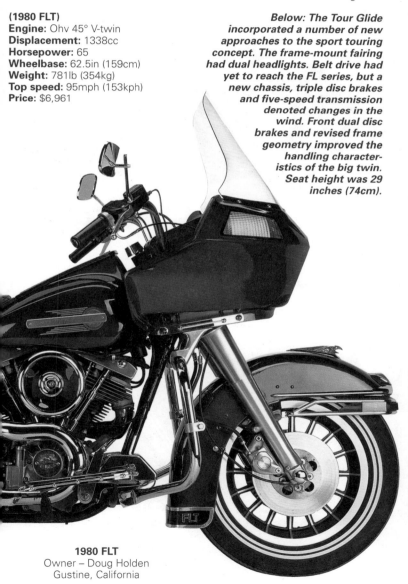

1980 FLT
Owner – Doug Holden
Gustine, California

Below: Footboards enhanced the nostalgic theme invoked by the Heritage Edition. Ham can air cleaners were growing even larger.

1981 FLH
Owner – Trev Deeley Museum
Vancouver, British Columbia

Milwaukee's intent to compete more forcefully with Honda's Gold Wing touring model. The initial objective was to quell some of the big twin's vibration, thus the new mounting system. The next consideration was improved low-speed handling, which was addressed with new frame geometry. And measures were underway to improve engine reliabilty.

The Wide Glide carried the factory custom banner another mile with a kicked out Electra Glide fork and flame paint job. The custom/cruiser motif was showing signs of infinite variation, but the corporate problems at AMF/Harley-Davidson soon prevailed over design decisions. A group of managers bought the company from AMF in 1981, and the '81 FLT would be the final Electra Glide to wear the combined company logo. And there were still hard times ahead. ▶

Below: The Heritage Edition FLH was the final Electra Glide built under the AMF banner. The run was limited to 784 copies.

(1983 XR-1000)
Engine: Ohv 45° V-twin
Displacement: 1000cc
Horsepower: 71
Wheelbase: 60in (152cm)
Weight: 490lb (222kg)
Top speed: 125mph (201kph)
Price: $6,995

1983 XR-1000
Owner – Oliver Shokouh
Glendale, California

*Above: The XR-1000 was a serious
effort at a factory hot-rod, but was
more expensive than its counterparts
and had some hard edges.*

On the eve of its rebirth as a privately-held company, Harley-Davidson faced a sharply falling market for heavyweight motorcycles. But improvements to the products were already well underway. The Super Glide II featured a new frame and rubber-mount engine layout. Designated the FXR, the new Glide carried a five-speed transmission, while the standard FX remained a four-speed with solid-mount engine. The new chassis made the FXR one of Milwaukee's best handling machines.

The XR-1000 was built in reponse to hot rodders' requests for a street-legal version of the XR 750. While that prospect was prohibitively expensive, race chief Dick O'Brien and marketing director Clyde Fessler teamed up to create a street racer based on the XLCR chassis. With trick alloy heads modified by respiration specialist Jerry Branch, the 70-horsepower engine had plenty of punch. But the XR-1000 was a bit temperamental for the average civilian rider, and still too expensive at $7,000. The model was produced ▶

Below: The Super Glide II appeared in 1982, with a new box-section frame, rubber-mount engine and five-speed transmission.

1982 FXR
Owner – Ginger Gammon
Cranleigh, England

1984 FXST
Owner – Dudley Perkins Company
San Francisco, California

only for 1983–84.

The real big gun in Milwaukee's arsenal had been in continuous development, and after a seven-year process, the V2 Evolution engine appeared in the 1984 FXST Softail. Although it was Harley's first all new engine in 50 years, the Evo was still an air-cooled, big-bore V-twin. So the first of the new generation of Harley-Davidson's was, by design, traditional in appearance but far more contemporary in terms of performance. The Evolution engine did not furnish the reborn company with instant success, but did set the foundation for its ensuing salvation and prosperity. ▶

Left: The Softail had its engine solidly mounted to the frame in traditional fashion, but the hardtail-style frame hooked to shock absorbers hidden below the transmission.

(1984 FXST)
Engine: Ohv 45° V-twin
Displacement: 1338cc
Horsepower: 55
Wheelbase: 66.3in (168cm)
Weight: 628lb (285kg)
Top speed: 110mph (177kph)
Price: $7,999

Below: The urban/suburban/rural cruiser was steadily being refined in Milwaukee. The FXST's new Evolution engine retained four-speed transmission. The Softail marked the next generation of retrograde progression in the future of past styles transmogrified by contemporary technology.

The Evolution continued to evolve in the FL rendition of the Softail, designated the FLST. (There is some sense in the lettering system if one pays attention.) The Shovelhead had been shuffled off to history, and by 1985 the Evo was the big twin engine from Harley-Davidson. The Electra Glide became the FLHTC Electra Glide Classic, with five-speed transmission, solid-mount engine and belt drive. The next chapter in Milwaukee's new book of modern engineering and nostalgic styling was the FLST Heritage Classic in 1986.

The retro look was enhanced by the 1950s-style Hydra Glide front fork, jumbo headlight and deeply valenced fenders. The Heritage would be the first in a running series

(1986 FLST)
Engine: Ohv 45° V-twin
Displacement: 1338cc
Horsepower: 55
Wheelbase: 62.5in (159cm)
Weight: 650lb (295kg)
Top speed: 112mph (180kph)
Price: $9,099

Below: The Heritage Softail also kept the solid-mount engine, but was granted the five-speed transmission. But the Look was pure fifties. Disc brakes were at odds with the retro architecture, but helped get the 650-pound (295kg) machine slowed down in modern fashion.

of nostalgic design themes for the FL series, the next of which would be the Classic model in 1987. The FX received similar treatment in 1988, with the release of the FXSTS Springer Softail. The twin-girder springer fork recalled the Knuckle-head era, and Milwaukee continued to expand the scope of its motorized memorabilia.

The next iteration was the FLSTF Fat Boy in 1990. This was one of Willie G.'s favorite designs and one that achieved instant popularity. The monochromatic paint scheme, highlighted with a bit of orange, and the disc wheels combined to evoke an image of forties' futurism and industrial engineering. The Fat Boy remains in production. ▶

Below: The headlight nacelle and aluminum fork cover recalled the Hydra-Glide of 1955. Period trim included the hubcap.

1986 FLST
© Harley-Davidson Archive photo
Milwaukee, Wisconsin

1988 FXSTS
© Harley-Davidson Archive photo
Milwaukee, Wisconsin

(1988 FXSTS)
Engine: Ohv 45° V-twin
Displacement: 1338cc
Horsepower: 55
Wheelbase: 64.5in (164cm)
Weight: 635lb (288kg)
Top speed: 114mph (183kph)
Price: $10,279

Left: The Springer brought the Softail theme half-circle, to the front of the motorcycle. Old-fashioned looks combined with current performance.

Below: The Fat Boy combined styling cues from Flash Gordon, Buck Rogers and Captain Video. "American industrial art," by Willie G.

1990 FLSTF
Owner – Bartels' Harley-Davidson
Marina Del Rey, California

Below: The new, improved Sturgis featured the Dyna Glide chassis and a simplified but more effective belt-drive system.

1991 FXDB
Owner – Bartels' Harley-Davidson
Marina Del Rey, California

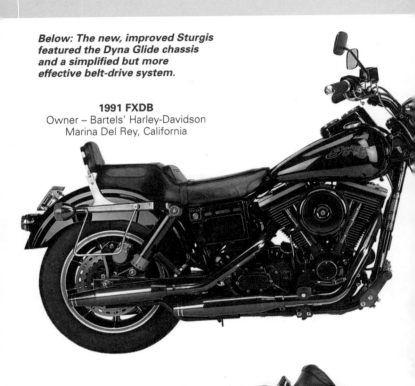

Right: The Electra Glide Ultra Classic had plenty of luggage capacity. The large tail trunk was hinged on the left side; a luggage rack was optional. The cushy seat offered a detachable backrest. Passenger accomm odations included separate controls for the stereo.

1993 FLHTC
Owner – Bartels' Harley-Davidson
Marina Del Rey, California

In 1992 the Sturgis was revived in more modern dress, with a new "computer-aided" design frame and two-point rubber-mount Evo engine. This marked the entry of the Dyna Glide chassis, with square-section frame backbone and swingarm, and all the major frame junctions forged rather than stamped. And the new Sturgis boasted a belt-drive system both simplified and improved. The FXDB was designed with the oil tank situated below the transmission.

In 1993 the factory fat bob reappeared as the FXDWG Wide Glide, and one of six Harley-Davidson 90th anniversary special editions. The FLHTC Electra Glide Ultra Classic was also offered in anniversary trim, with silver/gray paint scheme, new cruise control and new brake and clutch levers. The $16,000 tourer also featured air-adjustable suspension for both wheels, and hinged saddlebag lids with new latches and chromed guard rails. The FL series also had the ▶

(1993 FLHTC)
Engine: Ohv 45° V-twin
Displacement: 1338cc
Horsepower: 72
Wheelbase: 62.9in (160cm)
Weight: 774lb (351kg)
Top speed: 110mph (177kph)
Price: $15,349

Below: The front fork is built by Ohlins; brake calipers are six-piston units from Willwood. Front wheel travel is 4.7 inches (12cm).

oil tank under the transmission and the battery located below the seat.

The VR 1000 was one of those rare Milwaukee gambles, all the more risky given the highly competitive state of Superbike racing. But given its phenomenal market success with road models over a period of five years, Harley-Davidson could afford to take a flyer on a pure-bred racing machine. The VR was new from the ground up, and was five years in the making. The engine was a 60-degree double-overhead cam V-twin, with four valves per cylinder, Weber fuel injection, liquid cooling and five-speed transmission. The development program continues.

(1994 VR 1000)
Engine: Dohc 60° V-twin
Displacement: 1000cc
Horsepower: 135
Wheelbase: 55.5in (141cm)
Weight: 390lb (177kg)
Top speed: 170mph (274kph)
Price: $49,490

Below: The VR 1000 Superbike engine is a liquid-cooled 1000cc 60° V-twin, with dual overhead cams, fuel injection and about 140 horsepower.

1994 VR 1000
Owner – Petersen Automotive
Museum
Los Angeles, California

The concept of traditional styling and contemporary performance was applied to the FLHR in 1994. Replacing the Electra Glide Sport, the Road King featured an air-adjustable fork and dual disc brakes at the front. An improved wiring harness had waterproof connectors, and the motorcycle had taller gear ratios and detachable saddlebags and wind-shield. The passenger saddle could be removed easily as well. So the Road King was positioned as a combination cruiser and touring machine. In 1996 the FLHR was fitted with fuel injection.

The Weber Marelli injection system came standard on the 30th Anniversary Ultra Classic Electra Glide in 1995. The system allowed the

(1995 FLHR)
Engine: Ohv 45° V-twin
Displacement: 1338cc
Torque: 77lb-ft @ 4000rpm
Wheelbase: 62.9in (160cm)
Weight: 719lb (326kg)
Top speed: 112mph (180kph)
Price: $13,475

Below: For 1996 the Road King received the optional fuel injection system for the 1340cc Evolution V-twin engine. Saddlebags and windshield were also easy-off and -on items. Air-adjustable fork and front dual disc brakes were standard equipment. The Road King paid styling tribute to the original Electra Glide of 1965. The passenger seat was quick-detach for solo rides.

Milwaukee tourers to pass California's stringent emission standards without catalytic converters. And fuel mileage was also improved. The big tourer also featured standard spotlights, four-speaker AM/FM/cassette stereo with separate passenger controls and a citzen's band radio with helmet-mount headsets and voice-activated intercom.

The Sportster had undergone incremental changes since 1986 when it received the Evolution engine. In 1996 the XL 1200S Sportster Sport edition featured adjustable suspension front and rear, a 3.3-gallon fuel tank and Dunlop Sport Elite tires. The more aggressive configuration brought the price close to $8,000. ▶

1995 FLHR
Owner – Mike Lady
Arroyo Grande, California

(1996 FLHTC UI)
Engine: Ohv 45° V-twin
Displacement: 1338cc
Torque: 77lb-ft @ 4000rpm
Wheelbase: 62.7in (159cm)
Weight: 781lb (354kg)
Top speed: 110mph (177kph)
Price: $17,500

1996 FLHTC UI
Owner – Los Angeles Harley-Davidson
South Gate, California

Below left: The 30th anniversary Ultra Classic Electra Glide was the first fuel-injected tourer from Milwaukee. Cruise control and 80-watt stereo were standard.

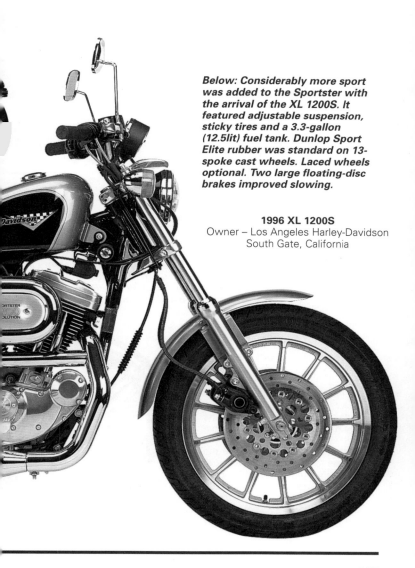

Below: Considerably more sport was added to the Sportster with the arrival of the XL 1200S. It featured adjustable suspension, sticky tires and a 3.3-gallon (12.5lit) fuel tank. Dunlop Sport Elite rubber was standard on 13-spoke cast wheels. Laced wheels optional. Two large floating-disc brakes improved slowing.

1996 XL 1200S
Owner – Los Angeles Harley-Davidson
South Gate, California

Hawthorne (1911-1912)

Engine: IOE single
Displacement: 376cc
Horsepower: 3
Wheelbase: 53in (135cm)
Weight: 150lb (68kg)
Top speed: 35mph (56kph)
Price: $200

The Hawthorne was a re-branded Armac that came on the market near the end of the Chicago company's decade in the business. The motorcycle was also available as an AMC, from the Allied Motors Corporation. The later models did not have the exhaust-through-frame feature and were offered only with belt drive. V-belt tension was controlled by lever on the left side of the tank; a sight-glass lubication dispenser was fitted to the rear downtube. The leading-link parallel-strut front fork was an improvement over the original item. The Hawthorne was sold by Montgomery Ward, a large mail-order house in Chicago.

Right: The Montgomery Ward rendition of the Armac single was sold in the Chicago company's mail order catalog as the Hawthorne.

Henderson (1912–1931)

The brothers Henderson, Tom and William, took up the manufacturing trade in 1911, the same year Ignaz Schwinn acquired Excelsior. After five years of independent manufacture, the Henderson Motorcycle Company would also be absorbed by the Chicago industrialist.

The first Henderson Four, which appeared in 1912, was long. As the ads stated: "The long wheebase of the Henderson, 65 inches, permits the riders to sit between the wheels, reducing road shocks to the minimum." On the first seven-horsepower model in 1912, the passenger seat was fitted to the top frame tube just above the footboard. This was changed to a rear tandem the following year.

"Owing to the extreme wheelbase, the tandem saddle is still located with the load center directly over the rear axle, thus giving the ▶

Below: "It is a motorcycle with classy lines, style, and plenty of speed. A machine that is sassy and snappy in action, without the usual vibration."

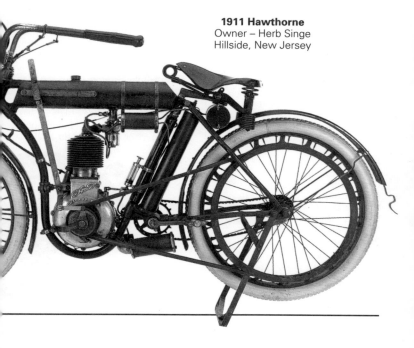

1911 Hawthorne
Owner – Herb Singe
Hillside, New Jersey

1912 Henderson
Owner – Jim Lattin
Encinitas, California

greatest degree of comfort to the passenger and greatly facilitating the steering and control." The four was then up to eight horsepower and 1065cc, with a stronger front fork and new rear brake. The upper frame tube now curved down at the rear, and enclosed the new squared off fuel tank, with three-gallon (11.35lit) capacity. Tire widths went from 2.5 to 3 inches (6.35 to 7.62cm).

The contracting band rear brake appeared in 1913, operated by a pedal on the footboard. The Henderson four-cylinder engine used four individually cast iron cylinders on an aluminum crankcase, with a one-piece crankshaft on three main bearings. The engine was fitted with an Eclipse clutch, Bosch magneto and Schebler carburetor. The motor came to life car-style, with a hand crank. The tubular fuel tank held 2.25 gallons (8.5lit) of gas and two quarts (1.9lit) of oil. An elegant, seven-horsepower touring machine, it sold for $325.

(1913 Four)
Engine: IOE inline four
Displacement: 965cc
Horsepower: 7
Wheelbase: 65in (165cm)
Weight: 310lb (141kg)
Top speed: 55mph (89kph)
Price: $325

Below: The Henderson Four set the standards for length and motoring excellence. The two-wheeled version of a touring car.

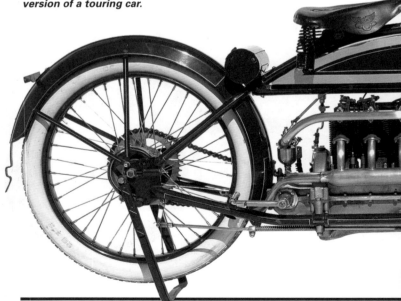

Below: The cylindrical fuel tank was gone in 1913, replace by a more streamlined container filling the space between the new upper frame tubes.

1913 Henderson
Owner – Otis Chandler
Ojai, California

1913 Henderson
Owner – Vince Martinico
Auburn, California

231

Henderson's place in two-wheeled history was assured in 1913, when young Carl Stearns Clancy became the first person to circumnavigate the planet on a motorcycle, riding a 1912 Henderson.

In 1914 Henderson introduced the Model C, with lighter pistons, two speeds and adjustable seat springs. The company took some effort in its advertising to explain the differences in the kinds of power delivered by motorcycle engines. "It is four cylinder or continuous power that alone can give you all you would seek in your power plant." Some of the ad copy described the difference in this fashion: "The single cylinder motorcycle 'jerks' itself along. You can fairly see each separate 'jerk.' In a twin the same is true, except it has twice as many jerks."

There was no denying the smoothness of a four-cylinder engine, but likewise the motorcyclist faced added complexity, weight and cost. The Thor two-speed hub added $40 to the cost of the machine, and with the advent of war in Europe, the costs of materials and production were rising. Work was also begun on a short-wheelbase model in 1914, in response to requests from dealers.

(1917 Four)
Engine: Inline four
Displacement: 990cc
Horsepower: 12
Wheelbase: 58in (147cm)
Weight: 310lb (141kg)
Top speed: 75mph (121kph)
Price: $295/325

Below: The three-speed Model G would be among the last Detroit-built Hendersons. Early 1918 models were released before the move to Chicago.

Below: Illinois dealer Dale Walksler's Wheels Through Time Museum displays many American classics, including this 1917 Henderson cross-country special.

1917 Henderson
Owner – Dale Walksler
Mt. Vernon, Illinois

1917 Henderson Model G
Owner – Frank Westfall
Syracuse, New York

233

For 1915 the company introduced a two-speed hub of its own manufacture, improved Eclipse clutch, a stronger crankshaft, larger front fork, new seat and longer starting crank. The clevis arrangement on the intake rocker arms was replaced with a ball joint system. And despite the costs of such improvements, the price was dropped to $295 and the two-speed marked at $335. Hendersons sagging fortunes were boosted by a large order from Italy, which could no longer get British or German machines because of the war. The short-wheelbase Model E appeared in the spring of 1915, with a reduction of seven inches (18cm) between the axles and 1.5-inch (3.8cm) lower seat height. The center footboard gave way to side footboards on the short-coupler. Both models (D long, E short) were offered in single or two-speed versions, with no change in the prices.

By 1916 only the shorter model was in production, and the prices were lowered once again; $265 for

(1927 Four)
Engine: Inline four
Displacement: 1168cc
Horsepower: 10-14
Wheelbase: 58in (147cm)
Weight: 325lb (147kg)
Top speed: 75-90mph (121-145kph)
Price: $380/435

the one-, 295 for the two-speed. Henderson, among other manufacturers, was now on hard times and doing everything possible to maintain the company's viability. The advent of war brought material shortages and higher costs in labor and production. In January of 1916, Henderson raised the price of both models by $30. "The Henderson Company emphasizes the fact that it did not decide upon the increased prices until it became evident that it would be impossible to continue production on the present high standard without an actual loss on every machine." (*MotorCycle Illustrated.*)

At this low ebb in Henderson's economic situation, in stepped Ignaz Schwinn. With his acquisition of Excelsior five years prior, the former bicycle mechanic had become a significant force in the motorcycle industry. But Indian and Harley-Davidson had grown stronger yet, and Schwinn reasoned that it was time to expand the line. And the distress in ▶

Below: Frank Westfall's Henderson is set up for the annual Great Race from coast-to coast. In 1997, the engine was rained out on the last day.

1928 Henderson
Owner – Frank Westfall
Syracuse, New York

Detroit complemented his timing.

The 1917 model year would be the last for Henderson as an independent company. The new G model of 1917 featured a three-speed transmission, new intake manifold and improved fork. That summer, Henderson rider Alan Bedell set a new transcontinental record of 7 days, 16 hours, breaking Cannonball Baker's previous cross-country mark by nearly four days. Roy Artley also broke Baker's Canada-to-Mexico record by nearly nine hours, making the run in just under 72.5 hours. And Henry Ford himself bought an electrically equipped Henderson Four, at the full price of $370. (Henry asked for a discount, but was refused.)

But all the good news or record-breaking didn't alleviate the company's economic dilemma, and by the end of the year 1917 William and Tom Henderson were on their way to Chicago. The Excelsior con-nection saved Henderson, and both brothers were hired to facilitate the shift to production in the new plant. But after a year the Hendersons decided to go

Right: On one of Chicago's wide new super-highways (four lanes wide), racer Joe Petrali ran the Henderson Special up to 116mph (187kph).

Below: With removal of the bracket bolts, the rear fender could be rotated upward to facilitate tire changes.

1930 Henderson KJ
Owner – Robert Beard
Courtesy of AMA Museum
Pickerington, Ohio

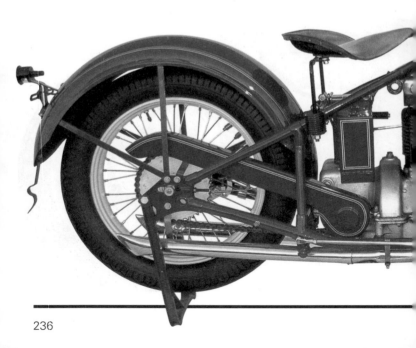

their separate ways; Tom resigned in 1919 to sell motorcycles in Europe and William left to build another motorcycle to be called the Ace.

Production of the Chicago Excelsior-Hendersons continued for another 12 years. The machines adopted heavier frames, pressurized lubrication system and side-valve cylinders. In 1920 the carburetor, now built by Zenith, moved to the middle of the manifold. The K model had larger bore and stroke for a displacement of 1310cc and 18 rated horsepower. The drive chain was fully enclosed.

In its final years (1929–1931), the Henderson gained weight, power and adopted the new streamlined styling of the era. San Francisco's Joe Petrali, who later became a Harley racing star, helped develop the machines. But the Depression put Excelsior out of play in 1931, ending the storied history of Henderson and the Super X.

Below: Streamlining styles of the 1930s reached the Henderson just in time for the final chapters. But the design would survive under the Indian flag.

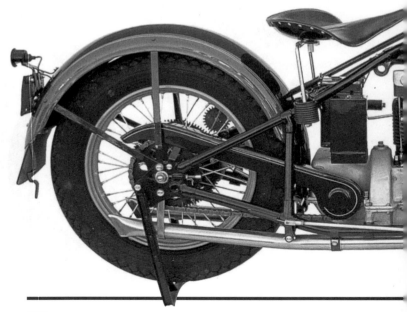

1931 Henderson KL
Owner – Sylvester Boyachek
Courtesy of AMA Museum
Pickerington, Ohio

Hercules (1902-1903)

Engine: IOE single
Displacement: 500cc
Horsepower: 2.5
Wheelbase: 58in (147cm)
Weight: 130lb (59kg)
Top speed: 45mph (72kph)
Price: $200

Below: The first Curtiss was called a Hercules, until a California company laid claim to ownership of the name. After some urging, Curtiss agreed to the use of his own name.

The Hercules was the original machine built by Glenn Curtiss (see also pp.34-35). He began with the Hercules bicycle, built in Addison, New York in 1900. By 1902 he had developed his first motorcycle and applied to it the same name.

Young Glenn blistered the backroads on his prototypes, and developed a knack for fast riding. With investments from local wine financier J.S. Hubbs, and the Masson brothers of France, Curtiss built a V-twin and immediately began winning races. When a California company claimed priority on the Hercules trademark, the motorcycles took Curtiss's own name.

Holley (1902-1911)

George Holley began racing motorcycles as a teenager in his home town of Bradford, Pennsylvania, and caught the bug, which also affected his younger brother, Earl. Together they started to build motorcycles. In 1897 they created a single-cylinder three-wheeler, The Runabout, from plans that George, at only 19 years of age, had drawn himself, having been to a pattern shop to learn how to develop patterns for a single-cylinder motor. The Runabout could reach a respectable speed for the time of 30 miles an hour.

Although a racer, George's first love was building engines, and in 1899 he and Earl set up a company (Holley Motor Co.) with the intention of supplying engines to the evolving motor and motorcycle trade. George was chairman, responsible for engineering and sales; Earl was president, handling the business and ▶

Below: The Holley crankcase was integral with the frame. The one-into-two seatpost tubing was used by several early builders.

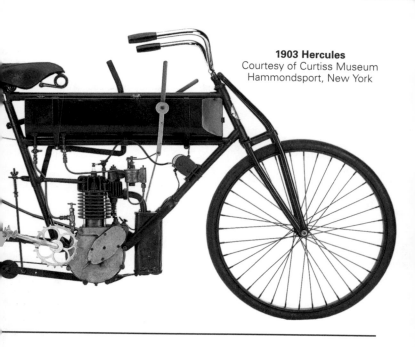

1903 Hercules
Courtesy of Curtiss Museum
Hammondsport, New York

1903 Holley
Owner – Jim Dennie
Palmyra, New York

finance aspects. Demand was still slow in the unproven market, however, so they undertook the manufacture of complete motorcycles.

In 1901 the Holley brothers negotiated a license to produce and sell the French Longuemare carburetor in the United States, and this refocused the business back to engines, and the motor trade.

Meanwhile, George kept racing, and in 1902 won America's first Motorcycle Endurance Contest, and went on to set a series of world speed records for motorcycles at the Pan American Exposition in Buffalo, New York.

In 1903 the company built a small car, the Holley Motorette, with a

Engine: IOE single
Displacement: 220cc
Horsepower: 2.25
Wheelbase: 46in (117cm)
Weight: 110lb (50kg)
Top speed: 35mph (56kph)
Price: $200

1905 Holley
Owner –Herb Singe
Hillside, New Jersey

5.5hp single-cylinder engine, tilt steering wheel with lock, and front and rear kerosene lamps. It sold for $550, and over 600 were built during a three year period.

Success on the track and in the factory brought the Holleys to the notice of Henry Ford who asked them to build a carburetor for the Model T. This convinced the brothers that their future should be geared to production of carburetors and other components, which they went on to make for various car makers, including Pierce-Arrow, Winston, Buick, Chevrolet and, of course, Ford. The company evolved in various ways, became part of Ford Motor Company toward the end of World War I, and remains in business today.

Below: The forward-mount engine and seating position indicate that the former model's aft weight bias may not have offered adequate handling. In 1905 the Holley appeared with a new front fork, fuel tank and transposed frame tubes and engine.

Indian (1901~1953)

George Hendee and Oscar Hedstrom, both former bicycle racers, met in 1900 at the Madison Square Garden wheelman event. Hedstrom was building motorized pacers for bike races, and Hendee was manufacturing Silver King bicycles in Middletown, Massahusetts. Their meeting would create the Hendee Manufacturing Company and Indian motorcycles.

Hedstorm had settled on the diamond-frame chassis with the IOE single engine integral with the seat post. Some controversy attended the claims for and against bicycle-style frames versus loop frames, each side claiming the other's set-up to be inherently unstable. The loopers would eventually win out, but Indian kept the bicycle style for seven years, when it became apparent that racing speeds required stronger chassis.

Hedstrom had the first Indian prototype up and running in less than five months. The premier

(1901 Single)
Engine: IOE single
Displacement: 213cc
Horsepower: 1.75
Wheelbase: 47in (119cm)
Weight: 110lb (50kg)
Top speed: 25mph (40kph)
Price: $200

(1903 Single)
Engine: IOE single
Displacement: 213cc
Horsepower: 1.75
Wheelbase: 48in (122cm)
Weight: 115lb (52kg)
Top speed: 25mph (40kph)
Price: $200

1901 Single
Owner – Otis Chandler
Ojai, California

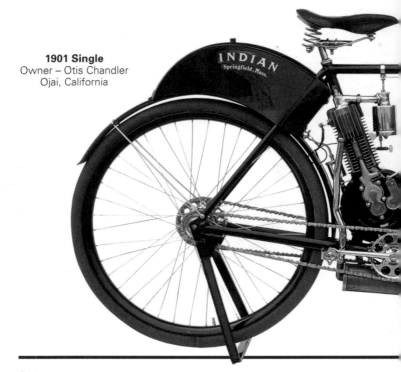

1903 Single
Owner – Jim Lattin
Encinitas, California

Above: By 1903 Indian was a power player in the growing motorcycle market. The Hedstrom-designed engine was built by Aurora in Illinois.

Below: The 213cc single was rated at 1.75 horsepower. Indian decided on chain drive only at the beginning, and only slipped once.

demonstration on Cross Street Hill in Springfield was eminently successful, and well-attended by the public and press. Indian motorcycles, or motocycles as they were then called, were off to a quick start. Hendee engaged the Aurora Automatic Machine Company of Illinois to build engines, while Hedstrom set to work on refinements to both the engine and chassis.

Springfield produced 377 motorcycles in 1903, and by 1904 production was up to almost 600. And it would nearly double the following year. Horsepower was up to 2.25 from the 213cc single, which in 1905 still sold for $200. Hedstrom then turned his engineering focus to development of the V-twin engine. The Hendee Manufacturing Company was rolling strong. ▶

Right: The company apparently built six motorcycles in 1901. Natural rubber tires were butt-glued to the wooden rims.

Below: By 1905 the Indian single had gained another half-horsepower, by virtue of more precise cam and valve timing. Twist grip controls for both the throttle and spark appeared in 1905. Keeping both hands on the bars also improved the safety factor.

1905 Single
Owner – Mort Wood
Marathon, Florida

In 1907 the V-twin arrived, with slightly larger cylinder bores it shared with the new single. The 633cc twin was rated at four horsepower and the single at 2.25. Oscar Hedstrom also produced a racing V-twin, with 698cc and seven horsepower. The front fork was given a longer cartridge spring. The smaller twin gained only about 15 pounds (7kg) on the single, but cost 20 percent more at $240.

Hedstrom had been working on improvements to his carburetor, and on the conversion to mechanical intake valves. Atmospheric valves couldn't meet the high performance demands of a newly competitive racing scene, which was heating up. Motorcycle racing was fast becoming a popular entertainment among the new sophisticates of motoring technology, and a dandy way to sell motorcycles.

In 1907 the enthusiasm to pit man and machine against like-

(1907 Twin)
Engine: IOE 42° V-twin
Displacement: 633cc
Horsepower: 4
Wheelbase: 51in (130cm)
Weight: 135lb (61kg)
Top speed: 45mph (72kph)
Price: $240

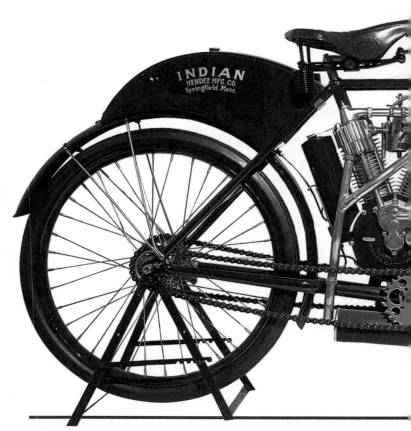

Right: The Hedstrom carburetor set the early standards for accurate mixture of air and fuel. Exhaust plumbing was fundamental.

Below: The first Indian V-twin came to market in 1907. The four-horsepower engine still had atmospheric intake valves.

1907 Twin
Owner – Mike Parti
North Hollywood, California

minded competitors created two contests that have survived to this day. The Tourist Trophy event on the Isle of Man and the 1000-Mile Reliability Trial in England set the stage for a century of global motorcycle competition. The trial, which would evolve as the International Six Days Trial, was won in its inaugural event by Teddy Hastings of New York, riding a stock Indian V-twin. And in 1908 he did it again, this time with factory support.

French-Canadian Jake DeRosier had apprenticed with Oscar Hedstrom, and risen to the top as a championship motorcycle racer. By 1908 he was fully sponsored by the Indian factory, and would achieve national and international fame within the next few years.

(1908 Racer)
Engine: IOE 42° V-twin
Displacement: 1000cc
Horsepower: 7
Wheelbase: 51in (130cm)
Weight: 130lb (59kg)
Top speed: 70mph (113kph)
Price: $350

Right: The "monkey-on-a stick" racer wasn't built for comfort, but it would pull to about 70mph (113kph).

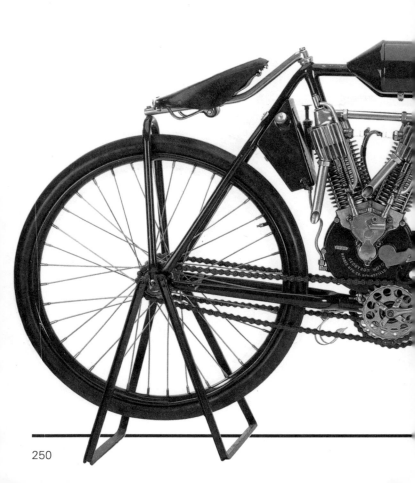

1908 Racer
Owner – Tony Penachio
Millwood, New York

Below: The torpedo tanks were built in three different sizes, and fitted according to the different race distances. The oil tank and hand pump fit behind the engine.

The last of the diamond-frame Indians were built in 1909, as options to the new loop frame. Boardtrack speeds were now pushing 80mph (129kph) and a half-dozen of the new motorcycle companies were spending money to develop racing machines. The race was on to be first to the 100mph (161kph) mark. Between 1909 and 1912 the construction of boardtrack motordromes was a national growth industry in the big cities, and the

banking quickly increased from 25 to 60 degrees. "Neck & Neck on the Wall of Death!" blared the headlines. Humans had yet to travel this fast, in the air or on the ground.

In 1910 Indian introduced a leaf-spring front fork that would become a lasting trademark, and also offered a two-speed transmission. Production for 1909 fell just short of 5,000 machines, and in 1910 rose to more than 6,000. Indian had quickly established itself as a primary player

(1910 Single)
Engine: IOE single
Displacement: 316cc
Horsepower: 5
Wheelbase: 56in (142cm)
Weight: 175lb (79kg)
Top speed: 45mph (72kph)
Price: $215

Right: By 1910 the single was offered in either a single-speed or two-speed with clutch. The cartridge spring fork was replaced by the leaf-spring unit.

Below: The five-horsepower 633cc engine was designated the Light Twin. This example has been fitted with a later model fuel tank.

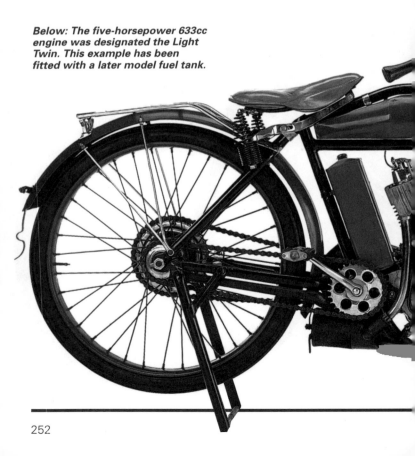

1910 Single
Owner – Marv Baker
Vallejo, California

1909 Light Twin
Owner – Chuck Vernon
La Mirada, California

in the international motorcycle market, and was rapidly expanding its dealer network at home and abroad.

Jake DeRosier continued to set speed records on the boardtracks, as the level of competition rose with entries from Merkel, Excelsior, Reading-Standard, NSU and Thor. DeRosier traveled to the Isle of Man for the first Tourist Trophy to be held on the 37-mile (60km) island circuit.

(1911 8-valve Racer)
Engine: Ohv V-twin
Displacement: 1000cc
Horsepower: 14-17
Wheelbase: 53in (135cm)
Weight: 245lb (111kg)
Top speed: 100mph (161kph)
Price: $350

Although the factory star had problems on the island, Indian riders finished 1-2-3 on the demanding course. A month later at Brooklands in England, DeRosier set a new mile record at 88mph (142kph).

But upon his return to Springfield, DeRosier was not granted a ride on the new 8-valve racer developed by Hedstrom. DeRosier quit immediately and signed a contract with Excelsior.

Right: The big-base overheads had one throttle position, wide open. Speed was controlled by a kill switch. Direct drive, no brakes, lord have mercy.

Below: Oscar Hedstrom was determined to establish Indian's domination on the racetracks. The big-base 8-valve was a major weapon.

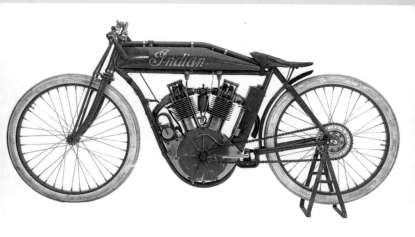

1912 Big-base 8-Valve
Owner – Jim Dennie
Palmyra, New York

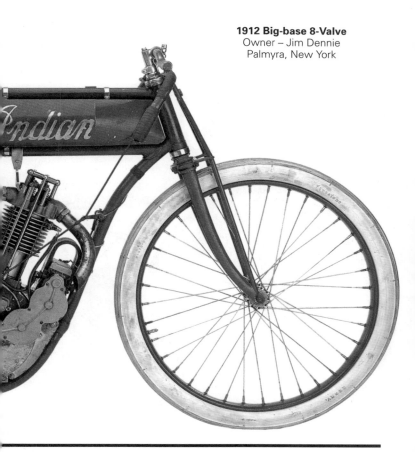

(1912 Boardtrack Racer)
Engine: IOE V-twin
Displacement: 1000cc
Horsepower: 12
Wheelbase: 53in (135cm)
Weight: 240lb (109kg)
Top speed: 90mph (145kph)
Price: $235

Right: Steep-bank boardtrack racing reached its popularity peak in 1912. When eight people died at a New Jersey motordrome, the sport faded quickly.

(1912 Single)
Engine: IOE single
Displacement: 500cc
Horsepower: 4
Wheelbase: 56in (142cm)
Weight: 230lb (104kg)
Top speed: 45mph (72kph)
Price: $215

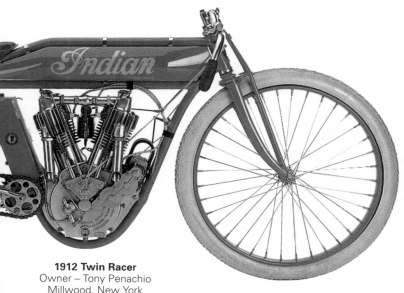

1912 Twin Racer
Owner – Tony Penachio
Millwood, New York

Below: The only belt-drive Indian was produced in 1911, but met with little success. Leftover machines were sold as 1912 models.

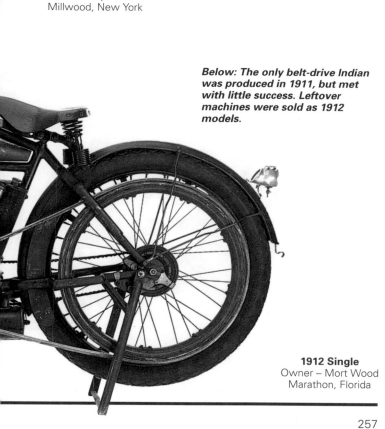

1912 Single
Owner – Mort Wood
Marathon, Florida

Although Oscar Hedstrom was firmly convinced of the superiority of chain drive, Indian dealers were lobbying for a belt-drive model. The factory obliged in 1911, but the machine failed to generate the interest the dealers had expected and it became a one-year model. On the other hand, Springfield production reached nearly 20,000 machines in 1911 and profits rose to record highs.

This was to be Indian's Golden Era, dominating the dawn of motorcycling on the road and track, with a broad network of dealers at home and abroad and a reputation for advanced engineering and performance. But it would also be the end of the daredevil era of motordrome racing, as the escalating speeds brought more fatalities among both ridsers and spectators. In 1912, the deaths of Indian riders Eddie Hasha, Johnnie Albright and six spectators at a New Jersey boardtrack signaled the

(1913 Twin)
Engine: IOE V-twin
Displacement: 1000cc
Horsepower: 7
Wheelbase: 59in (150cm)
Weight: 355lb (161kg)
Top speed: 55mph (89kph)
Price: $250

end of the steeply-banked motor-dromes.

By 1913 Indian motorcycle production approached 32,000 machines for the year, the best figure Springfield would ever have. On the flip side, Hendee and Hedstrom had come to disagree on the future of motorcycle design and marketing. Hedstrom decided to retire to pursue other engineering challenges, and when Jake DeRosier died of racing injuries in 1913, the chief engineer submitted his resignation.

Hedstrom's reputation as an engineer would serve Indian well for many years thereafter. His racing engines had set the standards for others to match, and the cradle spring frame proved his talents in designing a motorcycle with power and handling in dynamic balance. And the athletic abilities of Erwin "Cannonball" Baker would publicize the results around the world. ▶

Below: Indian was one of the first major builders to adopt rear wheel suspension. The leaf-spring system was patterned on automobile engineering. Indian suspension components were well tested during cross-country record runs by one Erwin "Cannonball" Baker.

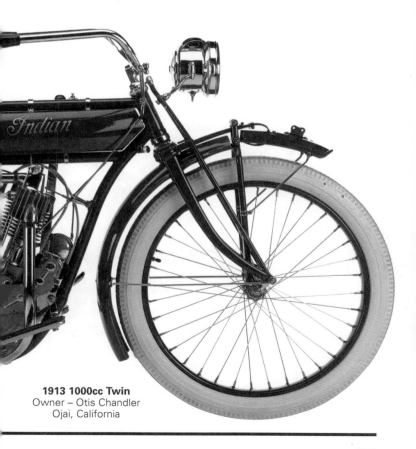

1913 1000cc Twin
Owner – Otis Chandler
Ojai, California

Within two years George Hendee also retired and Indian came under the control of an investment group. Both Hedstrom and Hendee had achieved a comfortable level of prosperity, and both moved to large estates in the country. The motorcycle market itself remained strong; Harley-Davidson production had quadrupled in two years. Indian maintained a strong position in the market, but would never again reach the production levels of 1913.

The 1915 Indians were the final renditions of the Hedstrom F-head engines, offered in big twin (1000cc) and little twin (700cc) versions. A three-speed transmission was off-

(1915 8-valve Racer)
Engine: Ohv V-twin
Displacement: 1000cc
Horsepower: 18-20
Wheelbase: 53in (135cm)
Weight: 240lb (109kg)
Top speed: 100mph (161kph)
Price: $350

(1915 Big Twin)
Engine: IOE V-twin
Displacement: 1000cc
Horsepower: 15
Wheelbase: 59in (150cm)
Weight: 370lb (168kg)
Top speed: 55mph (89kph)
Price: $275

Right: The 8-valve came in response to racing performance challenges from Excelsior and Harley-Davidson. Glory days of daring.

Below: The three-speed transmission debuted on the Big Twin. The clutch was more stout and had dual controls, and a new magneto was fitted. The pillion attachment was a popular accessory, and was fully equipped with its own suspension.

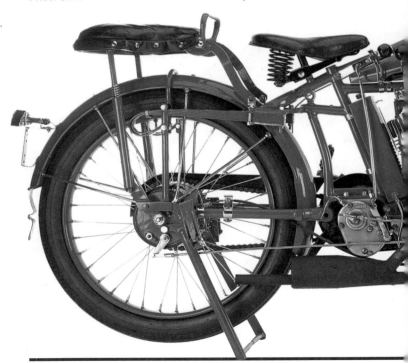

1915 8-valve Racer
Owner – Stephen Wright
Morro Bay, California

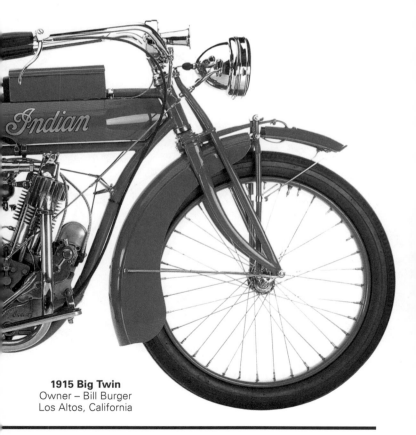

1915 Big Twin
Owner – Bill Burger
Los Altos, California

ered for the first time as optional equipment, and a new kickstart mechanism was fitted. Generators were included on the electric light models, and Schebler carburetors replaced the Hedstrom units.

Ireland's Charles Franklin replaced Hedstrom as chief engineer, and with the help of former Reading-Standard engineer Charles Gustafson, designed the side-valve engine that would be called the Powerplus. The engine, with slightly smaller bore but longer stroke, was a bit more powerful than its predecessor. The bottom end, clutch and transmission were strengthened. Most of Springfield's production for 1916 was devoted to military models ordered by the government.

(1916 Powerplus)
Engine: Side-valve 42° V-twin
Displacement: 1000cc
Horsepower: 18
Wheelbase: 59in (150cm)
Weight: 405lb (184kg)
Top speed: 60mph (97kph)
Price: $350 (with sidecar)

Right: Sidecars remained popular in the teens, and figured strongly in the export trade for both Indian and Harley.

Below: A number of Powerplus export models were sold in 1915. The front wheel stand and aluminum footboards were standard.

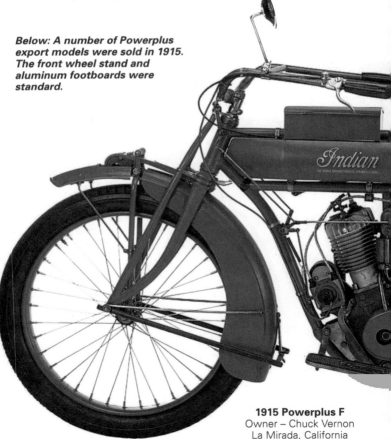

1915 Powerplus F
Owner – Chuck Vernon
La Mirada, California

1916 Powerplus F
Owner – Bob Romig
Pottstown, Pennsylvania

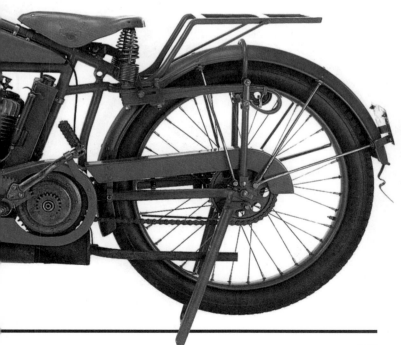

In 1913 it became more apparent that Europe would go to war, and that for the first time in the history of armed combat, men would take to the air in flying machines and shoot at one another. American aircraft development had been hobbled by patent litigation between the Wright brothers and Glenn Curtiss. Motorcycle advancement had continued unconstrained, though two-wheelers would prove considerably less effective as weapons of war.

(1917 Model O)
Engine: Opposed side-valve twin
Displacement: 257cc
Horsepower: 2.75
Wheelbase: 49.5in (126cm)
Weight: 235lb (107kg)
Top speed: 45mph (72kph)
Price: $180

But as swift and agile couriers (and smaller targets), motorcyclists could contribute to the cause of victory. Thus, in 1916, the U.S. War Department ordered 20,000 Indian motorcycles in military dress. The Indian Powerplus and its Harley counterpart the Model J were both drafted into service. Both companies needed the financial boost, but Indian turned more of the production to the military bikes and neglected their civilian dealers and customers. With

Right: The Model O opposed twin was another attempt to create a lightweight market. The machine was most popular in Britain and Europe.

1917 Model O
Owner – Otis Chandler
Ojai, California

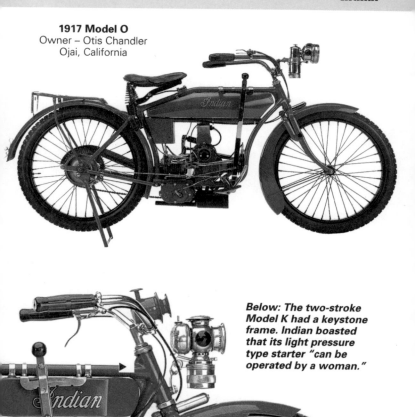

*Below: The two-stroke
Model K had a keystone
frame. Indian boasted
that its light pressure
type starter "can be
operated by a woman."*

1916 Model K
Owner – Paul Pearce
Oxford, Michigan

America's relatively short involvement in the war, this would become a costly mistake.

Neither of Springfield's new lightweights, the Model K two-stroke or Model O opposed twin, found much success in the market. American riders seemed stubbornly resistant to small motorcycles. The Powerplus was still available in either cradle-spring or rigid frame models, and the single remained in the lineup. With the end of World War I the racing scene was soon revived, and Indian's Gene Walker won four of the nine dirt-track championship events in 1919.

(1919 Powerplus Model F)
Engine: Side-valve 42° V-twin
Displacement: 1000cc
Horsepower: 18
Wheelbase: 59in (150cm)
Weight: 430lb (195kg)
Top speed: 60mph (97kph)
Price: $290

Below: The Powerplus V-twin was rated at 18 horsepower. Speeds were up and Cannonball Baker continued setting endurance records for Indian. The Indian leaf-spring fork was a durable system, and found application on racing and hillclimb machines as well as road models. The compression release, clutch and transmission levers juggle for space beside the fuel tank. The Powerplus had three-speed transmission, and a dry clutch.

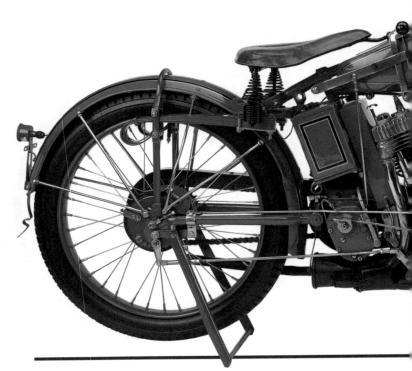

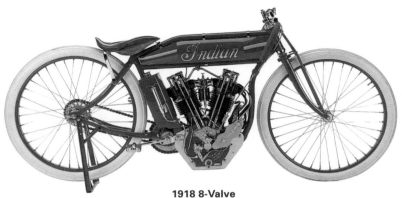

1918 8-Valve
Owner – Daniel Statnekov
Tesuque, New Mexico

*Above: The 8-valve's 20-plus
horsepower would propel man
and machine to more than
100mph (161kph), for those who
could handle the ride.*

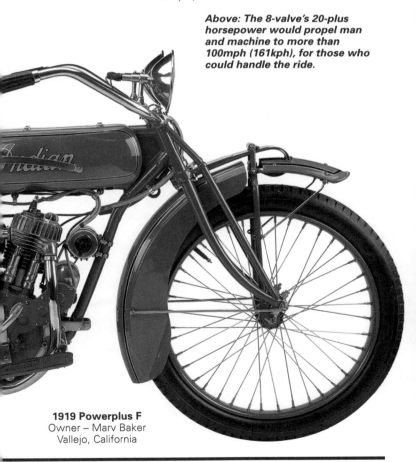

1919 Powerplus F
Owner – Marv Baker
Vallejo, California

267

The racing motorcycles built between 1915 and 1925 represented the leading edges of motorcycle engineering, design, style and performance. These machines, mostly Indians, Excelsiors and Harleys, were built to the optimum balance between velocity and durability, and the fellows who rode them at the limit were courageous souls. The names Jake DeRosier, Cannonball Baker, Percy Coleman, Gene Walker and Shrimp Burns were carved into legend.

Indians captured 14 of the 17 national title events in 1920, but once again Harley-Davidson won the long races and with them the championship. The following year, the last for Harley's factory team, the Milwaukee riders won all the national championship events. Indian had finally been humbled.

But 1920 was also the year that Charles Franklin's engineering prowess was certified with the release of the 600cc Scout. Franklin had remained convinced, despite considerable evidence to the contrary, that

(1920 Daytona Twin)
Engine: Side-valve 42° V-twin
Displacement: 1000cc
Horsepower: 22
Wheelbase: 53in (135cm)
Weight: 270lb (122kg)
Top speed: 106mph (171kph)
Price: $300

Below: The Daytona Twin was one of the dominant racing motorcycles of the period. Indian riders won 14 of the 17 national meets in 1920. Gene Walker set numerous records on the 8-valve and the standard side-valve models. On the latter he recorded 107mph (172kph) at Daytona Beach.

1920 Daytona/Flxi
Owner – Tony Penachio
Millwood, New York

Above: Sidecar racing on fairground ovals was one of the most popular forms of racing. Floyd Dreyer of Indianapolis was a leading rider.

1920 Daytona
Owner – Tom Hensley
Highland Park, California

American riders would accept a middleweight machine. The two-cam side-valve made about ten horsepower, and could be readily tweaked for more urge. With gear-drive primary and three-speed transmission, the Scout was good for about 60mph (97kph) in stock trim.

(1923 Scout)
Engine: Side-valve 42° V-twin
Displacement: 596cc
Horsepower: 11
Wheelbase: 54.5in (138cm)
Weight: 340lb (154kg)
Top speed: 55mph (89kph)
Price: $325

Below: The new Scout was basically a downsized Powerplus. The 600cc side-valve V-twin employed helical gears for the primary drive.

And the machine handled far better than the Powerplus.

Dirt-track racing was growing in popularity, and the Flxi sidecar appeared in competition at a New York event in 1920. The leaning hacks were built by the FlxibleCompany in Loudonville, Ohio.

Right: The Scout exceeded nearly everyone's expectations for performance. The two-cam engine was rated at a modest 11 horsepower.

1923 Scout
Owner – Eric Vaughan
Monrovia, California

The next task at hand for Indian was a new big twin to replace the aging Powerplus. The older model, now called the Standard, remained in production for three more years, but the new side-valve Chief became the premier model. The Chief, with 1000 or 1200cc engine, was derived from the Scout and built as direct competition with the Harley big twin.

(1923 Big Chief)
Engine: Side-valve 42° V-twin
Displacement: 1200cc
Horsepower: 34
Wheelbase: 60.5in (154cm)
Weight: 440lb (200kg)
Top speed: 75mph (121kph)
Price: $435

The Chief was well suited to the needs of touring riders and sidecarists, but the Scout remained the popular choice among sporting riders. The 1200cc Chief, which first appeared in 1923, featured improved carburetion and reinforcements to the frame. The Big Chief was naturally more powerful than the smaller version, and soon passed the Scout in

Right: The sidecar market in the states began to dwindle in the 1920s, as automobiles got cheaper. European markets remained strong.

Below: The Big Chief had a stronger frame and plenty of torque. The machine was well received by police riders and hillclimbers.

1923 Big Chief
Owner – Rocky Burkhart
Birdsboro, Pennsylvania

1923 Chief
Owner – Vince Spadaro
Burlingame, California

overall sales figures. In 1924 the factory went to a new front fork and larger wheels and tires. The Chief was especially popular with police departments around the country.

Charles Franklin had not abandoned the hope for a popular lightweight machine. The single-cylinder Prince, a 350cc side-valve, appeared in 1925, and was available in an overhead-valve version the following year. But the Prince met the same fate as most earlier attempts to sell Americans on the lightweight concept, and the machine was discontinued in 1928.

(1928 Prince)
Engine: Vertical side-valve single
Displacement: 350cc
Horsepower: 7
Wheelbase: 54in (137cm)
Weight: 265lb (120kg)
Top speed: 55mph (89kph)
Price: $195

Below: The Prince, a 350cc side-valve single was introduced in 1925. A few overhead-valve versions were made, even fewer with overhead cam.

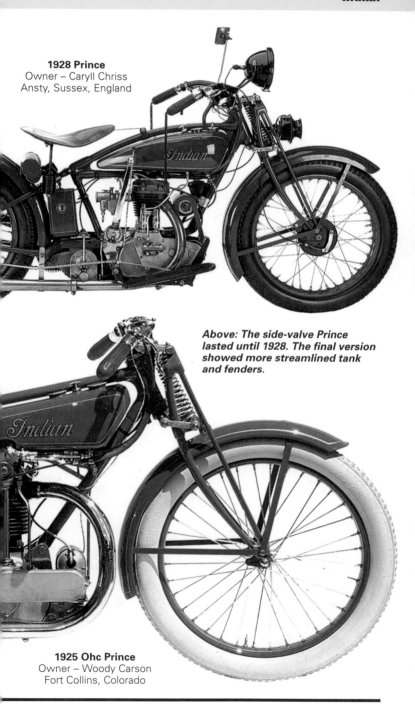

1928 Prince
Owner – Caryll Chriss
Ansty, Sussex, England

Above: The side-valve Prince lasted until 1928. The final version showed more streamlined tank and fenders.

1925 Ohc Prince
Owner – Woody Carson
Fort Collins, Colorado

The national economy improved in the mid-twenties, and Indian production began to rise accordingly. President Frank Weschler was determined to expand the company's product line, and spent considerable effort in 1926 to buy the assets of the now defunct Ace Motorycle Company. By year's end he had made a deal with then owner Michigan Motors, and the Ace inventory and tooling was transfered to Springfield.

Just when Indian and Harley had settled on standard engine sizes for singles and twins, Excelsior confused the issue with the 750cc Super X. When the new twin began winning races against 1000 and 1200cc machines, Indian and Harley undertook development of 750cc twins.

Hedstrom's reply was the 101

(1928 Ace Four)
Engine: IOE inline four
Displacement: 1265cc
Horsepower: 35
Wheelbase: 59in (150cm)
Weight: 395lb (179kg)
Top speed: 80mph (129kph)
Price: $425

Right: Sidecar rigs for export had the chair on the left side. Domestic models were fitted to the opposite side, with the kickstarter on the left.

Below: The purchase of the Ace inventory and tooling gave Indian the most comprehensive line of motorcycles in the industry.

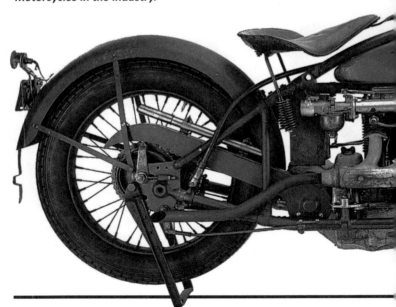

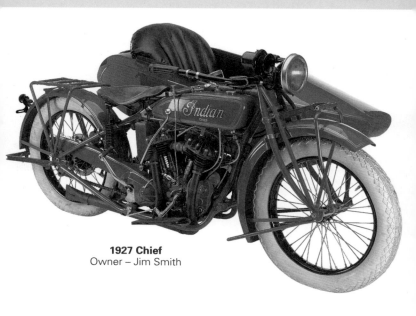

1927 Chief
Owner – Jim Smith

1928 Indian Ace
Owner – Mort Wood
Marathon, Florida

Scout, a longer and lower version of his original design. The new Scout was heavier than its predecessor, but it also had more power, a front brake and superior handling. The machine generated enthusiastic response at home and abroad, and soon showed up on racetracks. The factory built two dozen overhead-valve versions

(1929 101 Scout)
Engine: Side-valve 42° V-twin
Displacement: 750cc
Horsepower: 22
Wheelbase: 57in (145cm)
Weight: 370lb (168kg)
Top speed: 75mph (121kph)
Price: $300

for flat track and hillclimb.

The Indian/Ace Four came to market in the same configuration it had under William Henderson. In succeeding years it would appear with an Indian fork, frame and fuel tank. By 1929 the four would have a complete Springfield chassis, and extensive engine modifications.

Right: The 101 Scout proved to be an exceptionally well balanced motorcycle for all-round use. And with a stroker kit it was quite fast.

Below: The 101 Scout was met with suspicion by Sport Scout enthusiasts. But the new model soon proved its merits on the road and track. Despite some added weight, the 101 Scout had the distinction of a front brake, which made its debut in 1928.

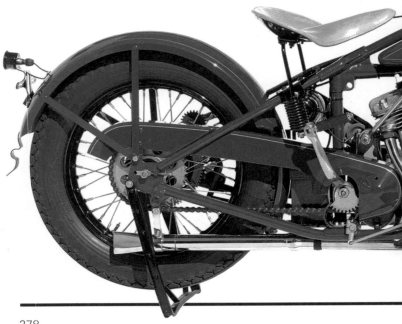

1929 101 Scout
Owner – Vince Martinico
Auburn, California

The Indian double-downtube frame replaced the Ace tubing in 1929. The leaf-spring fork held a twin-shoe drum brake, and the rear frame section was patterned on the 101 Scout. The wheelbase was up by 1.5 inches (3.8cm). The three-main bearing Ace crankshaft was supplanted by a five-main Springfield crank, and the engine carried new pistons and cylinder heads. The Four was rated at 30 horsepower and had also grown some 60 pounds (27kg) heavier.

The heavier-duty Indian four was a sophisticated sport-touring machine in 1929, but the price of $445, and the advent of the Great Depression, kept it to limited production. No changes were made to the four in the next two model years.

Indian was still committed to racing in the dirt-track and hillclimb categories. The 26 overhead-valve V-twin engines were used in all forms of competition, and would pull past 125mph (201kph) on a long straight-away. The side-valve Altoona motor, so named for its success on the

Below: Indian singles remained a force on the dirt tracks. The factory built 500cc overhead-valve models in two- and four-valve trim.

1929 Ohv Racer
Owner – Tony Penachio
Millwood, New York

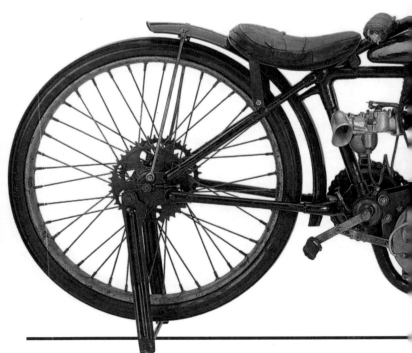

1928 Hillclimber
Owner – Tony Penachio
Millwood, New York

Above: This hillclimber is fitted with the 1000cc Altoona engine with dual carburetors. On the board track it was good for 120mph (193kph).

Pennsylvania boardtrack, had taken Curley Fredericks to a 120mph (193kph) boardtrack record in New Hampshire.

The same engine was used in national championship hillclimb events, with considerable success.

(1929 Four)
Engine: IOE inline four
Displacement: 1265cc
Horsepower: 30
Wheelbase: 59in (150cm)
Weight: 460lb (209kg)
Top speed: 80mph (129kph)
Price: $445

These were high-compression engines running on alcohol, and they made serious power. Hillclimbing was established as grassroots racing at the fundamental level, and several young Indian riders would rise to fame as the most fearless of "slant artists."

Right: The leaf-spring fork and front brake were among the first Springfield additions to the Four.

Below: The Ace frame was replaced by a double-downtube cradle in 1929. The three-main-bearing crankshaft was supplanted by a five-main shaft. The Four was already gaining weight in its Springfield configuration, but it also looked more like a traditional Indian.

1929 Four
Owner – Larry Struck
Groveland, California

By 1930 the economic depression had taken its toll on the Indian Motocycle Company. After three short-term shifts in management groups and investors, and increasing apprehension among stockholders, the company was sold to E. Paul DuPont. The wealthy industrialist undertook the rebuilding project in Springfield, and appointed Loren Hosley the new production chief.

Faced with a diminished market and necessary cost-cutting measures, the new owners had to make cuts in production. This led to a decision to discontinue the 101 Scout, much to the dismay of many Indian fans. Few could understand why the company would abandon such a popular model, especially when the limited-production Four was only marginally profitable. Many enthusiasts would look back on this as the first crippling wound in the company's battle for survival.

So 1931 was the last year for the 101, but the Scout name was applied in 1932 to the model 203, which was the Scout engine in a Chief frame. A heavier machine by about 60 pounds (27kg), the new Scout was not the agile sportster of the past. But despite its moderate power, the 203 scored well as a police model in the big cities where its reliability and handling ease were appreciated.

(1930 Four)
Engine: IOE inline four
Displacement: 1265cc
Horsepower: 35
Wheelbase: 59in (150cm)
Weight: 460lb (209kg)
Top speed: 80mph (129kph)
Price: $445

Below: The Four was a relatively compact motorcyle for a four. With a 59-inch (150cm) wheelbase, and 27-inch (69cm) seat height, it was almost nimble.

1930 Four
Owner – Mort Wood
Marathon, Florida

1931 101 Scout
Owner – Edwin Aucott
Green Lane, Pennsylvania

*Above: The last of the Scouts had
the Indian face horn and new
headlight. The rear brake and
sprocket stayed in place for wheel
removal.*

1932 Scout
Owner – Rocky Burkhart
Birdsboro, Pennsylvania

(1932 Scout)
Engine: Side-valve 42° V-twin
Displacement: 750cc
Horsepower: 22
Wheelbase: 61in (155cm)
Weight: 430lb (195kg)
Top speed: 75mph (121kph)
Price: $295

*Left: Lacquer paint was replaced
by enamel in 1931. Multiple hues
were available from the sizeable
DuPont catalog.*

*Below: The Scout-as-Chief was a
popular machine, despite the
additional weight. Handling ease
helped make up for the lack of
power. The Scout engine had
about two-thirds the horsepower
of the big twin, but was still
serviceable for most utilitarian
chores.*

Springfield's motorcycle production had been dropping steadily for four years, and fewer than 1,700 machines were made for 1933. The cost-cutting measures had, however, eliminated the deficit and Indian showed a slight profit.

Another encouraging result of budget consciousness was the development of the new Sport Scout. The new model borrowed from the Prince, 101 Scout and Junior Scout to become a machine with performance that seemed more than the sum of its parts. Though heavier and longer than the 101, with a keystone rather than

Right: Some motorcycles display a balance of engine and running gear that states they can get down the road smartly. This is one of them.

Below: The Four grew larger, added wheelbase and evolved with more streamlined tank and fenders. Weight gain was about 60 pounds (27kg).

1932 Four
Owner – Luke Walker
Newport, Rhode Island

1933 Four
Owner – Jim Smith

cradle frame, the Sport Scout combined speed, handling and practical efficiency. The gear-drive primary was replaced by chain, but the motorcycle was easy to ride, and easily made to be ridden faster.

With Harley-Davidson's emphasis on the 750cc side-valve RL series, the two company's established the racing formula called Class C, which would define American dirt-track from then on. Within a few years, the new production-based racing would revive the flagging fortunes of professional dirt-track racing.

The Four gained the streamlined tank and fenders that accompanied the Art Deco trend in motor-styling for cars and motorcycles. The 403 series, begun in 1932, also had a new longer and stronger frame, and shared many components with other models in the line. The cost-effectiveness of the Four remained only marginal, but more improvements were planned.

(1934 Sport Scout)
Engine: Side-valve 42° V-twin
Displacement: 750cc
Horsepower: 22
Wheelbase: 56.5in (144cm)
Weight: 450lb (204kg)
Top speed: 70mph (113kph)
Price: $300

1934 Sport Scout
Owner – Mort Wood
Marathon, Florida

Below: At first the Sport Scout appeared to be a seriously compromised version of the 101 Scout. But it became an all-round performance champion. The Sport Scout was a multiple hybrid of several preceding models.

But the additional weight and length were compensated by the handling. Many an adventuresome lad learned to go fast on the back roads with a Sport Scout. And Class C dirt-track racing began to grow.

The Depression lifted slightly in 1935, and Indian was encouraged to bring out a re-designed four. In an attempt to improve engine cooling, the new cylinders had the exhaust valves at the top and the intakes on the side. This would come to be known as the "upside-down" four. The model was only produced for two years.

(1934 Dispatch Tow)
Engine: Side-valve 42° V-twin
Displacement: 750cc
Horsepower: 22
Wheelbase: 57in (145cm)
Weight: 630lb (286kg)
Top speed: 65mph (105kph)
Price: $375

The styling of the motorcycles now moved to the forefront, with the elaboration of streamlined shapes and a broad selection of colors. The fenders had added valence, and the forms were outlined and enhanced by pin striping. In times of extraordinary economic stress, folks seem to like getting dressed up.

Below: The Dispatch Tow was powered by a Sport Scout engine, with lower compression and gearing.

Right: The tow bar was handy for auto mechanics, who could pick up and deliver the customer's car, and go for a ride.

1934 Dispatch Tow
Owner – Mike Tomas
Riverside, California

293

In 1936 a new distributor ignition replaced the previous wasted-spark system. The distributor drove off the rear cylinder camshaft, and proved itself a reliable provider of sparks. The lubrication system was improved to offer added life to the valve train.

The Indian lineup for 1936, excepting the misguided reconfig-uration of the four, offered a colorful selection of well-engineered motor-cycles. To their misfortune, it was also the year Harley-Davidson presented the long-ballyhooed overhead-valve 1000cc Knucklehead.

It was at this historical juncture that American motorcycling entered the musclebike era.

(1936 Chief)
Engine: Side-valve 42° V-twin
Displacement: 1200cc
Horsepower: 34
Wheelbase: 61in (155cm)
Weight: 490lb (222kg)
Top speed: 85mph (137kph)
Price: $340

Right: The lubrication system was improved in the mid-1930s. Indian script was also cast into the Chief sidecovers.

Above: In 1936 Springfield switched to an automobile-type distributor ignition. This is a stylish three-passenger three-wheeler.

1936 Chief
Owner – Robin Markey
Etters, Pennsylvania

The inverted four-cylinder saw its final year in 1937, with the option of dual Zenith carburetors. The motorcycle was faster but remained an aesthetic disappointment, and the engine configuration switched back to the earlier design in 1938.

(1937 Sport Scout)
Engine: Side-valve 42° V-twin
Displacement: 750cc
Horsepower: 22
Wheelbase: 56.5in (144cm)
Weight: 450lb (204kg)
Top speed: 70mph (113kph)
Price: $315

So the new Indian four was the old Indian four, still at 1265cc, and once again with a Schebler carburetor. (Schebler Deluxe with Heat Control.) One new feature was the casting of cylinders in pairs, to improve engine cooling. The saddle was also larger

Right: Sport Scout fenders got more swoopy, and buyers could chose a three- or four-speed transmission. An optional magneto was $25 more.

Above: In 1937 this rig would set you back $530. But for style like this, who would niggle over the price?

1937 Four
Owner – Jim Smith

1937 Sport Scout
Owner – Bob Stark
Perris, California

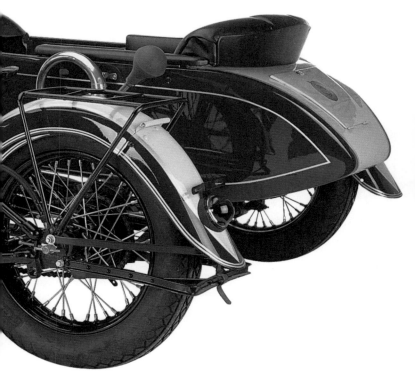

and allowed some adjustment fore and aft. The Indian head tank design was now painted in full color. No magneto model was offered in 1938.

The last of the rigid-frame fours, 1938 and '39, have become prized collectibles based on the combination of beauty, performance and rarity. Fewer than 700 were built over the two years.

The best news for Indian in 1937 came from Florida, where California's Ed Kretz won the inaugural Daytona 200 on a Sport Scout. Rollie Free ran a similar bike up to 111mph (179kph) on the beach, and Fred Ludlow later rode a Sport Scout to 115mph (185kph) at Lake Bonneville, Utah. The following year Kretz won the 100-mile national at Langhorne, Pennsylvania, and the inaugural 200-mile TT at Laconia, New Hampshire.

(1938 Four)
Engine: IOE inline four
Displacement: 1265cc
Horsepower: 45
Wheelbase: 59in (150cm)
Weight: 540lb (245kg)
Top speed: 95mph (153kph)
Price: $425

Right: In certain quarters, including this one, this is considered a genuinely handsome motorcycle.

Below: In 1938 the Four got a larger saddle with fore and aft adjustment. The luggage rack and saddlebags were a $13 option. No magneto ignition was offered in 1938. But the engine was right-side up again and it looked swell. Cylinders were cast in pairs.

1938 Four
Owner – Elmer Lower
Etters, Pennsylvania

(1939 Four)
Engine: IOE inline four
Displacement: 1265cc
Horsepower: 45
Wheelbase: 59in (150cm)
Weight: 540lb (245kg)
Top speed: 95mph (153kph)
Price: $425

Below: An option for 1939 was the World's Fair paint scheme, available on all models. This Four is the original metallic blue and silver.

(1938 Sport Scout)
Engine: Side-valve 42° V-twin
Displacement: 750cc
Horsepower: 35
Wheelbase: 56.5in (144cm)
Weight: 320lb (145kg)
Top speed: 105mph (169kph)
Price: $315

Below: The Sport Scout of the one and only Ironman Ed Kretz. "He was so strong," said one competitor, "he could carry the bike across the line." American dirt track had grown to be an exciting and popular sport after the Depression. Soon it would be postponed by war.

1938 Sport Scout
Owner – Ed Kretz, Jr.
Monterey Park, California

1939 Four
Owner – Leon Blackman
Emmaus, Pennsylvania

*Left: The venerable racer was
updated regularly over the
years. The frame was chromed
only after retirement.*

Although production dropped by nearly 40 percent from 1937 to 1938, and Indian was once again in the red (so to speak), they had a national hero in Ed Kretz. And for five years he would be the dominant racer in the country, even though he was not destined to repeat his victory at Daytona.

Springfield was not shy about proclaiming Kretz's prowess, and by association the sterling performance of the Indian motorcycle. The factory, of course, emphasized the latter, although it was popularly given that Ed Kretz would have won on anything. And speculation always surfaced that the California rider might well have achieved even greater success

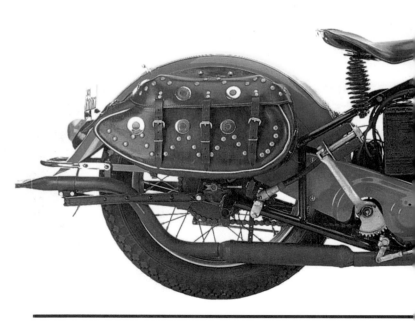

aboard the more reliable Harley-Davidson. When Indian folded in 1953 he was still racing, and switched to Triumph twins.

Other riders who put the Sport Scout out front were Lester Hillbish, the Castonguay brothers of Springfield, Massachussets, and Rollie Free. Bobby Hill and Bill Tuman would carry

the Indian banner successfully well into the fifties. Unlike the early days of professional racing, the Class C riders tended to be loyal to one manufacturer.

And by this time, Indian and Harley-Davidson were the only two left. The British invasion, however, was forthcoming. ▶

Left and below: The civilian Sport Scout was also a stylish piece of roadware. The upswept tail pipe, a distinctive Indian feature, was also on the Chief.

1939 Sport Scout
Owner – Eric Vaughan
Monrovia, California

In 1940 the Indian motorcycles appeared with fully skirted fenders, and created something of a fashion dilemma. Motorcycles had, concurrent with automobiles, developed increasingly stream-lined styling through-out the thirties. But no one had yet considered covering up the wheels. There was talk of heresy in some quarters, and some pestiferous pettifogging regarding the manhood of Springfield designers.

On the other side of the beauty beholding spectrum, many eyes held the skirted Indians in almost reverential awe. This was more than just a motorcycle; it was the style of the future. Art on wheels. So the

Below: The World's Fair paint scheme was also available on the Dispatch Tow. This was a popular color combination.

1939 Dispatch Tow
Owner – Jill Baker
Coatesville, Pennsylvania

camps were fairly evenly divided between the pro and con elements. But the issue was soon shelved, as economic and industrial attention turned to preparations for another global war. Motorcycle styling would be put on hold for five years.

The Four would not survive the war. The Sport Scout was to return stronger than ever, but for the time being it had to shed its pretty skirts for olive drab fatigues and adornments of military hardware. Plans were already underway for a racing version of the Scout, and several prototypes were built and raced in 1941. Another six years would pass before more racing models were built. ▶

(1940 Four)
Engine: IOE inline four
Displacement: 1265cc
Horsepower: 45
Wheelbase: 59in (150cm)
Weight: 575lb (261kg)
Top speed: 95mph (153kph)
Price: $425

Below: The Four got a seatpost spring in 1940. The fork was two inches (5cm) longer and overall weight had reached almost 600 pounds (272kg).

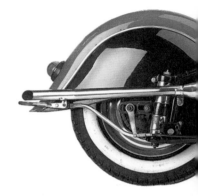

(1940 Sport Scout)
Engine: Side-valve 42° V-twin
Displacement: 750cc
Horsepower: 22
Wheelbase: 58in (147cm)
Weight: 485lb (220kg)
Top speed: 90mph (145kph)
Price: $390

Below: Covered fenders created quite a controversy when they appeared in 1940. The likers and dislikers were about evenly divided. Some observers felt that motorcyles had to have the wheels showing, and not look like automobiles. Others didn't feel that way at all.

1940 Four
Owner – Larry Struck
Groveland, California

1940 Sport Scout
Owner – Jeff Sierck
Plymouth, California

Springfield's first military contract was to build Chiefs for the French army, and the deal offered Indian a welcome injection of working capital. The last few civilian Chiefs were built in 1941 for the 1942 model year. Both Indian and Harley-Davidson accepted the call from the war department for development of a shaft-drive motorcycle for military use. Indian designed and built the 841, a 750cc transverse V-twin with foot shift, but only about 1,000 were built. The project was canceled when the military shifted its emphasis to the Jeep.

The other models produced by

(1940 Police Chief)
Engine: Side-valve 42° V-twin
Displacement: 1200cc
Horsepower: 40
Wheelbase: 62in (157cm)
Weight: 625lb (283.5kg)
Top speed: 75mph (121kph)
Price: Negotiable

Right: Fully rigged for duty, this 1940 Chief saw service with the California Highway Patrol. Hot rod hooligans arrived in force after the war.

(1942 640B)
Engine: Side-valve 42° V-twin
Displacement: 750cc
Horsepower: 22
Wheelbase: 58in (147cm)
Weight: 485lb (220kg)
Top speed: 75mph (121kph)
Price: Unknown

Below: Fully rigged for dispatch or reconnaisance duty, the 640 was a workhorse of the first order. Many stayed in Europe.

1942 640B
Owner – Robin Markey
Etters, Pennsylvania

1940 Police Chief
Owner – Bob Stark
Perris, California

Indian during the war were, by government order, restricted to civil defense and police markets. Springfield produced more than 16,000 machines in both 1942 and 1943, nearly all military bikes, most of which went to England and Europe. Many of the thousands of young men introduced to motorcycling during the war, came home with the intent to have one of their own. So the Indian vs. Harley dialogue would continue

into the 1950s. As would the racing.

Although the 841 never reached production as a military machine, its development contributed to the post-war civilian models. The hydraulic girder-spring fork was adapted to the Chief in 1946, and the plunger suspension was dialed in during endurance testing on the 841. Ed Kretz assisted in the tests of the 841, and trained military personnel in both riding and repairing the motorcycles.

Above right: A modified version of the 841 fork would be adapted to the Chief after the war. This was the first Indian to have foot shift.

Above: Barrels and heads from the Sport Scout were grafted to the transverse V-twin. Moto Guzzi later used this layout with greater success.

1944 841
Owner – Bob Stark
Perris, California

Although the Henderson/Ace-design four was gone, Indian was at work on two other quadruples during the war. The X44 was an overhead-valve motor in an 841 chassis, complemented by a telescopic fork. The compact, shaft-drive machine was built only as a prototype, as was the Torque four designed by Briggs Weaver. This engine was a double-up of the vertical twin that would become the next Indian Scout.

But Indian was bogged in another transfer of ownership, and in no position to finance new models. DuPont sold the company to Ralph Rogers in 1945, and the new owner bought the Torque Engineering Company. The intent was to develop a line of lightweight motorcycles designed by former Indian engineer Briggs Weaver. The re-shuffling left the Chief as Indian's only production model for 1946 and 1947.

The racing effort, on the other hand, was off and running as if nothing had happened. Ed Kretz won the Laconia 100, and when the Daytona 200 resumed in 1947, Johnny Spiegelhoff won it on a big-base Scout. His was one of the prewar prototypes, but for 1948 the factory built 50 of the racers to meet the rules of the American Motorcycle Association.

In the storybook finish, Floyd Emde took the lead at the start in the 1948 Daytona 200 and held it all the way to the checkered flag.

Above right and below: The Four that never was. A prototype was built by Torque Engineering, but only the single and twin reached production.

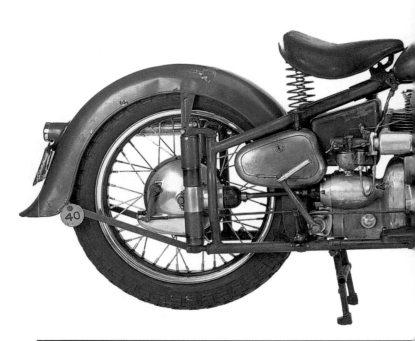

1943 Torque Four
Owner – Dr. John Patt
Gilbertville, Pennsylvania

(1947 Chief)
Engine: Side-valve 42° V-twin
Displacement: 1200cc
Horsepower: 40
Wheelbase: 61in (155cm)
Weight: 560lb (254kg)
Top speed: 85mph (137kph)
Price: $475

1947 Chief
Owner – Bob Stark
Perris, California

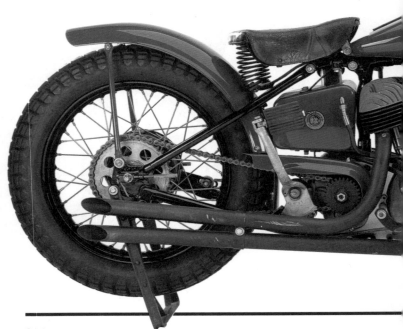

Left: By 1947 the wartime shortages had ended. Two-tone paint returned to the roster, and chromed accessories were *available. Indian script replaced the Indian head tank emblem. Chromed front and rear safety guards were popular additions.*

(1948 Big-Base Scout)
Engine: Side-valve 42° V-twin
Displacement: 750cc
Horsepower: 40-45
Wheelbase: 58in (147cm)
Weight: 325lb (147kg)
Top speed: 115mph (185kph)
Price: $750

Below: In 1948, Floyd Emde took off first from the line in the annual Daytona 200-mile race, and he stayed out front all the way. Several of the big-base Sport Scouts were raced successfully before the war. Afterwards, Indian built 50 to meet the homologation rule. The magneto was moved atop the oil pump. The engine was massaged for improved lubrication and more horsepower, and it went fast.

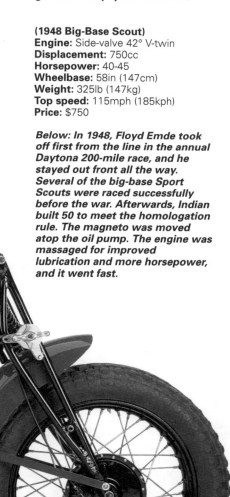

1948 Big-base Scout
Owner – Jim Smith

The attempt to bring the lightweight Torque twin and single to market consumed more time and money than Springfield had expected. Not only had the machines been inadequately developed and tested, the prices had to be higher than anticipated. So Rogers' attempt to enlighten the American ridership with European-style motorcycles was doomed to failure. And production of the Chief had been suspended in 1949.

The Arrow and Scout might well have been sorted out in time, but the expense had already been too great. Ralph Rogers chose to import British motorcycles and accepted financial investment from John Brockhouse of England. Rogers would be forced out in 1950, and Indian divided into separate manufacture and marketing

(1949 Scout)
Engine: Ohv vertical twin
Displacement: 440cc
Horsepower: 20
Wheelbase: 51in (129.5cm)
Weight: 295lb (134kg)
Top speed: 75mph (121kph)
Price: $350

Below: The new Scout looked nothing at all like the old. The vertical twins were part of Ralph Rogers' plan to revive the company.

Right: The Torque engines were beset with mechanical problems, most created by rushed development and insufficient testing.

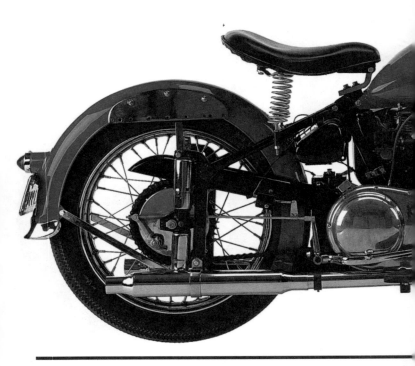

1949 Arrow
Owner – Trev Deeley
Vancouver, British Columbia

1949 Scout
Owner – Bob Stark
Perris, California

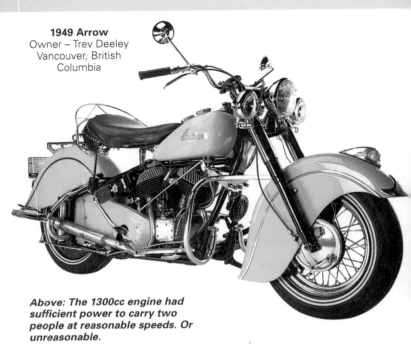

1949 Arrow
Owner – Trev Deeley
Vancouver, British
Columbia

Above: The 1300cc engine had sufficient power to carry two people at reasonable speeds. Or unreasonable.

entities, the latter run by Brockhouse.

The Chief was back in production for 1950, with a traditional side-valve V-twin stroked to 1300cc. The big twin now had a telescopic front fork and the right-hand throttle was standard. A number of design changes were made in the last few years, but Brockhouse had little interest in refining the Chief to match the efforts of Harley-Davidson. His primary goal was in the employment of Indian dealers in selling a line of British motorcycles. ▶

(1950 Chief)
Engine: Side-valve 42° V-twin
Displacement: 1300cc
Horsepower: 40
Wheelbase: 62in (157cm)
Weight: 560lb (254kg)
Top speed: 95mph (153kph)
Price: $750

Below: Sunshine yellow was among the popular post-war colors, although most Chiefs were painted red or black. The 5.00 x 16 tires were now the only size offered. Indian fans were relieved to witness the return of the Chief.

1950 Chief
Owner – Bob Mercer
San Jose, California

The final iteration of the Torque twin was the Warrior, offered in street or trail trim for 1951. Most of the mechanical problems had been rectified in these models, but that wasn't enough to make them survive another year.

Few changes were made to the Chief. Riders could still choose between a three- or four-speed transmission and distributor or magneto ignition. A spring-loaded "Torque Evener" engine sprocket was added to cushion the primary drive. Footboard extenders for the passenger were now made of aluminum rather than iron.

The 1952 Chief was given several new styling touches to dress it up even more. The front fender had a slightly revised profile and a new panel was fitted ▶

Right: Suspension at both ends of the Warrior TT had increased travel, to better handle the rigors of scrambles and enduro competition.

Below: The traditional Chum-Me seat shown was joined in 1950 by an optional bench-style for a tad less chumminess.

1950 Warrior TT
Owner – Bob Stark
Perris, California

1951 Chief
Owner – Bob Stark
Perris, California

(1953 Chief)
Engine: Side-valve 42° V-twin
Displacement: 1300cc
Horsepower: 40
Wheelbase: 62in (157cm)
Weight: 560lb (254kg)
Top speed: 95mph (153kph)
Price: $960

Left: The Antique Motorcycle Club of America has chapters throughout the country. Shows, auctions and swap meets are held throughout the year.

between the upper fork tubes, which were now finished in chrome. The fuel tank, now more tapered at the rear, had the Indian script logo on a wing-shaped background. The word "Eighty" was added to note the number of cubic inches. A new cowling fit between the exhaust pipes, covering the oil pump and distributor.

The combustion chambers were slightly reshaped on the late models and compression was also higher. The handlebars, low-rise or Western-style, now had external cables for the throttle, choke and spark advance. ▶

Below: Final renditions of the Chief had chromed upper fork legs, and the horn was moved up near the steering head. "Eighty" indicated cubic inches. Exhaust header pipes were lengthened to circumvent the engine cover. The exhaust pipe now carried straight back.

1953 Chief
Owner – Elmer Lower
Etters, Pennsylvania

(1968 Scout)
Engine: Side-valve 42° V-twin
Displacement: 750cc
Horsepower: 28
Wheelbase: 57in (145cm)
Weight: 425lb (193kg)
Top speed:110mph (177kph)
Price: Unknown

1968 Clymer Scout
Owner – David Manthey
Portage, Wisconsin

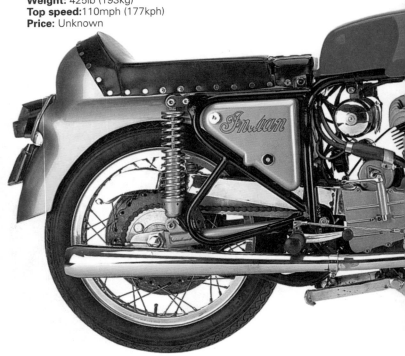

The last of the Chiefs, and the end of Indian, came in 1953. The arguments and opinions over the demise of the Indian Motocycle Company have continued to rattle back and forth for nearly 50 years. Some of them are persuasive, other less so. It's inarguable that Harley-Davidson's technology did improve more steadily than did Indian's, and that even Milwaukee's progress was cautious at best.

But although both companies built large V-twins, their management and engineering were different in nearly every respect imaginable. And the combined effects of those dissimilarities saw one prevail and the other decline and fail.

Indian showrooms were soon filled with AJS, Royal Enfield, Norton and Matchless motorcycles from England. Some dealers added Triumph, BSA or Velocette machines, and others even switched to Harley-Davidson at the risk of social ostracism. In 1959 a few took on an obscure Japanese brand named Honda.

In the mid-sixties, Floyd Clymer attempted to revive Indian. He imported several Italian minibikes to be marketed as Indians, and commissioned a sport model with a Velocette engine and Italian chassis. But his prime goal was to bring back the Scout in an updated version. Designed by Germany's Friedl Münch, a prototype was produced in 1967. The bike pictured here was the only one made.

Left: Floyd Clymer's attempt to revive the Indian produced several hybrids. Perhaps the most promising was the model designed by Friedl Münch.

Iver Johnson (1907-1916)

(V-Twin)
Engine: Side-valve V-twin
Displacement: 1020cc
Horsepower: 7-8
Wheelbase: 58in (147cm)
Weight: 265lb (120kg)
Top speed: 65mph (105kph)
Price: $225

Iver Johnson's Arms and Cycle Works had been building bicycles for 23 years when they entered the motorcycle business. The Massachussetts firm had started manufacturing firearms many years earlier.

The Iver Johnson was uncon-ventional in many respects. The top and middle frame tubes were bent to arch over the engine, and the front fork was an interesting leading link, leaf spring design. Customers could choose either rigid or swingarm rear suspension. This was known as a keystone frame, one that employs the engine as a stressed member.

The Iver Johnson's side-valve singles and twins had two different valve mechanisms. The belt-drive single featured a longitudinal cam-shaft driven by worm gears, the shaft extending forward through the case to drive the magneto. On the V-twin

Below: "The Iver Johnson motorcycle is a wonderful example of engineering, design and construction. It has tremendous speed, very flexible control, and rides like a touring car." The leading-link spring fork was an interesting piece of work. Iver Johnson credited the keystone frame for the machine's supple handling.

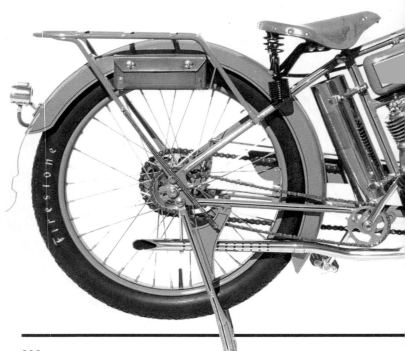

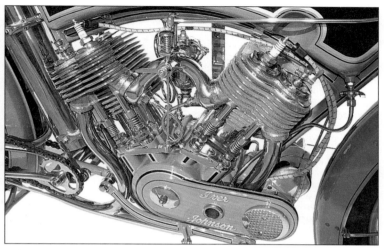

Above: The Iver Johnson twin was a handsome piece of craftwork, although it did not produce much in the way of horsepower.

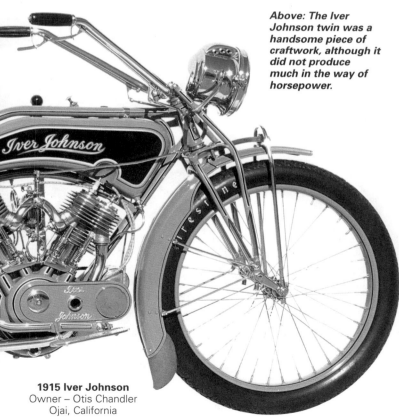

1915 Iver Johnson
Owner – Otis Chandler
Ojai, California

and chain-drive single, the cams were incorporated in a large ring gear driven by a pinion gear on the crankshaft. The magneto on these engines was chain-driven.

The V-twin was designed with offset crankpins which provided evenly spaced combustion strokes; so the Iver Johnson exhaust note sounded like a vertical twin. The engine featured both mechanical and hand oil pumps. The final versions of the twin were equipped with a planetary clutch, with either an

Below: Iver Johnson offered a 500cc single with either chain or belt drive. The engine was rated four to five horsepower.

Eclipse two-speed hub or a single speed. The twin was rated at eight horsepower, and the single at 4.5hp.

In 1916 the final chain-drive V-twin was $250 for the two-speed, and $225 for the single-speed; the single-cylinder was priced at $200 and $175 respectively. The single was also offered in a belt-drive version for $150. In that year, the market for weapons began to seriously outsrip the prospects for motorcycle sales, so Iver Johnson turned its attention to firearms and tools.

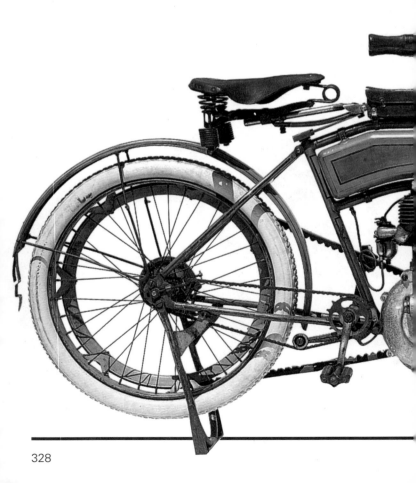

Right: The camshaft was fitted longitudinally, amidships. The bevel drive shaft extended forward to power the magneto.

1913 Iver Johnson Single
Owner – Jim Lattin
Encinitas, California

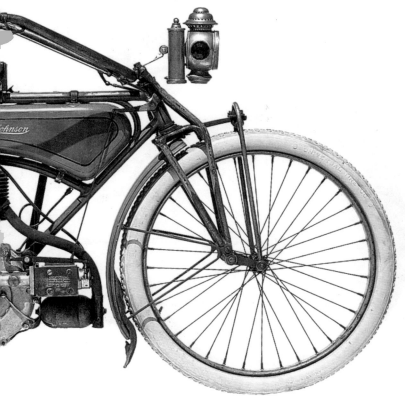

Kokomo (1909-1911)

Engine: IOE single
Displacement: 346cc
Horsepower: 4
Wheelbase: 57in (145cm)
Weight: 175lb (79kg)
Top speed: 45mph (72kph)
Price: $200

The Kokomo had a relatively short run under the name of its hometown in Indiana, but it would carry on under the Shaw imprint in 1912. The belt-drive single was housed in a loop frame with a leading-link, leaf-spring front fork. The engine

was positioned mid-way between the axles, and the centerline of the crankshaft was slightly below the axles' plane. Some thought was given to the design and engineering.

The company was purchased by the Shaw Manufaturing Company of Kansas, which sold the Kokomo in conjunction with their engine attachment kits for bicycles. Shaw later suspended motorcycle production to manufacture farming implements. It is not known how long the Kokomo was built in Kansas, but it's not in Kansas anymore.

Below: The Kokomo was built back home in Indiana, in sweet home Kokomo. But that train doesn't stop here anymore. Play the blues. Both the drive belt and rear pulley were stout-looking items. The drive hoop was affixed to the rim by nine mounts.

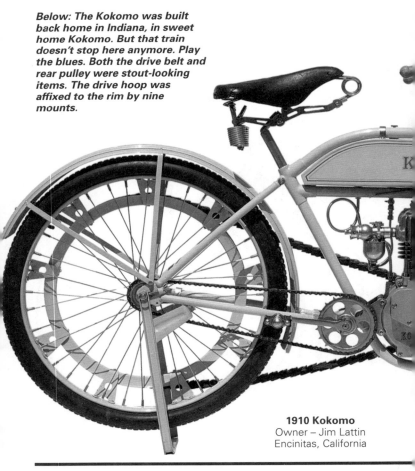

1910 Kokomo
Owner – Jim Lattin
Encinitas, California

Above: The Kokomo's gear-driven magneto was fitted at the front of the engine. The interesting muffler was positioned well away from the rider's feet.

Light (1901-1911)

Engine: IOE single
Displacement: 213cc
Horsepower: 2.25/3.0
Wheelbase: 48.5in (123cm)
Weight: 115lb (52kg)
Top speed: 35mph (56kph)
Price: $185/225

The Light Manufacturing and Foundry Company bought en-gines from Aurora, and the early versions were almost identical to the Indian of the period. Imitation was a popular trend at the time, and it was too early in the motorcycle era for trademarks or copyrights to be resolved. A wide open market, in other words.

Later, when Indian began building their own motors, Aurora released their own motorcycles under the Thor brand. The same engine was employed by a half-dozen other man-ufacturers until motorcycle prod-uction was abandoned in 1916, owing largely to the coming war. Thor continued for many decades in the power tool business.

Below: The Light was also sold as the Thor-Bred, for its Thor engine. Two years later the machine had a loop frame, leading-link fork and a vertical engine.

Light began marketing their machines rather more aggressively in 1907, dropping the Thor-Light des-ignation. Two models were offered; the 2.25-horsepower machine with chain drive, and the three-horse engine with Thor's new internal pinion gear in lieu of a countershaft. The Sager-cushion spring fork was standard, and the exhaust system included the Light Radio muffler with 18 small tubes within the cannister.

According to The Bicycling World and Motorcycle Review, "The whole design of the Light and the arrangement of its equipment gives it an appaearance of lightness and indicates the result of experience and a practical turn of mind." In 1908 Light acquired the Merkel Motor Company and changed the name to Merkel Light, with production still in Pottstown, Pennsylvania. Three years later the company was sold to the Miami Cycle and Manufacturing Company, production transfering to Middletown, Ohio.

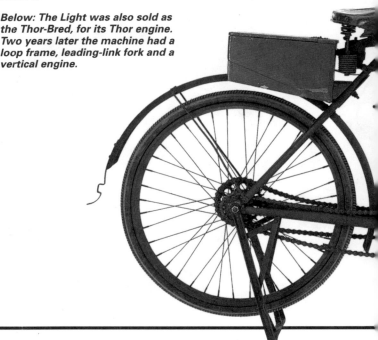

Right: The Thor engine, built by the Aurora Automatic Machinery Company of Illinois, was the most widely used proprietary engine in the early days of American motorcycling.

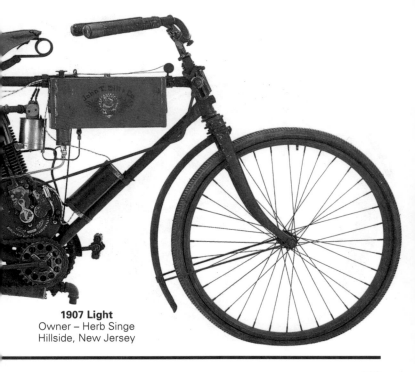

1907 Light
Owner – Herb Singe
Hillside, New Jersey

Marsh (Marsh & Metz M.M.) (1900-1913)

(Single)
Engine: IOE single
Displacement: 510cc
Horsepower: 3.5
Wheelbase: 53in (135cm)
Weight: 150lb (68kg)
Top speed: 40mph (64kph)
Price: $175

The Marsh brothers built their first motorized bicycle in 1899. The single horsepower single soon grew to 1.75 ponies, and the Marsh Motor Bicycle was shipped to market with a one-year guarantee.

General Manager W.T. Marsh and his brother A.R. were confident in the quality of their product. With E.R.

Thomas, theirs were among the first machines built as a motorcycles rather than as adapted bicycles. The frame joints were heavier drop forgings, and the fork was beefier than most of their counterparts. The engine was fitted at first forward of the seat post, then integrated with the frame in the 1902 production model.

As early as 1902 the Marsh boys had built a short-coupled racer with a loop frame, heavy duty truss fork, lowered handlebar and seat. This was a big-base, six-horsepower single that was good for nearly 60mph (97kph); the rear belt pulley was nearly the same diameter as the wheel.

Below: A forward mounted muffler helped keep heat from the rider's legs. But it was also out in harm's way. The tubular fuel tank held 1.5 gallons (5.7lit); the aft section carried two quarts (1.9lit) of oil.

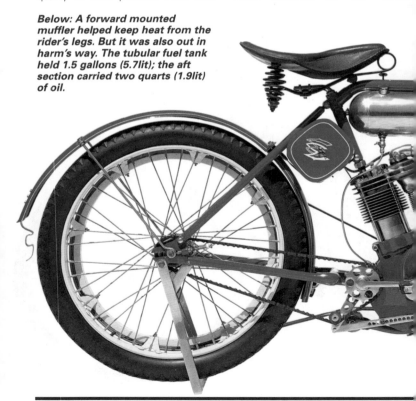

Right: The Roadster engine was rated at three horsepower. The M.M. float feed carburetor sat directly in front of the intake valve.

1909 M.M. Roadster
Owner – Jim Lattin
Encinitas, California

According to *Cycle and Automobile Trade Journal* of 1902, "Mr. W.T. Marsh states that the thrilling excite-ment of riding this mon-ster on the state roads at between 50 and 60 miles an hour is (for lack of better words) grand.

"He also states that he was very much amused on one occasion, when he perceived in the distance, far ahead of him, a man on a footpower machine, who evidently belonged to the sprinting class. As the

Above: M.M. built a 90° twin in 1909. "Forty-five degrees, the angle so generally used in motorcycle construction, is the worst possible angle, being always out of reciprocating balance."

(Twin)
Engine: IOE 90° V-twin
Displacement: 1087cc
Horsepower: 10
Wheelbase: 58in (147cm)
Weight: 230lb (104kg)
Top speed: 65mph (105kph)
Price: $275

Right: The 90° V-twin first appeared in 1908. The Massachusetts company had offered a 45° V-twin for two years previous.

racer is fitted with a large pulley in front which measures about 10 inches, and makes about the same number of explosions at 50 miles an hour as the 1-3/4 horsepower motor does at 25 miles an hour, the man evidently figured that there was a bit of pace behind and put down his head to get speed on to tack on behind. It is needless to say that the sprinter was disappointed when the catapult shot by him and disappeared in a cloud of dust."

· Marsh did not continue racing efforts into the professional era that blossomed near the end of the decade. In 1905 they joined forces with Charles Metz, of Orient bicycle and motorcycle fame, to form the American Motor Company. The Marsh & Metz, or M.M. became a stronger force in the market, and developed the first 90-degree V-twin in the country. In addition to their own models, Marsh & Metz sold engines to the trade, which appeared under other brand names such as Peerless, Arrow and Haverford. The American Motor Company, like so many of its counterparts, would not see a second decade in business and folded in 1913. Charles Metz carried on with his Metz automobile, "the car you'll be proud to own."

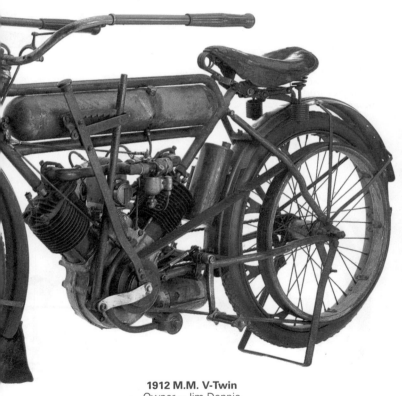

1912 M.M. V-Twin
Owner – Jim Dennie
Palmyra, New York

Marvel (1910~1913)

Engine: Ohv single
Displacement: 500cc
Horsepower: 4-5
Wheelbase: 57in (145cm)
Weight: 155lb (70kg)
Top speed: 55mph (89kph)
Price: $225

The Marvel was the final iteration of the Curtiss motorcycle. By 1910, Glenn Curtiss was heavily involved in airplane projects, and had entered into partnership with Agustus Herring, who had experimented with heavier-than-air flight before the turn of the century. (For details of Curtiss's career, see Glenn Curtiss, Pioneer of Flight by C.R. Roseberry, Syracuse University Press.)

The Marvel was advertised as a four to five horsepower 500cc overhead-valve single with more power than most twins. "By Brake Test it shows over one horsepower

Below: One element that distinguished the Marvel was its single pushrod operating both the intake and exhaust valves.

338

Above: The Marvel represented the end of the Curtiss motorcycle genealogy. Quite an interesting chapter for students of moto-history.

1911 Marvel Single
Owner – Wes Allen
Yuba City, California

more than any previous Motor of equal cylinder capacity. On hills it shows up as good as the large doubles and ahead of the smaller ones. It is not such a wonder as a racer but for ordinary road work it has not an equal in any Motor ever built."

The Marvel was "guaranteed to climb a hill steeper than any other."

The Marvel employed the large frame tubes as fuel and oil containers. The engine was lubricated by a splash system, regulated by a cork float in the sight glass. The first engine had

Below: The overhead-valve engine was 50 percent more powerful than its Curtiss pocket-valve predecessor. The oil tank held 2.5 quarts (2.1lit).

its 1⁵/₈-inch (41mm) overhead valves disposed at 30 degrees; both intake and exhaust were controlled by a single pushrod. In 1911 the valves grew to 1³/₄ inches (44mm) and a more substantial front fork was fitted.

The Marvel disappeared under the weight of a grim legal battle between Agustus Herring and Glenn Curtiss. The matter was settled in 1923, in favor of Curtiss, but the decision was overturned in 1928.

1910 Marvel
Owner – Wes Allen
Yuba City, California

Merkel (1902-1915)

(1905 Single)
Engine: IOE single
Displacement: 233cc
Horsepower: 2.25
Wheelbase: 50in (127cm)
Weight: 85lb (38.5kg)
Top speed: 30mph (48kph)
Price: $155

(1908–09 Single)
Engine: IOE single
Displacement: 500cc
Horsepower: 3
Wheelbase: 54in (137cm)
Weight: 150lb (68kg)
Top speed: 40mph (64kph)
Price: $185

The motorcycles built by Joseph Merkel set the high performance standards in the century's first decade. The engines and suspension invited high-speed exercises, and Indian soon followed suit with race-bred improvements. With the addition of Excelsior and Harley-Davidson, the American motorcycle racing scene attracted large crowds and sizeable profits for promoters and riders.

A few of the 500cc belt-drive singles were built as racers at the original Merkel plant in Milwaukee. When the company was purchased by the Light Manufacturing and Foundry Company and moved to

Below: The early Merkels employed the frame's front downtube as part of the exhaust system. A half-dozen other manufacturers used the same technique.

1905 Merkel
Owner – Herb Singe
Hillside, New Jersey

1909 Light Single
Owner – Herb Singe
Hillside, New Jersey

Above: During the transition period in 1909, the Light Manufacturing & Foundry Company still offered machines bearing the Light brand. Singles and twins were Thor engines.

Pennsylvania in 1909, one of the bikes came to young test rider Maldwyn Jones. An inventive mechanic and racer, Jones set up the bike and defeated Cannonball Baker in 10-mile race in Ohio. The following year he turned pro and won three of his first four races on a second-generation Pottstown leftover, which now bore the Flying Merkel logo on the tank.

Jones went on to become a champion racer, and his abilities helped Merkel achieve lasting status among motorcycle performance enthusiasts. The Merkel front fork was the instrument of choice on racing bikes of other builders, and the single-shock rear suspension was an advanced concept. "All roads are smooth to the Flying Merkel." When ownership shifted to the Miami Cycle

Below: By 1910 Merkel production had been merged with the Light brand in Pottstown, Pennsylvania. This was the first year that the name Flying Merkel was used. The Flying Merkel was flashy, fast and it flew down the road.

Right: Most of the credit for Merkel's racing success goes to the innovative Maldwyn Jones, who joined the company as a mechanic in 1910. This frame was fitted with several singles and a V-twin between 1910 and 1914.

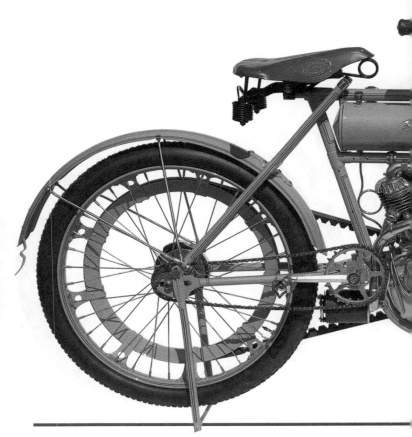

1912 Merkel Twin
Owner – Jim Lattin
Encinitas, California

1910 Flying Merkel Twin
Owner – Mike Parti
North Hollywood, California

(1915 V-Twin)
Engine: IOE V-twin
Displacement: 1000cc
Horsepower: 7-9
Wheelbase: 54in (137cm)
Weight: 280lb (127kg)
Top speed: 60mph (97kph)
Price: $240-275

1912 Merkel Twin
Owner – Jim Lattin
Encinitas, California

Left: Although the Ohio-based Merkel had no official racing department, racing employees continued to receive support.

Below: The Flying Merkel was a pioneer in the use of swingarm rear suspension. Springs were housed inside the upper rear fork tubes. The Flying Merkel V-twin was offered in both 885cc (V) and 1000cc (VS) versions. The big-bore engine was rated at seven horsepower.

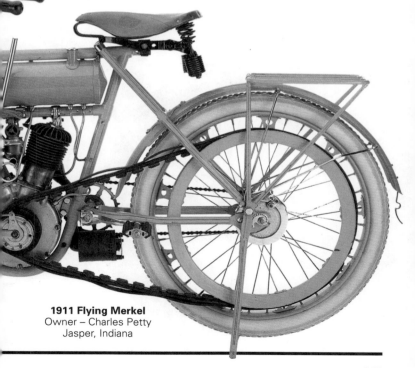

1911 Flying Merkel
Owner – Charles Petty
Jasper, Indiana

Below: The last of the Merkels had a right-side kickstarter. A two-speed planetary transmission was available as an option.

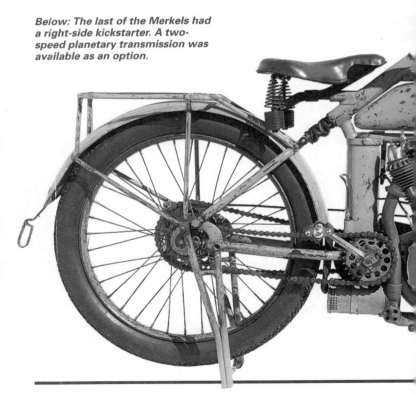

and Manufacturing Company of Ohio in 1911, the factory racing team was abandoned, though Jones and several other riders were provided machines.

By 1913 the Ohio Flying Merkels had mechanical intake valves, chain drive was an option and the oil tank and seat post were integrated. The engine was steadily refined and in 1915, the final model year, it received a

Left: "If it passes you it's a Flying Merkel," read the ads. In the early days, when high-performance motorcycling was a wonderful new adventure, the Cyclone and Flying Merkel V-twins were the fastest machines on the road and track.

kickstarter. A two-speed planetary transmission was optional.

Merkel was the least conservative of the pioneer motorcycle companies. They tried more engineering innovations than most, took more chances and gave Indian and Harley fits on the racetracks. But a contracting market left them, as so many others, in the historical heyday of motorcycling.

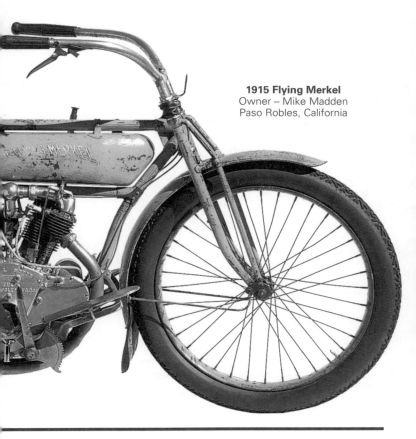

1915 Flying Merkel
Owner – Mike Madden
Paso Robles, California

Miami (1915-1916)

Engine: Side-valve single
Displacement: 236cc
Horsepower: 2.5
Wheelbase: 50in (127cm)
Weight: 125lb (57kg)
Top speed: 35mph (56kph)
Price: $115

The Miami was a Merkel by another name. Sold as the Miami Power Bicycle, the belt-drive side-valve single was housed in a Merkel-style loop frame. The lightweight machine sold for $115. The motorcycles were in production for little more than a year, and very few examples remain.

Right: The Miami Power Bicycle lasted only briefly. A magneto system appeared in 1916; this engine has a drive mechanism built by its owner.

Militaire/Militor (1911-1922)

Engine: Inline IOE four
Displacement: 1145cc-1435cc
Horsepower: 11-14
Wheelbase: 65in (165cm)
Weight: 400lb (181kg)
Top speed: 60mph (97kph)
Price: $335

Now for something completely different. The Militaire Autocycle Company built its first machines in Cleveland, Ohio. The motorcycle departed sharply from conventional forms in design and construction, and was apparently conceived as a two-wheeled car. The original vehicle, powered by a single-cylinder, had hub-center steering, a steering wheel and retractable outrigger wheels at the rear.

The Cleveland operation expired in 1913, but was resuscitated a year later in Buffalo, New York by owner N.R. Sinclair. The single had been replaced by a four-cylinder engine,

Right: The gearshift lever rose directly from the three-speed transmission. As a motorcycle/automobile, the Militaire was better than neither.

1915 Miami Single
Owner – Shorty Tomkins
Sacramento, California

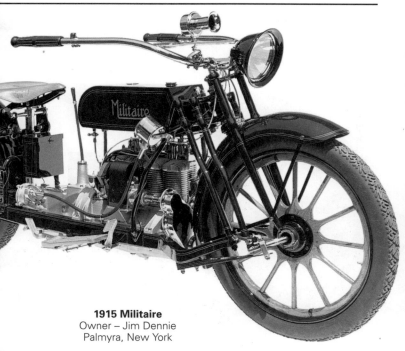

1915 Militaire
Owner – Jim Dennie
Palmyra, New York

and the steering wheel was supplanted by handlebars. The automotive-style frame and rear idler wheels remained. The 1065cc engine delivered better than 11 horsepower through a three-speed floorshift transmission and shaft drive. The wheelbase, like the early Henderson, was 65 inches (165cm). The wooden artillery wheels carried 28-inch Goodyears.

Given the name, the Militaire was surely intended as a military device from the beginning. But it was too long and heavy for a motorcycle and too unstable for a car. The army did buy a few examples for use in France in 1918, but the machines were immobilized by mud. The Buffalo enterprise had also succumbed, and Sinclair reformed the company in New Jersey and changed the name to Militor.

N.R. Sinclair was obviously not one to retreat in the face of adversity. When the Jersey City operation floundered, he set up shop again in the Knox Motors factory, an automobile company in Springfield, Massa-chussetts, a stone's throw

Below: The F-head four held a sizable multi-plate clutch and an electric starter. The seat put the rider a considerable distance from the front wheel. The wooden artillery wheels enhanced the Militaire's stately appearance. Warfare had now shifted from mounted cavalry to tanks and aircraft. Outrigger wheels were lowered by a pedal on the footboard. Gentleman riders were not obliged to put their feet down on dirty roads.

Right: One of the more complex steering systems in the motorcycle catalog. High-speed handling, such as it was, could be dicey. Low-speed agility was mostly absent.

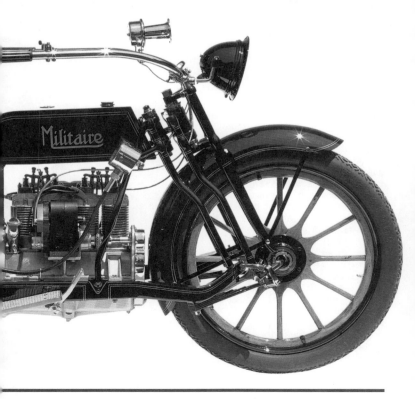

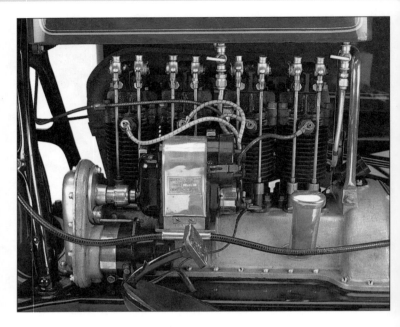

from the Indian factory. But this association also failed within a year, and Sinclair relocated in Bridgeport, Massachussets under the banner of the Bullard Machine Tool Company.

The Militaire was arguably ahead of its time (or its time never came), but as an engineering exercise it was an interesting device. As a hybrid, the machine was subject to numerous mechanical faults given the complex systems and overall length. Many of the motorcyles were returned for repairs, and the company would eventually fold under the burdens of warranty work and poor development.

In the Bridegeport chapter, the final three years of Militor production, the machine had an 1435cc overhead-valve engine. The latter renditions were sold only as sidecar units, and anticipated the arrival of art deco styling for motorcycles. Unfortunately the ohv engine was subject to lubrication problems, which pushed the company off the roster for good.

Left: With the shift to Militor came an overhead-valve engine, displacing 1435cc. The length of the pushrods indicate the long-stroke (3.5in/8.9cm).

Below: Since the Militor was outfitted with a sidecar, the idler wheels were deleted. The front end and steering system were simplified. Production ended in 1922.

1920 Militor
Owner – Otis Chandler
Ojai, California

Minneapolis (1908-1914)

Engine: IOE single
Displacement: 591cc
Horsepower: 5-6
Wheelbase: 57in (145cm)
Weight: 190lb (86kg)
Top speed: 55mph (89kph)
Price: $300

An alphabetical coincidence, but the Minneapolis was originally produced by the same company that produced Michaelson motorcycles. The early Minneapolis used the proprietary Aurora single, and were all but identical to the Thor model. In 1911 the Minneapolis had its own side-valve single and a leading link spring fork. The engine featured an internal two-speed planetary transmission.

The Mineapolis Big 5 Auto-Cycle

Below: Motorcycles figured strongly as service vehicles in the early days. Most were used for light deliveries, postal or police work.

1911 Minneapolis Tri-car
Owner – Otis Chandler
Ojai, California

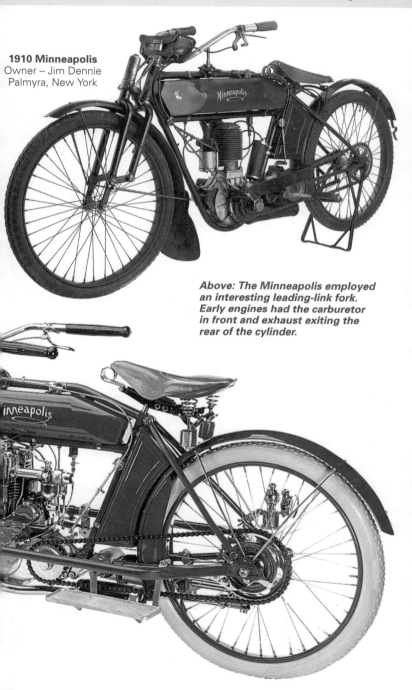

1910 Minneapolis
Owner – Jim Dennie
Palmyra, New York

*Above: The Minneapolis employed
an interesting leading-link fork.
Early engines had the carburetor
in front and exhaust exiting the
rear of the cylinder.*

was rated at 11.5 horsepower, with performance that was "reliable – quick – efficient." And the Unit Power Plant was a significant selling point. Unlike most American singles, the Minneapolis displaced its valves and exhaust pipe on the left side of the engine.

The late-series Minneapolis featured a swingarm rear suspension with an interesting monoshock system.

Toward the end of their production, the Minneapolis utilized the DeLuxe engine built by the Spacke Machine Company of Indianapolis, Indiana.

Right: The Minneapolis was advertised as "an automobile on two wheels." The big single was rated by the manufacturer at 11.5 horsepower. The Big 5 was one of the first side-valve engines in use, and was unusual in having the valve gear arranged on the left side.

Monarch (1912-1915)

Engine: IOE V-twin
Displacement: 1200cc
Horsepower: 10
Wheelbase: 59in (150cm)
Weight: 340lb (154kg)
Top speed: 65mph (105kph)
Price: $275

The Monarch was built by the Ives Motorcycle Corporation in western New York. The Monarch Big 5 (horsepower), a belt-drive single, was fitted with a leading-link, parallel strut front fork. The company also produced a V-twin, an F-head engine with pushrods driven by the right-side camshaft. Though a stoutly built machine, the Monarch was another marque that faded from the market within a few years.

Right: The Monarch big twin carried a leading-link spring fork. The oil tank was fitted in front of the seat post; a tool box at the rear. Note unique "leaf spring saddle suspension."

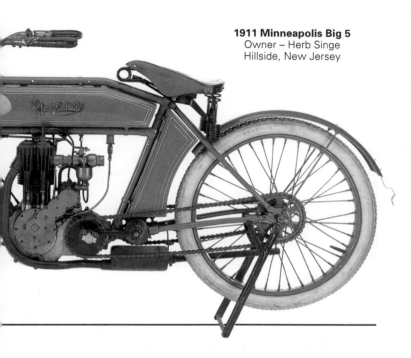

1911 Minneapolis Big 5
Owner – Herb Singe
Hillside, New Jersey

1912 Monarch
Owner – Bud Ekins
North Hollywood,
California

Mustang (1946-1967)

Another of the rapidly-rising post-war scooter outfits was Mustang of California. Designed by racer/engineer Howard Forrest, a sprint car racer, the Mustang became the original hot rod of scooterville. In association with financier John Gladden, Forrest introduced the first Villiers-powered Mustang in 1946.

The two-stroke was soon dropped in favor a four-stroke flathead. The Mustang, overgrown scooter or mini-motorcycle, was easily the king hot rod musclebike of the post-war utility machines. With wheels sightly larger than the average scooter, a telescopic fork and industrial horsepower, the Mustang, in the vernacular of the period, hauled ass.

With some cam and head work, and a bit of reinforcement on the frame, the Mustang could be hustled smartly around a short dirt track. When Walt Fulton and other west coast racers began beating full-size motorcycles in Class C competition, the American Motorcycle Association frowned upon them. The Mustang was subsequently disqualified from sanctioned competition, an action that some said resulted from pressure exerted by Harley-Davidson on the AMA.

So the Mustang returned to its role of pit bike, commuter and all-around work pony. Cushman responded to its success with the Eagle, another scooter dressed in motorcycle styling of the period. The Eagle became Cushman's best seller, but neither company would survive the 1960s, a time of uncertainty in Scooterville and elsewhere.

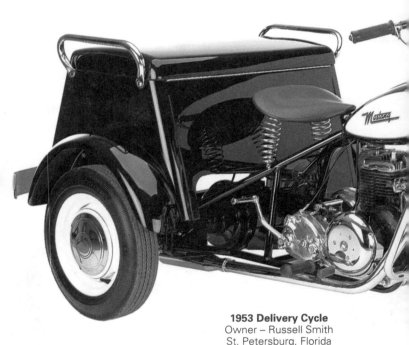

1953 Delivery Cycle
Owner – Russell Smith
St. Petersburg, Florida

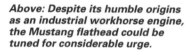

Above: Despite its humble origins as an industrial workhorse engine, the Mustang flathead could be tuned for considerable urge.

Left: The Delivery Cycle was a miniature version of the Harley-Davidson Servi-Car. The tow bar was handy for picking up and returning vehicles for repair.

1961 Mustang Thoroughbred
Owner – anonymous

Engine: Side-valve single
Displacement: 318cc
Horsepower: 12.5
Wheelbase: 50in (127cm)
Weight: 260lb (118kg)
Top speed: 70mph (113kph)
Price: $540

Left: The Thoroughbred, the Mustang version of a touring machine, appeared in 1960 and stayed until the end of the tour in 1965.

Below: Basic 1940s' motorcycle styling in a small package made the Mustang a popular choice. Mustang was one of the first, and few, scooter manufacturers to use telescopic forks. Disc wheels would later come back on custom Harleys.

1959 Mustang Pony
Owner – Russell Smith
St. Petersburg, Florida

Below: The Stallion was introduced in 1959 and remained in production for seven years. The Mustang Stallion sold for about $500 in 1961. Price increases and Japanese imports put the little horses out to pasture in 1966.

Right: The stout little flathead singles were producing 12 horsepower. Engines were made in the U.S., but three- and four-speed transmissions were British.

1961 Stallion
Owner – Stan Stanton
Overland Park, Kansas

Nelk (1905-1912)

Engine: Overhead-cam single
Displacement: 220cc
Horsepower: 2
Wheelbase: 45in (114cm)
Weight: 110lb (50kg)
Top speed: 35mph (56km/h)
Price: $225

Not much is known of the Nelk. Although the California company was in business for seven years, this is the only known example. Designed and built in Palo Alto by a Mr. Nelk, the motorcycle is quite unlike anything else built in the early 1900s. The overhead-cam single was water-cooled and rubber-mounted, and featured a clutch in the rear hub.

Cooling water was carried in the stylish tank in the upper frame section, and the fuel tank was fitted to the rear fork. The engine had external flywheels and curved battery box located below the engine. The craftsmanship, fit and finish of the components is well above average at this stage of motorcycle evolution. And it had a front brake.

Below: The overall configuration of the Nelk suggests "bicycle," but the two horsepower engine was able to propel it to quite a respectable 35mph (56kph).

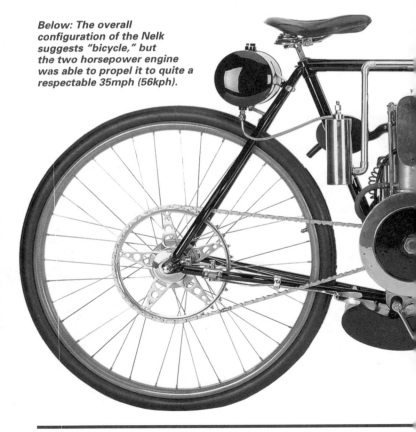

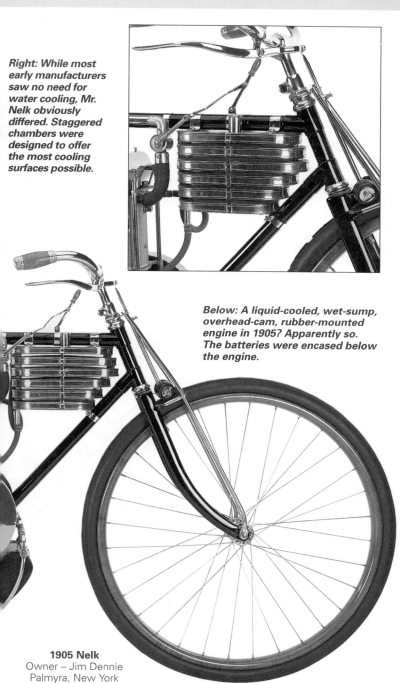

Right: While most early manufacturers saw no need for water cooling, Mr. Nelk obviously differed. Staggered chambers were designed to offer the most cooling surfaces possible.

Below: A liquid-cooled, wet-sump, overhead-cam, rubber-mounted engine in 1905? Apparently so. The batteries were encased below the engine.

1905 Nelk
Owner – Jim Dennie
Palmyra, New York

Neracar (1920-1927)

Engine: Two-stroke single
Displacement: 221cc
Horsepower: 2.5
Wheelbase: 57in (145cm)
Weight: 175lb (79kg)
Top speed: 40mph (64kph)
Price: $225

In the tradition of the Militaire and New Era, albeit on a smaller scale, the Neracar emerged from Syracuse, New York in 1920. The name was double wordplay; almost like a car and a twist on the name of its designer, Carl Neracher. Maybe they should have just called it Carl.

By most motorcycle standards, the Neracar was a genuine oddball. With its monocoque chassis, hub center steering and a transverse-mount two-stroke single amidships, the Neracar was well outside the mainstream. Power transfered from the flywheel to a friction disc, then by chain to the rear wheel. The front wheel pivoted on a kingpin, with a compression and rebound spring on either side of the lower arms. Low-speed handling was comfortable, but steering lock was limited.

The Neracar had limited success at home, but the marque was carried on by licensed production in England from the Sheffield Simplex Company. The British used a larger 285cc two-stroke engine, and later added a 350cc side-valve Blackburne engine with a three-speed transmission. An overhead-valve version came out in 1925.

The Syracuse operation called it quits in 1924, but the British rendition lasted through 1927, when the Sheffield Simplex concern could no longer support, car, truck and nearly-a-car production.

Right: The two-stroke cylinder emerged from the middle of the amphibian body work. The company hired the legendary Cannonball Baker as a spokesman.

Right: The Neracar was one of the most popular versions of the combined car/scooter/motorbike configurations for getting about town.

1923 Neracar
Owner – Dale Walksler
Mt. Vernon, Illinois

1921 Neracar
Owner – Doc Batsleer
New Smyrna Beach, Florida

New Era (1909-1913)

Engine: IOE single
Displacement: 475cc/623cc
Horsepower: 4/6
Wheelbase: 62in (157cm)
Weight: 215lb (97.5kg)
Top speed: 50/60mph (80/97kph)
Price: $285/300

Another of the early cruisers was the New Era, a motorcycle version of the town car. The machine, termed an Auto-Cycle, was built by the New Era Gas Engine Company of Dayton, Ohio. The intitial version of 1909 had 60 inches (152cm) of wheelbase and a 3.5-horsepower pocket-valve single. The debut model was fitted with a truss fork and an Indian-style fuel tank on the rear fender.

The ensuing models featured a new frame, leading-link spring fork, lower footboard and cylindrical fuel tank. The oil tank was cast into the frame. Power went up to four horsepower, and an optional larger bore and stroke engine offered six horsepower. The New Era retained its automotive heritage in the hand crank starter. Wheelbase on the latter frame was 62 inches (157cm). Once underway, with its clutch and two-speed transmission, the machine delivered a stylish ride in town or country.

The Roadster was offered in solo

Below: The 500cc single was offered in four- and six-horsepower versions. The latter with magneto sold for $325. The leading-link fork acted on a single enclosed spring. The tires were 28 x 2.5 inches. Automotive touches were apparent in the flat floorboard and hand

crank starter. Fuel capacity was 1.75 gallons (6.6lit); oil, 3 pints (1.4lit). The fuel tank was moved aft on the two-passenger Roadster model, making space for the passenger's grab handle.

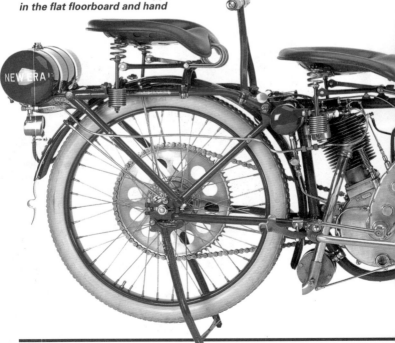

Above: The New Era's single footboard was an 11 x 17-inch (28 x 43cm) aluminum casting. The oil tank was incorporated with the seatpost tube.

1911 New Era
Owner – Shorty Tomkins
Sacramento, California

1912 New Era
Owner – Jim Dennie
Palmyra, New York

371

or passenger trim, with the promise of its ability to go "Anywhere Under Any Condition." Comfort was the primary appeal offered by its makers, "None of those small pains across the small of your back – no saddle soreness – no cramps in the toes – nothing but a keen delight in the pleasure of motorcycling and the desire to keep riding."

From the 1911 brochure: "A 62-inch wheelbase does away with the excessive jolting of the rider on rough roads, and on paved streets, with a short wheelbase, the jolting of the rider is very noticeable and very objectionable. A long wheelbase not only adds greatly to the comfort of the rider, but also increases the life of the tires and lessens the amount of repairs on the Auto-Cycle.

"Of what use are pedals if the motor will not run, and how much easier and simpler to start a motor by means of a crank than to pedal against a strong compression in the cylinder of a motor? Some motor-cycle riders say thay pedaled their motor-cycles a mile or more, but did not get over the exertion for many days; and this feature of being compelled to pedal the old style motor-cycle is the means of disgusting many a rider, who, after once riding the New Era Auto-Cycle, will not part with it."

Despite its sterling qualities, and high-grade mechanical components, the New Era Auto-Cycle went to history in 1913.

Above right: New Era took pride in the use of German Hess-Bright ball bearings for the crankshaft, and roller bearings at the connecting rod. The stroke on both engines was 3.75 inches (95.25mm); the four-horsepower had a bore of 3.25 (82.6mm), while the six-horse engine was 3.625 (92mm). The battery box held two #6 dry cells.

Right: The tandem Roadster had "ample power to take two riders up any grade that traction can be found for the rear wheel."

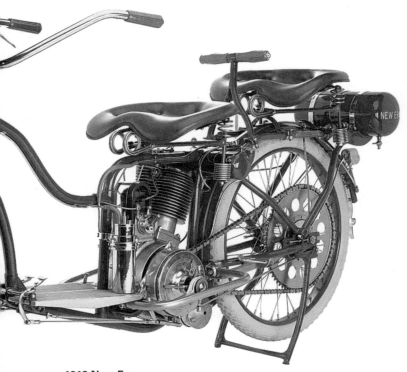

1912 New Era
Owner – Jim Dennie
Palmyra, New York

Orient (1900-1905)

Engine: IOE single
Displacement: 376cc
Horsepower: 1.75-3.5
Wheelbase: 48in (122cm)
Weight: 165lb (75kg)
Top speed: 30mph (48kph)
Price: $250-300

Right: The Metz-design engine appeared in 1903. Similar to the Aster, the cases were aluminum and the cylinder head was reconfigured.

Here is one of the originals. Before Metz met Marsh, he developed the Orient motorcycle using the French Aster engine. Charles Metz had formed the Waltham Manufacturing Company in 1893, to manufacture Orient bicycles. Five years later he caught the motor fever and designed a new frame to fit the Aster single, with an underslung fuel tank and a top speed of 30mph (48kph). The engine was distinguished by fluted copper flanges on the cylinder rather than cast fins, a claimed improvement in heat dissipation.

Metz built his own version of the Aster engine, using aluminum instead of bronze cases, and improved heads and cylinders for more power. When his associates wanted more attention given to the automobile arm of the company, Metz left to build motorcycles under his own name. The Orient remained in production for another three years, when it was dis-continued in favor of cars.

Panzer (1997-)

Engine: Ohv V-twin
Displacement: 1377cc
Horsepower: 68
Wheelbase: 62in (157cm)
Weight: 660lb (299kg)
Top speed: 120mph (193kph)
Price: $24,432

1998 Panzer Tourister
Courtesy of Panzer M/C Works
Canon City, Colorado

The Panzer is a retro Harley Panhead replica built with contemporary components. The Neo-Pan is a 1377cc engine with STD cases and heads, S&S cylinders, Truett & Osborne stroker flywheels and Andrews cam. Panzer offers four models with different trim in the $21-25,000 range. All are rubber-mount engine versions with five-speed transmssion.

Right: The Panzer represents the marriage of contemporary V-twin engineering and traditional 1950s design and styling.

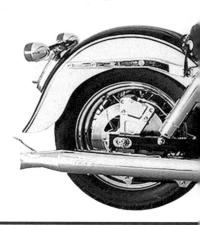

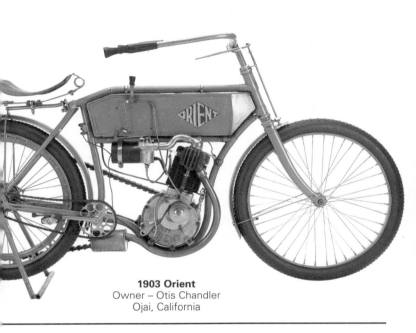

1903 Orient
Owner – Otis Chandler
Ojai, California

Pierce (1909-1913)

(Four)
Engine: Inline T-head four
Displacement: 696cc
Horsepower: 7
Wheelbase: 65in (165cm)
Weight: 275lb (125kg)
Top speed: 55 mph (89kph)
Price: $325-400

George Pierce founded the Pierce Great Arrow Motor Car Company and the Pierce Cycle Company in Buffalo, New York. His cars and bicycles were built to high standards and commanded premium prices. When Pierce put his son Percy in charge of the bicycle division in 1908, the young man added motorcycles to the roster. He had recently returned from Europe with an FN four, designed by Paul Kelecom of Belgium.

Pierce did not build a copy of the FN, but its influence on the first American four-cylinder motorcycle was apparent. While the FN was an IOE design, the Pierce employed a ▶

Below: Pierce used the FN Four of Belgium as a basic pattern, but departed with regard to frame construction and the engine's valve mechanism. Pierce frame tubes were 3.5 inches (8.9cm) in diameter.

1911 Pierce Single
Owner – Herb Singe
Hillside, New Jersey

Above: The five-horsepower Pierce single claimed the "efficiency of a twin with the the simplicity of single-cylinder construction."

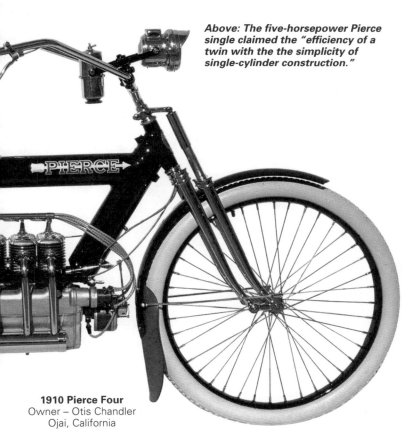

1910 Pierce Four
Owner – Otis Chandler
Ojai, California

377

side-valve arrangement, with intake valves on one side of the engine and exhausts on the other. This two-cam system was called a T-head engine. And rather than suspend the engine in a loop frame, Pierce adopted the keystone system with the engine as part of the frame. Like the FN, the Pierce used enclosed shaft drive to the rear wheel, and was the first American motorcycle to fit the automotive-style final drive mechanism.

The other distinctive aspect of the Pierce was the use of the frame tubes to carry fuel and oil. The tubes were 3.5-inch (8.9cm) 18-gauge steel, copper plated on the inside. The upper and rear frame tubes held seven quarts (6.6lit) of gasoline, while the front downtube carried five pints (2.36lit) of oil. The original 1909 model was genuine direct drive, with no clutch or gearbox; so the rider had to be ready to go when the engine fired up. In its second model year the four was fitted with a multi-disc clutch and two-speed transmission. The Pierce "vibrationless motorcycle" would give "motor car comfort and travel comfortably from a mere walking pace up to the speed of the motor car."

(Single)
Engine: Side-valve single
Displacement: 592cc
Horsepower: 5
Wheelbase: 57in (145cm)
Weight: 235lb (107kg)
Top speed: 55mph (89kph)
Price: $250

1912 Pierce Single
Owner – Jim Lattin
Encinitas, California

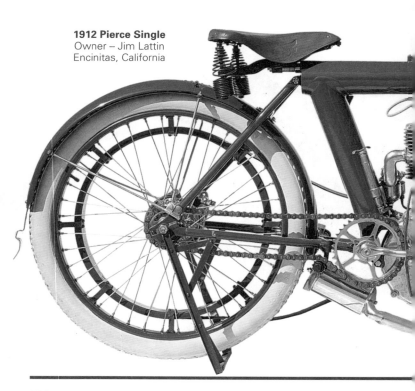

378

1912 Pierce Single
Owner – Otis Chandler
Ojai, California

Above: "Pierce motorcycles are not made to compete in price but to surpass in quality," read the ads of 1912. "It is a deluxe motorcycle for discriminating riders."

Below: "The Vibrationless Motorcycle" was exported to 14 foreign countries. The 1912–13 models, the final editions, were two-cam engines.

Pope (1911-1918)

(Single)
Engine: Ohv single
Displacement: 623cc
Horsepower: 5-8
Wheelbase: 56.5in (143.5cm)
Weight: 255lb (116kg)
Top speed: 50mph (80kph)
Price: $215

Lieutenant Colonel Albert Augustus Pope (Union Army, Civil War) was one of the American transportation pioneers. He began importing then manufacturing bicycles in the 1870s, and undertook building automobiles ▶

Below: The Model M for 1913 was the top of the line single. Chain drive and a Bosch magneto added $15 compared to the belt-drive model. The Pope overhead-valve single for 1913 was a stately machine with chain drive, rear suspension and front leaf-spring fork.

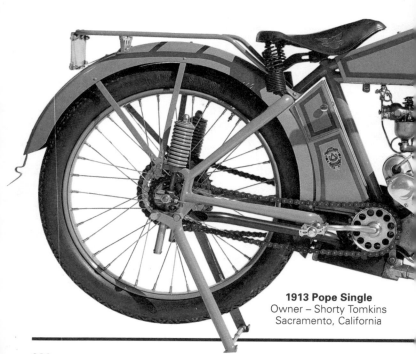

1913 Pope Single
Owner – Shorty Tomkins
Sacramento, California

1912 Pope Single
Owner – Shorty Tomkins
Sacramento, California

Above: The 1912 Pope single was touted as "light, silent, reliable. Pope quality has never been questioned."

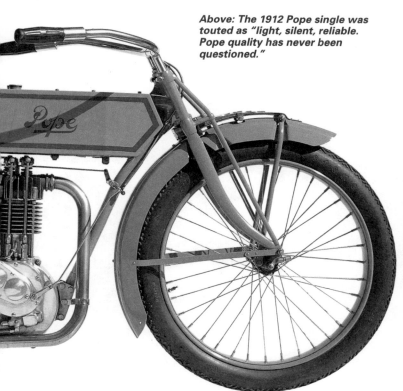

in 1896. Pope bicycles were sold under the Columbia brand, and also as Cleveland, American, Imperial, Crescent, Monarch and Tribune. The same names were attached to motorcycles built by the American Cycle Manufacturing Company.

Pope had factories in Connecticut, Indiana, Illinois and Ohio. He founded Wheelman magazine and was instrumental in the promotion of paved roads, but by 1908 his financial situation had seriously deteriorated. Pope's own name wasn't applied to the motorcycles until 1911, two years after his death. Motorcycle production was moved to Westfield, Massachussetts.

(Twin)
Engine: Ohv twin
Displacement: 1000cc
Horsepower: 12-18
Wheelbase: 56.5/58.5in
 (143.5/148.5cm)
Weight: 305lb (138kg)
Top speed: 65mph (105kph)
Price: $225/275

Right: In 1915 the Pope rear suspension was upgraded with twin shafts. Spring tension could be adjusted to match the rider's weight.

Below: The overhead-valve Pope twins were built from 1912 to 1918. The two-speed transmission and rear suspension were strong selling points.

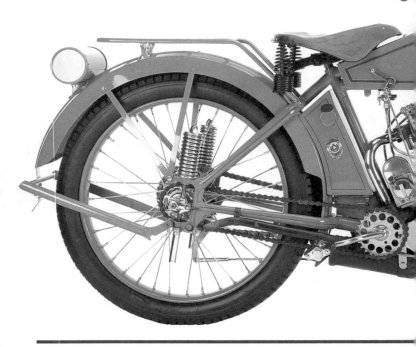

1915 Pope Twin
Courtesy of Mike Terry
Union, New Jersey

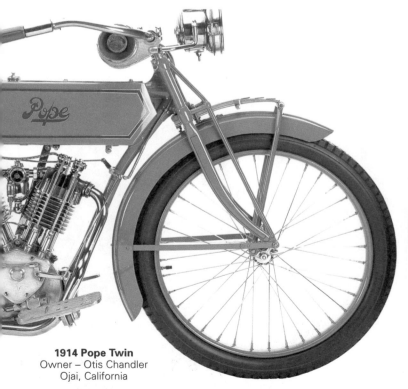

1914 Pope Twin
Owner – Otis Chandler
Ojai, California

1916 Pope Single
Owner – Dale Walksler
Mt. Vernon, Illinois

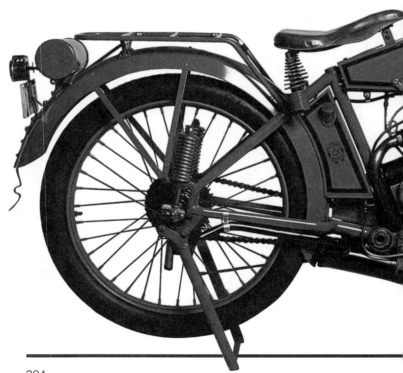

Left: 1916 was the final year for the belt-drive single. The economy model had changed little in six years of continuous production.

Below: Last of the Popes: the L-18 Special was a single speed. The three-speed was the T-18; both were 1000cc V-twins rated at 18 horsepower.

1918 Pope Special
Owner – Dale Walksler
Mt. Vernon, Illinois

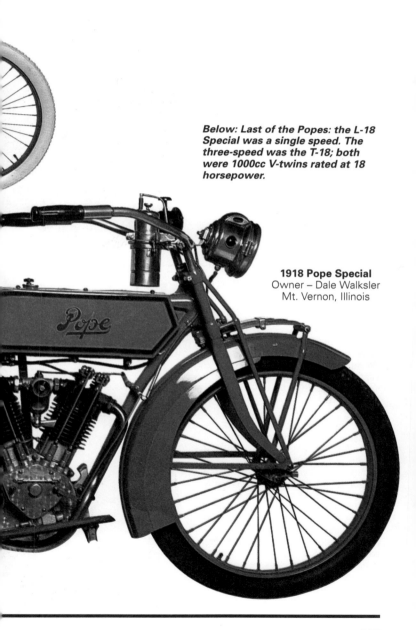

Pure Steel (1995-)

Engine: Ohv 45° V-twin
Displacement: 1573cc
Horsepower: 101
Wheelbase: 67.5in (171cm)
Weight: 485lb (220kg)
Top speed: 120mph (193kph)
Price: $33,900

Below: Staggered dual exhausts and velocity stack give the Scimitar the serious demeanor of a drag racing machine.

The Pure Steel customs are Harley-pattern V-twins, with a 1573cc S&S engine in Daytec chassis. The Scimitar employs a powder-coated Softail-style frame with a chrome swingarm. The engine carries Pure Steel's own Stage 4 heads; the Delkron gearbox holds Jims close-ratio gears. Pure Steel offers six models, including two rigid-frame versions. Engine options include 1753cc and 1852cc units.

Racycle (1905-1911)

(1907 Single)
Engine: IOE single
Displacement: 311cc
Horsepower: 2.25
Wheelbase: 48in (122cm)
Weight: 120lb (54kg)
Top speed: 30mph (48kph)
Price: $210

The first Racycle, from the Miami Cycle & Manufacturing Company of Ohio, was a re-labled Indian. The Thor engine was used by several other manufacturers until 1908, when the Aurora Automatic Machinery Company brought to market a complete machine under the Thor brand.

The second generation of Racycle singles lasted until 1911, when Miami bought out the Merkel-Light company. Still an intake-over-exhaust engine with atmospheric intake valve, the new single was a larger engine set vertically in a keystone frame. The new chassis featured a leading-link, ▶

1998 Pure Steel Scimitar
Courtesy of Pure Steel
Phoenix, Arizona

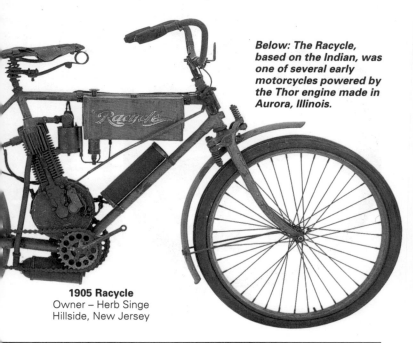

Below: The Racycle, based on the Indian, was one of several early motorcycles powered by the Thor engine made in Aurora, Illinois.

1905 Racycle
Owner – Herb Singe
Hillside, New Jersey

(1910 Single)
Engine: IOE single
Displacement: 475cc
Horsepower: 4
Wheelbase: 60in (152cm)
Weight: 175lb (79kg)
Top speed: 40mph (64kph)
Price: $210

Below: The Racycle still employed the Thor engine in 1910. The 1911 model retained the rear exit exhaust, but the carburetor moved aft of the cylinder. Production of the Thor-engine Racycle ended in 1911,

when the Miami Cycle and Manufacturing Company acquired Merkel-Light. The penultimate rendition of the Racycle was issued in 1910. The 1911 model woul have a reinforced, and heavier, frame.

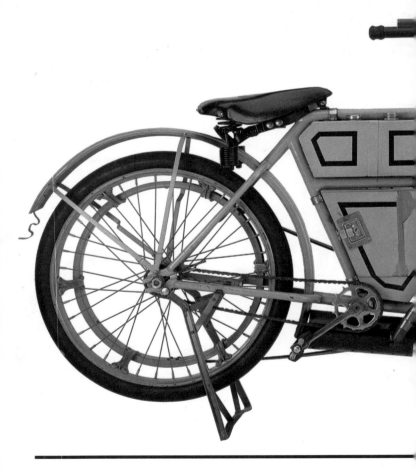

parallel-strut fork with a single cartridge spring, quite similar in design and construction to the New Era front suspension.

In its final rendition, the Racycle engine had the carburetor fitted aft of the cylinder and the spark plug in front. The frame was also modified, with a second rear downtube and seatpost suspension. Production was discontinued when Miami switched to the Merkel design.

1910 Racycle
Owner – Herb Singe
Hillside, New Jersey

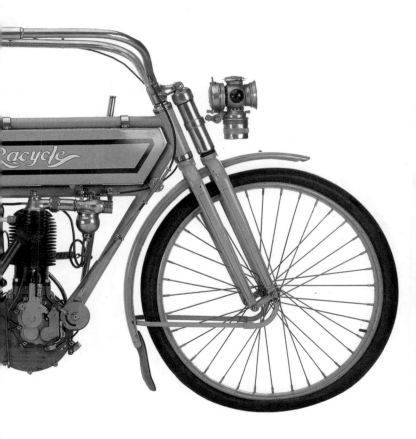

Reading-Standard (1903-1922)

(Single)
Engine: Side-valve single
Displacement: 361cc
Horsepower: 3
Wheelbase: 51in (130cm)
Weight: 150lb (68kg)
Top speed: 30mph (48kph)
Price: $200

The early Reading-Standards were also Indian replicas using the Thor engine, but the Pennsylvania company soon made its own modifications. The first change was a spring fork of its own design, and the fuel tank moved to the upper frame tube.

The most significant revision came in 1906, when Reading-Standard released the first side-valve engine produced in the United States. Designed by engineer Charles Gustafson, the three-horsepower engine disposed the intake and exhaust ports 180 degrees apart in the cylinder head. The R-S, as it was called, also had a new oil tank on the rear fork just below the seat. Turning the lever one way released a measure of oil into the engine and shut off the tank; turned the other way the valve refilled the oil cup.

R-S produced their first twin in 1908, but it did not employ the single's side-valve configuration. The F-head twin was rated at six horsepower, and had the unusual feature of the valve gear on the left side of the front cylinder and the right side of the rear. The twin was raced with some success in the early teens, most notably by Paul "Daredevil" Derkum of Los Angeles. But it was soon outpaced by the larger manufacturers. Charley ▶

1906 Reading-Standard
Owner – Mike Parti
North Hollywood, California

Right: Early carbide headlamps retained the ornate craftsmanship developed for carriage lamps of the previous century. Their glow was minimal.

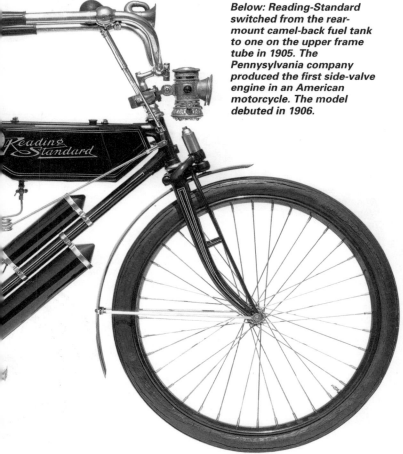

Below: Reading-Standard switched from the rear-mount camel-back fuel tank to one on the upper frame tube in 1905. The Pennysylvania company produced the first side-valve engine in an American motorcycle. The model debuted in 1906.

(1909 V-Twin)
Engine: F-head 45° V-twin
Displacement: 722cc
Horsepower: 6
Wheelbase: 51in (130cm)
Weight: 165lb (75kg)
Top speed: 45mph (72kph)
Price: $250

Right: The F-head V-twin carried its cams and valve gear on opposite sides of the cylinders. Racer Ray Seymour set a mile record of 76.7mph (123.4kph) in 1909.

Gustafson, their top engineer, went to work for Indian.

By the mid-teens R-S had reduced its output to three models; two twins (with or without electrics) and a single, all with side-valve engines. All had three-speed transmissions; the twin was rated at 12 horsepower and the single at six. These were larger engines, a 557cc single and 1100cc twin. But R-S faltered in the early twenties, and was sold to the Cleveland Motorcycle Manufacturing Company. The final editions in 1924 had a 1180cc twin with 16 horsepower, no match for the big Indian and Harley twins.

Reliance (1908-1915)

Engine: IOE single
Displacement: 425cc
Horsepower: 3
Wheelbase: 55in (140cm)
Weight: 125lb (57kg)
Top speed: 35mph (56kph)
Price: $175

The Reliance evolved from what was originally the Erie motorcycle made in Hammondsport, New York by the Motorcycle Equipment and Supply Company. Erie made a belt-drive and friction-drive motorcycle, and sold engine kits for bicycles. They also provided complete machines to the Reliance Motorcycle Company to market under their own name.

The three-horsepower engine, with Curtiss float-feed carburetor, was fitted low in a loop frame. The optional sidecar cost $38, and a cushion front fork was available for $3.50 extra. The Reliance was not widely distributed beyond the eastern U.S., and the company went out of business in 1915.

Right: The 1909 Reliance 850cc twin doubled up on the single-cylinder model. Both machines employed the spring fork and belt drive.

1909 Reading-Standard
Owner – Dale Walksler
Mt. Vernon, Illinois

1909 Reliance Twin
Owner – Bud Ekins
North Hollywood, California

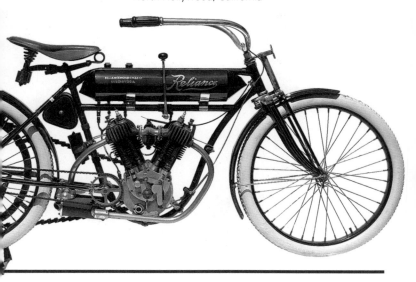

Rokon (1962–)

(RT-340)
Engine: Two-stroke single
Displacement: 335cc
Horsepower: 35
Wheelbase: 56.5in (143.5cm)
Weight: 260lb (118kg)
Top speed: 90mph (145kph)
Price: $1,660

The Rokon Trail-Breaker is a work-horse motorcycle of an entirely different order. The two-wheel drive machine was designed to go where other motorcycles, or even animals, could not. With chain drive to both wheels, the Rokon will ascend very steep slopes and plow through mud. When added traction is required, the aluminum wheels can be filled with water for more weight, or used as supplementary fuel tanks.

The Trail-Breaker is powered by a single-cylinder Chrysler two-stroke engine. In the mid-seventies the power was bumped from eight to ten horsepower, and a power take-off added. Popular with farmers, hunters, firefighters and mountaineers, the Trail-Breaker is still in production.

More conventional but still unusual was the Rokon RT-340, powered by a Sachs engine with automatic transmission. Developed as an enduro bike, the RT was also offered as a moto-crosser and dual-purpose motorcycle. Other uncommon features were disc brakes and optional magnesium wheels. The Rokon Automatic went out of production in 1979.

(Trail-Breaker)
Engine: Two-stroke single
Displacement: 134cc
Horsepower: 8
Wheelbase: 49in (124cm)
Weight: 185lb (84kg)
Top speed: 25mph (40kph)
Price: $695

Below: Aluminum drum wheels can carry 4.5 gallons (17lit) of gasoline, for added traction and/or mileage. With wheels empty, the machine will float.

1975 Rokon ST-340
Owner - John Cepek
Bridgeview, Illinois

Above: The Rokon ST-340 was a street legal version of the RT with battery, lights and horn. Magnesium wheels help keep the weight down.

1969 Rokon Trail-Breaker
Owner – Robert Sinclair

Royal (1901-1910)

(1903 Single)
Engine: IOE single
Displacement: 200cc
Horsepower: 1.5
Wheelbase: 48in (122cm)
Weight: 90lb (41kg)
Top speed: 20mph (32kph)
Price: $185

The Royal, designed by Emil Hafelfinger, was introduced in 1901 but was taken off the market in 1903. By 1907 it was back on the scene with belt rather than chain drive, larger engine, more substantial frame and front suspension. The Royal was quite similar to the early Indian, but the engine was not incorporated with the seat post. Instead, the post was joined to four smaller tubes that surrounded the engine and joined below it.

In 1909 the name was changed to Royal Pioneer, and the product was far more advanced. The engine featured horizontal overhead valves controlled by pull rods, and a hemispherical combustion chamber. Exhaust was routed through the frame, and the leading-link front fork had springs for compression and rebound. The Royal factory was destroyed by fire in December of 1909, and production was not resumed.

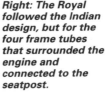

Right: The Royal followed the Indian design, but for the four frame tubes that surrounded the engine and connected to the seatpost.

Safti-Cycle (1946-1950)

Engine: Side-valve single
Displacement: 213cc
Horsepower: 1.5
Wheelbase: 56in (142cm)
Weight: 130lb (59kg)
Top speed: 35mph (56kph)
Price: $175

The Safti-Cycle combined elements of the bicycle and motor scooter to create a lightweight utility vehicle. Crash bars and a luggage rack were optional equipment, and a third-wheel delivery van was also available. The 1.5-horsepower Briggs & Stratton single would propel the unit in moderate safety to about 35mph (56kph). The powertrain employed an automatic clutch and chain drive. A lighting kit and generator were optional items. Ready for the road, the Safti-Cycle weighed in at 130 pounds (59kg), and made sufficient power for light delivery applications. And it also looked mighty keen on campus.

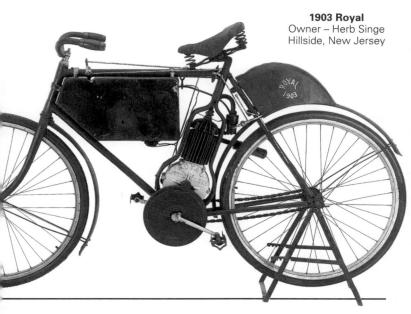

1903 Royal
Owner – Herb Singe
Hillside, New Jersey

1945 Safti-Cycle
Owner – Mark Buttles
Waupaca, Wisconsin

*Below: As a hybrid, the
Safti-Cycle employed
bicycle components at both
ends with a scooter box
and engine in between.*

Schickel (1912-1924)

(1912 Single)
Engine: Two-stroke single
Displacement: 495cc/695cc
Horsepower: 5/6
Wheelbase: 53in (135cm)
Weight: 190lb (86kg)
Top speed: 50mph (80kph)
Price: $210

The Schickel Motor Company was another pioneer in two-stroke technology. The Connecticut firm offered a choice of two engines, with chain or belt drive. The 695cc Big Six (horsepower) model with chain drive sold for $240 in 1914. The five-horsepower belt version was $20 less.

The Schickel magneto was enclosed in the crankcase. By 1916 the machine had added an Eclipse clutch and the price had dropped to $210. The belt-drive model sold for $200, and the Lightweight (290cc) version was offered at $109. At the end of Schickel production in 1924, only the Lightweight remained on the roster.

Below: Single-speed was standard with two-speed transmission an option. The Schickel was produced in both chain- and belt-drive models. The crankcase was stout and served as part of the frame. The crankshaft, crankpin and flywheel were cast in one piece.

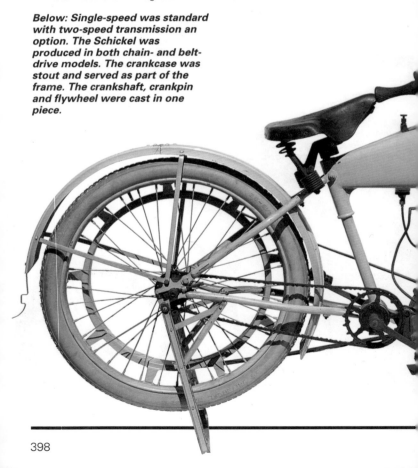

Right: Schickel was among the first to offer two-stroke engines in dimensions similar to their four-stroke counterparts. The Big Six displaced 695cc.

1912 Schickel Big Six
Owner – Bud Ekins
North Hollywood, California

Sears (1910-1916)

(1910 Single)
Engine: IOE single
Displacement: 492cc
Horsepower: 4
Wheelbase: 56in (142cm)
Weight: 200lb (91kg)
Top speed: 40mph (64kph)
Price: $189

The Sears Auto-Cycle was built for Sears, Roebuck and Company of Chicago by the Aurora Automatic Machine Company. This was the redesigned Thor engine, following the Illinois company's production of Indian engines. The Brown and Barlow carburetor was controlled by the left twistgrip, while the right regulated the spark. The keystone frame was fitted with a twin leading link fork.

In 1912 Sears switched suppliers, employing the Excelsior Cycle Company of Chicago, which was not

(1914 DeLuxe Single)
Engine: IOE single
Displacement: 578cc
Horsepower: 5
Wheelbase: 57in (145cm)
Weight: 220lb (100kg)
Top speed: 50mph (80kph)
Price: $197.50

associated with the Schwinn-owned company of the same city. This firm built the DeLuxe motorcycle, as well as the machines marketed by Dayton, Eagle and Crawford. The Sears DeLuxe Big Five was called "The Big Single With Nearly Twin Power."

The DeLuxe single featured a mechanical intake valve, Bosch magneto and Eclipse countershaft clutch. The loop frame carried a trailing-link leaf spring front fork, which appears identical to the Schwinn Excelsior fork of the period. Sears also offered the DeLuxe twin in seven- and nine-horsepower versions, with bore and stroke identical to the singles, for displacement of 1157cc. The singles and twins were built by F.W. Spacke of Indianapolis, Indiana.

Sears, Roebuck joined many other retailers in abandoning motorcycles with the advent of World War I.

Below: The DeLuxe Big Five was rated at 6.5 to seven horsepower at 2500rpm. "It will travel any road or climb any hill that the average twin can travel or climb."

Right: Second generation Sears featured the new Musselman air-cooled rear brake, and the seat post incorporated a double spring.

1910 Sears Auto-Cycle
Owner – Jim Harvison
Lombard, Illinois

Above: The first Sears models were belt-drive singles supplied by Thor. The 500cc "full 4 horsepower engine" had long stroke for torque and durability.

1914 Sears DeLuxe
Owner – Jim Harvison
Lombard, Illinois

Below: The trailing-link leaf-spring fork seems to be the same unit used on the Excelsior. It was billed as an "extra strong, suspension cradle fork."

Shaw (1903-1917)

Engine: IOE single
Displacement: 240cc
Horsepower: 2.5
Wheelbase: 48in (122cm)
Weight: 85lb (39kg)
Top speed: 35mph (56kph)
Price: $115

Stanley Shaw wasn't the first to offer engine kits for bicycles, but his company lasted longer than most of the other manufacturers. The Shaw Motorcycle Attachment was widely advertised and sold throughout the country for 12 years. The Shaw 240cc single fastened to the bicycle downtube, with belt drive to the rear wheel.

Shaw later produced a complete motorbike for the market, and continued to offer the engine in kit form. In its last years the machine had chain drive and magneto ignition, but remained an example of functional simplicity. Shaw suspended production in 1914, and later manufactured tractors.

Below: In 1910 the fuel/oil tank changed to a shorter, larger-diameter cannister. The front fender valance covered more of the tire.

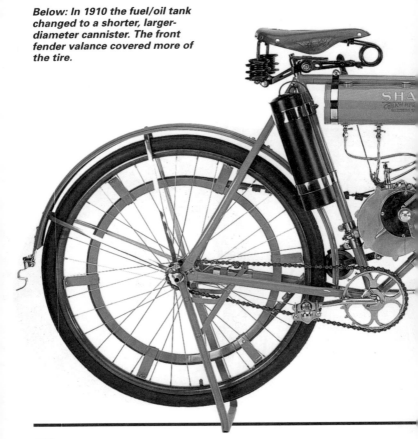

1909 Shaw
Owner – John Hasty
Galesburg, Kansas

Above: "Everything is complete and we send it to you all ready to attach to your bicycle in just a few minutes without the aid of an expert mechanic."

1910 Shaw
Owner – Jim Dennie
Palmyra, New York

Simplex (1935-1960)

Engine: Two-stroke single
Displacement: 125cc
Horsepower: 4
Wheelbase: 48in (122cm)
Weight: 150lb (68kg)
Top speed: 35mph (56kph)
Price: $249.50

The first Simplex was powered by a Peugeot V-twin back in 1902. This Simplex, also known as the Servi-Cycle, was built by the Simplex Manufacturing Company of New Orleans, Louisiana. Designer Joseph Treen mounted a simple two-stroke engine low in a lightweight motorcycle chassis, and also powered three-wheelers and scooters.

In its second generation the grown-up motorbike became the Simplex Automatic, for the automatic clutch. Simplex suspended production in 1942 because of the war, and resumed in 1946. The motorbike was virtually unchanged until 1953, when it was fitted with a kick starter, parallel strut leading-link spring fork and footboards. Despite its long life, the Simplex got "old fashioned" with the arrival of the Honda 50, and the company went out of business in the early sixties.

Below: The Simplex, which had by far the longest run of any American lighweight machine, changed very little over the years.

1956 Simplex Automatic
Owner –Dennis Boulis
Hudson, Michigan

*Above: The Automatic was
introduced in 1953 and and
remained in production for the
next seven years.*

1948 Simplex Servi-Cycle
Owner – Bill Erickson
Ottawa, Illinois

Spiral (1896?-1902)

Engine: IOE single
Displacement: 250cc approx.
Horsepower: unknown
Wheelbase: 51in (130cm)
Weight: 135lb (61kg)
Top speed: 30mph (48kph)
Price: Unknown

Records show that more than 300 American motorcycle companies came and went between 1900 and 1930. But no file has revealed the number of independent engineers and backyard tinkers who built motorcycles just for themselves. One such was Herman Jehle of New York, who began work on his own machine in 1896. His first effort, with belt drive and bicycle frame, evolved to chain drive. Then the frame was replaced by the more substantial piece shown here, probably around 1901.

The Spiral name came from the cylinder's continuous finning, app-

arently cut on a lathe. Jehle, formerly an instructor in machining and toolmaking, opened an auto parts store in Newark, New Jersey in 1902. For many years his motocycle was displayed in the store window.

Right: The Spiral is one of few remaining examples of early-American home-made motorcycles.

Surgical-Steeds (1989-)

(Quarterhorse)
Engine: Ohv 45° V-twin
Displacement: 1606cc
Horsepower: 110
Wheelbase: 70in (178cm)
Weight: 655lb (297kg)
Top speed: 120mph (193kph)
Price: $32,500

Surgical-Steeds builds six models of Harley-style V-twin customs on the Softail-style chassis. The company offers both complete machines and Monoglide frame kits. The Steeds Musclebike engine has T.P. Engineering cases and cylinders, S&S flywheels and RevTech dual-plug heads. The 1606cc motor runs a Mikuni carburetor and Crane ignition. The single gas-charged adjustable shock is by Progressive Suspension, and the four-piston brake calipers come from Willwood.

The Monoglide frame kit is $3,785, and the Steeds themselves are priced from $32,500-38,750.

Right: Surgical-Steeds builds five other models, and offers the Monoglide Frame Kit for customers who want to use their own engine.

c.1900 Spiral
Owner – Harry Buck
Pennsylvania

1998 Quarterhorse
Courtesy of Surgical-Steeds
Scottsdale, Arizona

Thor (1902-1917)

(Single)
Engine: IOE single
Displacement: 243cc
Horsepower: 3
Wheelbase: 56in (142cm)
Weight: 165lb (75kg)
Top speed: 40mph (64kph)
Price: $210

The Aurora Automatic Machinery Company entered the motorcycle game in 1902, as a supplier of engines for Indian. With the end of that contract in 1907, the Illinois firm brought to market its own machine under the Thor brand. It continued to market proprietary engines to other motorcycle companies such as Reading-Standard, Manson, Racycle and others.

Given its engine-building experience,

Thor was emboldened to participate in the racing game. While they did not enjoy broad success against veterans like Indian and Harley, Thor riders often did well. In 1915 Bill Briers on a Thor twin came second to Indian ace Glenn Boyd in the prestigious Dodge City 300. This race was a harsh test for man and machine.

The early Thor singles used the Indian-design engine, but by 1910 the company introduced its own motor. A new V-twin featured mechanical intake valves, and the next generation motor was enlarged to 76 cubic inches (1190cc). The Thor set several speed records on dirt tracks. By 1914 the roster include choices of single- or two-speed seven or nine-horsepower V-twin, and a four- or five-horsepower single.

1908 Thor Twin
Owner – Jim Lattin
Encinitas, California

1908 Thor Single
Owner – Marv Baker
Vallejo, California

Above: The first Thor engines were identical to the Indian powerplant designed by Oscar Hedstrom. Thor chose the vertical position.

Below: Thor chose to tilt the engine forward, providing space for the magneto. The seven-horsepower model was raced by Paul "Daredevil" Derkum of Los Angeles.

Right: Thor switched from curved to straight pushrods in 1912. The twins were offered in a nine-horsepower two-speed model, and a seven-horse version as either a two- or one-speed.

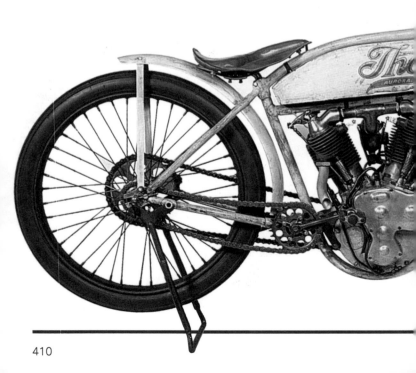

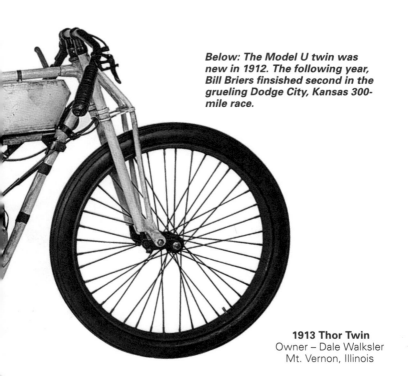

Below: The Model U twin was new in 1912. The following year, Bill Briers finsished second in the grueling Dodge City, Kansas 300-mile race.

1913 Thor Twin
Owner – Dale Walksler
Mt. Vernon, Illinois

In its last model year, 1917, Thor offered a 12- and 15-horsepower three-speed twin, with or without electrical equipment, a six-horse three-speed single and a four-horsepower two-speed Supersingle. The latter was $200, the top of the line twin sold for $285. The big twin was said to be good for 18 horsepower, but as civilized fellows the makers rated it at 15.

The intake valve springs were now enclosed in the head, and a front wheel stand was added. The lifter pivoted at the footboard mounts. The Lightweight twin, with smaller bore and stroke, displaced 633cc, and still had exposed intake valve springs. Wheelbase on the smaller version was 57 inches (145cm) compared to 59 (150cm) on the big twin.

In late 1916, Aurora sold all of its motorcycle inventory to the Standard Salvage Company of Detroit, and concentrated on air and electric powered tools.

Below: The Thor V-twin was developed by racing engineer William Ottaway, who by now had left to join Harley-Davidson. His success there is a matter of record.

Titan (1993-)

(Gecko)
Engine: Ohv 45° V-twin
Displacement: 1573cc
Horsepower: 94 @ 5250rpm
Wheelbase: 67.5in (171cm)
Weight: 590lb (268kg)
Top speed: 125mph (201kph)
Price: $29,065

The Titan Motorcycle Company of America produces an eight-model range of V-twin rubber-mount customs, divided four each between the RM twin shock frame and SX rigid-style torsion bar unit. The Titan Gecko employs a 1573cc S&S V-twin with Series E carburetor and 2 into 1 Supertrapp exhaust. The inverted fork carries dual discs and Performance Machine calipers; the rear shocks are adjustable for compression and rebound.

Titan motorcycles are priced from $26,000-40,000. Titan offers a three-year warranty that includes parts and labor.

Right: The Titan Gecko carries an S&S rubber-mount V-twin. Rake is 36 degrees and seat height is 24.5 inches (62.2cm).

1998 Titan Gecko
Courtesy of Titan Motorcycle Company
Phoenix, Arizona

1914 Thor Twin
Owner – Jim Lattin
Encinitas, California

413

Traub (1916)

Engine: Side-valve V-twin
Displacement: Approx 1300cc
Horsepower: 18
Wheelbase: 59in (150cm)
Weight: 375lb (170kg)
Top speed: 65mph (105kph)
Price: unknown

Little is known of this motorcycle. It is apparently one of one, built in Chicago by a fellow named Traub around 1916, and stolen shortly thereafter. Some 50 years later a plumber in Cicero, Illinois was working on repairs for the new owner of a house, and discovered the Traub under the front porch. A call to the previous owner revealed that his son had stolen the motorcycle, gone off to fight in World War I and never returned.

The owner of a Chicago motorcycle shop traded a Yamaha for the Traub, and eventually restored it. A decade later, Bud Ekins was in Chicago working as a stunt man on the "Blues Brothers" movie. He bought the Traub and later sold it to semi-legendary California collector Richard Morris. The machine returned

Ultra (1995-)

Engine: Ohv 45° V-twin
Displacement: 1573/1852cc
Horsepower: 96/105
Wheelbase: 66in (168cm)
Weight: 615lb (279kg)
Top speed: 120mph (193kph)
Price: $25,900

Below: The Avenger is one of seven Ultra QC Series customs with choice of two engines. Ultra offers a four-year unlimited mileage warranty.

The Ultra lineup includes eight Harley style V-twin customs, with a choice of 1573cc or 1852cc engines. The models include one rubber-mount, dual-shock chassis, hardtail frame and swingarm with torsion bar suspension. All models utilize an S&S engine, five-speed transmission and belt drive. The Ultra QC Series (Quality Custom) is distributed nationally through the Bikers Dream Superstores and selected dealers in 29 states. Ultra offers a four-year unlimited mileage warranty.

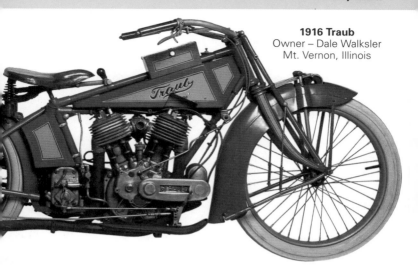

1916 Traub
Owner – Dale Walksler
Mt. Vernon, Illinois

to its home state when it was purchased by Harley dealer Dale Walksler. The Traub now resides in his Wheels Through Time Museum in Mt. Vernon, Illinois.

Above: Mr. Traub was apparently another independent thinker, but his machine had the refinements of a production motorcycle.

1999 Ultra Avenger
Courtesy of Ultra Cycles
Riverside, California

Victory (1998-)

Engine: Ohc 50° V-twin
Displacement: 1507cc
Horsepower: 75 @ 5700rpm
Wheelbase: 63in (160cm)
Weight: 665lb (302kg)
Top speed: 115mph (185kph)
Price: $13,000

The Victory is the first motorcycle produced by Polaris, a recreational vehicle company established in 1954. Known for its snowmobiles, watercraft and all-terrain vehicles, Polaris has now entered the V-twin cruiser fray. The Victory has a fuel injected 50-degree V-twin engine of 1507cc displacement. The overhead-cam powerplant is oil cooled, has four valves per cylinder and is rated at 75 horsepower. The wet sump engine carries six quarts (5.7lit) of oil.

The engine is solidly mounted in a stout cradle frame, with a gas-charged Fox shock absorber in back and 45mm Marzocchi fork up front. The single disc brakes on each wheel carry Brembo calipers, a four-piston in front and two in back. Harley-Davidson has another challenger.

Wagner (1901-1914)

(1909 Single)
Engine: IOE single
Displacement: 442cc
Horsepower: 3.5
Wheelbase: 53.5in (136cm)
Weight: 215lb (97.5kg)
Top speed: 40mph (64kph)
Price: $160

Below: The Standard Tourist was equipped with a 3.5-horsepower engine designed by George Wagner. Bore and stroke were both 3.25 inches (82.6mm).

George Wagner took a different approach to the bicycle/motor-cycle transmogrification. As a bicycle maker he recognized the design quality of the diamond frame, but also saw the value of weight distribution and strength afforded by a loop frame. So he designed a hybrid frame, grafting a forward loop on to a modified diamond chassis. In this stout platform he fitted an IOE single with atmospheric intake valve, and the exhaust routed through the front downtube.

The Wagner was offered with either V-belt or flat belt drive, and ▶

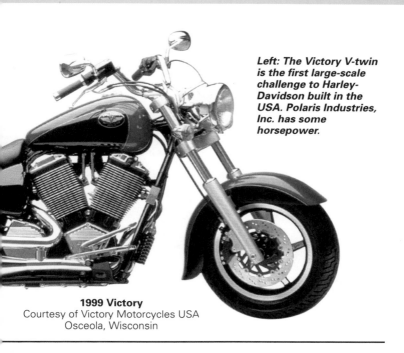

Left: The Victory V-twin is the first large-scale challenge to Harley-Davidson built in the USA. Polaris Industries, Inc. has some horsepower.

1999 Victory
Courtesy of Victory Motorcycles USA
Osceola, Wisconsin

1909 Wagner Standard Tourist
Owner – Dale Walksler
Mt. Vernon, Illinois

417

battery or magneto. Later deluxe models were equipped with a shock absorber between the seat and frame. After 1911 the exhaust system no longer used the frame as a pipe.

In 1909 Wagner also built a limited number of interesting tandem motorcycles using two engines. The upper belt run of the forward motor overlapped that of the rear, and the two were held in common tension by a twin-pulley idler arm. By 1914 motorcycles sales had dwindled, and George Wagner sold the company to an accessories firm.

(1911 Single)
Engine: IOE single
Displacement: 475cc
Horsepower: 4
Wheelbase: 55in (140cm)
Weight: 240lb (109kg)
Top speed: 50mph (80kph)
Price: $200

Right: In 1912 the Wagner no longer used the exhaust-through-frame method. Sales declined in 1914, and Wagner sold out to the Motorcycle Accessories Co.

Below: Exhaust exited the frame tube aft of the engine. The header pipe/clamp assembly also acted as an engine mount. The 4-11 was offered with battery or magneto.

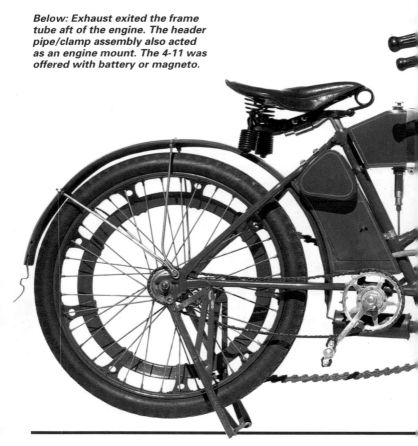

1912 Wagner 4-12
Owner – Herb Singe
Hillside, New Jersey

1911 Wagner Tourist 4-11
Courtesy of Mike Terry
Union, New Jersey

Whizzer (1939-1962)

(Pacemaker)
Engine: Side-valve single
Displacement: 138cc
Horsepower: 2-3
Wheelbase: 45in (114cm)
Weight: 105lb (48kg)
Top speed: 40mph (64kph)
Price: $199

The Whizzer properly belongs in the motorbike category, but the little tyke probably launched more motorcycling enthusiasts than any other vehicle. The 138cc side-valve single didn't generate much horsepower (about two), but it was enough to eliminate most of the pedaling its absence would require.

For many years the Whizzer engine and drive system were sold only in kit form, and were most widely attached to Schwinn bicycles. So for a kid with a bicycle, only about $80 stood between him and motorized freedom. In the 1940s the Whizzer Motor Company moved from Los Angeles to Pontiac, Michigan, and the post-war engines were larger and more powerful, up to three horsepower. Then the company offered a complete motorbike called the Pacemaker, and all the paperboys without toolkits or handy dads could buy one. And many did.

With the influx of imported scooters and mopeds in the 1960s, Whizzer went out of business.

1949 Whizzer Pacemaker
Owner – Stan Stanton
Overland Park, Kansas

1952 Whizzer 700
Owner – Kenneth Workman
Herrin, Illinois

Above: Also designated the Schwinn WZ, this stylish package featured swooping one-into-two twice pipes and various shiny accessories.

Below: The Whizzer Pacemaker inroduced more American youngsters to the sport of motorcycling than any other machine on two wheels.

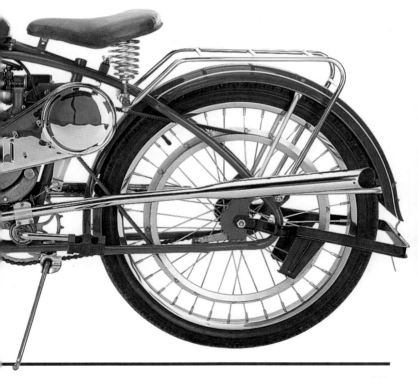

Williams (1912-1916)

Engine: Radial 3-cylinder
Displacement: 876cc
Horsepower: 9
Wheelbase: 60in (152cm)
Weight: 200lb (91kg)
Top speed: 55mph (89kph)
Price: Never sold

For something else completely different, we turn to the creation of Professor J. Newton Williams of Derby, Connecticut. In 1911 the professor came forth with a 360-degree three-cylinder engine with geared reduction drive. Mounted within the rear wheel, the engine rotated in unison on a fixed crankshaft/axle. The engine weighed 24 pounds (11kg), and according to Williams developed nine horsepower.

In 1908, Professor Williams demonstrated an experimental helicopter to the Aerial Experiment Association in Hammondsport, New York, in the company of Glenn Curtiss and Dr. Alexander Graham Bell. The radial engine was later adapted for motorcycle use, but apparently the machines never reached the production line stage. The machine shown here is designated number four.

The professor developed a three-valve induction/exhaust system; the intake valve was integrated with the piston and admitted the fuel charge through the crankshaft. The exhaust valve allowed gasses out through holes in the cylinder head; the third valve regulated the fuel-air mixture by throttle position. The starter and clutch were combined, and the engine was started by pedaling the treadles which also served as footboards. Professor Williams, fortunately, had made his money in the typewriter business.

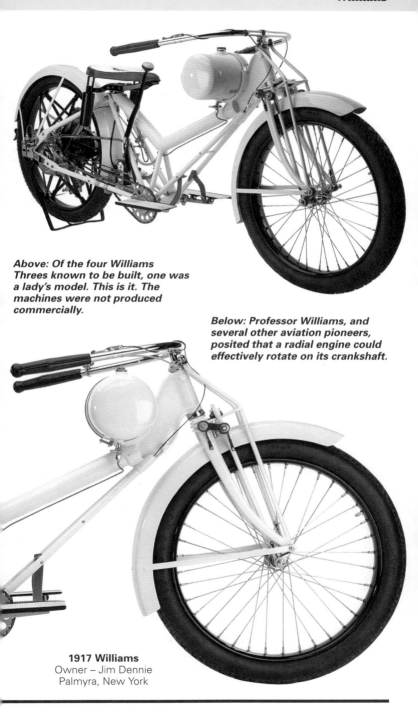

Above: Of the four Williams Threes known to be built, one was a lady's model. This is it. The machines were not produced commercially.

Below: Professor Williams, and several other aviation pioneers, posited that a radial engine could effectively rotate on its crankshaft.

1917 Williams
Owner – Jim Dennie
Palmyra, New York

Yale (1902-1915)

(1905 Single)
Engine: IOE single
Displacement: 292cc
Horsepower: 2
Wheelbase: 54in (137cm)
Weight: 125lb (57kg)
Top speed: 35mph (56kph)
Price: $165

Yale was a major player in the first decade of American motorcycling. The Consolidated Manufacturing Company of Toledo, Ohio was attracted to the market in 1902. Rather than start from scratch they bought the California Motorcycle Company in 1903, seeking to complement their lines of Snell and Yale bicycles. For its first five years, the motorcycle was sold as the Yale-California.

In 1908 the motorcycle gained a few pounds with an improved front fork, and a quarter-inch bigger bore that was good for another quarter-horsepower. The wheelbase had contracted to 51.5 inches (131cm). The tanned leather drivebelt was said to be good for 5,000 miles (8,000km). The following year the big single grew to a mighty 473cc in displacement, with a 3.5-horsepower rating. The three inches (7.62cm) of missing wheelbase were restored, and overall weight was up to 175 pounds (79kg). The flywheel, which prior to 1909 had ▶

Below: By 1909 the company had dropped the California tag and used Yale as the brand name. All of the early models were belt drive.

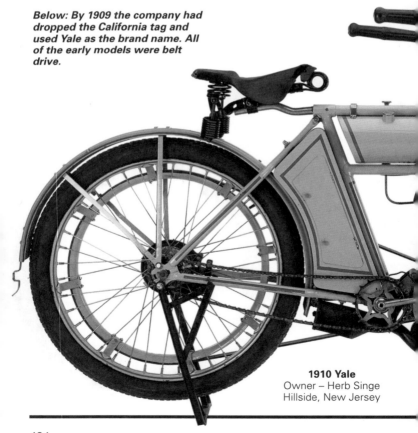

1910 Yale
Owner – Herb Singe
Hillside, New Jersey

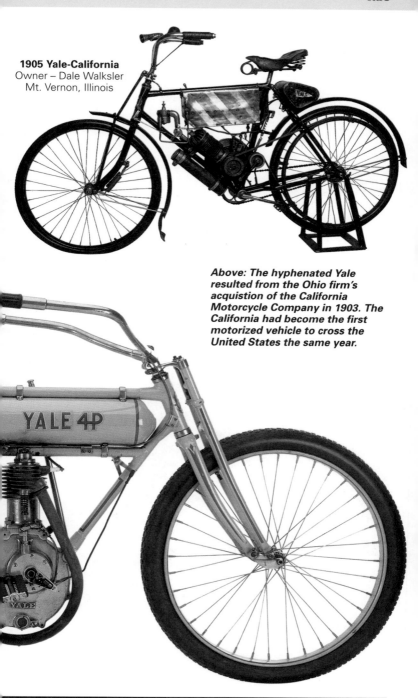

1905 Yale-California
Owner – Dale Walksler
Mt. Vernon, Illinois

YALE 4P

Above: The hyphenated Yale resulted from the Ohio firm's acquistion of the California Motorcycle Company in 1903. The California had become the first motorized vehicle to cross the United States the same year.

lived outdoors, moved within the crankcases.

Yale was not among the contenders in national championship racing, but it did compete in numerance endurance contests. In 1909 the first three riders home in the 600-mile Chicago Motorcycle Club endurance run were aboard Yales.

In 1912 the company switched to chain drive as standard equipment, with belt drive an option. The Yale V-twin was distinguished by the all-horizontal cooling fins, and the muffler remained at the front leading edge of the engine. The later models (1913–1915) had the exhaust pipe routed below the engine and the muffler fitted just forward of the rear wheel.

The engine in the last Yales was a 998cc V-twin with a two-speed planetary transmission. The new

(1913 Twin)
Engine: IOE twin
Displacement: 998cc
Horsepower: 8
Wheelbase: 57.5in (146cm)
Weight: 325lb (147kg)
Top speed: 55mph (89kph)
Price: $285

(1911 Single)
Engine: IOE single
Displacement: 473cc
Horsepower: 4
Wheelbase: 53.25in (135cm)
Weight: 165lb (75kg)
Top speed: 45mph (72kph)
Price: $235

frame had the upper tube angled down to the seatpost, and wheelbase had grown to 57.5 inches (146cm). The two-speed sold for $285 and the single with a two-speed was $235.

Although Yale was only in business for 13 years, it held the distiction of tracing its lineage to the first motorcycle to cross the country in 1902. By the end of 1915 the market for war materials looked more promising than that for motorcycles, and Yale suspended production.

1913 Yale Twin
Owner – Mike Parti
North Hollywood, California

1911 Yale
Owner – Mike Lange
Big Bend, Wisconsin

Above: Tandem passenger accessories gained popularity in the second decade of motorcycling. Weight distribution looks somewhat dodgy.

Below: 1913 was the last year for the option of belt drive, with the switch to chains. The top frame tube was no longer straight, and a new tank and logo appeared.

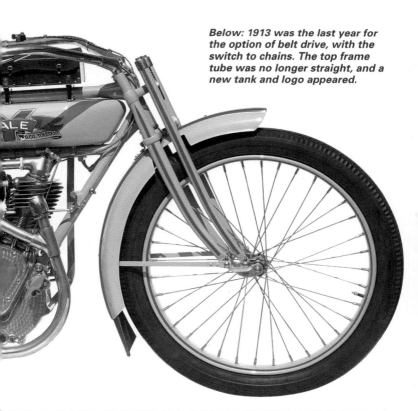

427

428

An A-Z of American Motorcycle Manufacturers

From 1898 to 1931, more than 300 American manufacturers built motorcycles for sale to the public. Most of them are listed here – we have attempted to include information for all bona fide marques for which there is some extant documentary evidence. Some of these builders were in business for a year or two, and several made fewer than a dozen machines. Others lasted a decade or more, but only Indian and Harley-Davidson made it past the Great Depression. A few brands listed here lack dates and locations, and beyond documented reference to several brand names, no other information was available on their histories. Readers with any documentation on the brand-only listings, or others not included here, are invited to submit it in printed (postal or faxual), or electronic form to the address below. The information will be updated in subsequent editions.

MotoArchival, P.O. Box 230, Santa Margarita, CA 93453, USA
fax: 805/545-7617 email: traff@thegrid.net

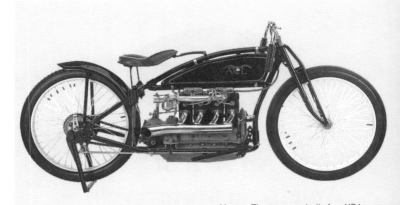

A

Ace (1920–1927)
Philadelphia, Pennsylvania
The Henderson brothers had originated the mighty Henderson Four in 1911. Their company was absorbed by Excelsior in 1917, and the Hendersons worked briefly for the Chicago firm under Ignaz Schwinn. William Henderson left in 1919 to build the Ace Four. During a test ride in 1922, he was struck and killed by an automobile. (See pages 10-17.)

Below: Early flyers extol the virtues of the American brand.

Above: The purpose-built Ace XP4 was designed for top speed records, and was good for 129mph (208kph).

Below: The Ace represented new hope for fans of powerful four-cylinder sporting motorcycles.

AMC (1912–1915)
Chicago, Illinois
The AMC may have been the first Harley clone. But for minor details, the machines were almost identical. This suggests that, given the patent constraints of the day, H-D may have sold components to the Chicago firm.

America (1904–1906)
La Porte, Indiana
Built by the Great Western Manufacturing Company, the America used a Thor engine. Early models employed a steering wheel rather than handlebars.

American (1902–1910)
Chicago, Illinois
The American Cycle Manufacturing Company sold machines under its own name, and supplied other companies such as Columbia, Tribune, Rambler and Crescent.

American (1911–1914)
Chicago, Illinois
The American Motor Cycle Company sold a belt-drive single built by the Thiem Manufacturing Company of St. Paul, Minnesota.

American (1921)
Louisville, Kentucky
This inline opposed twin was only on the market briefly.

American IronHorse (1995–)
Ft. Worth, Texas
This company makes five Harley-style V-twins with an S&S engine and aftermarket components. (See page 18.)

Anthony (1903)
Colorado Springs, Colorado
A motorized bicycle produced by E.J. Anthony. The engine was fitted behind the rear wheel, and employed belt drive.

Apache (1907–1911)
Denver, Colorado
The Brown & Beck Company sold Thor-powered singles in the still mostly-wild west. (See page 18.)

Argyle (1950–1961)
Memphis, Missouri
Argyle made a fold-up mini motor scooter called the Scooter Cub

Armac (1902–1913)
St. Paul Minnesota/Chicago, Illinois
Armac produced its own F-head single, with options of chain or belt drive. It also sold machines to AMC and Montgomery Ward. (See page 20.)

Below: The American Rocket of 1952 was a Sam Pierce special; mostly Indian with a little Ford and General Motors.

Above: M.M/Arrow was the first 90° V-twin. Owner – Mark Michel, Sterling Heights, Michigan.

Left: Arrow motorcyles with the "Aviation Type Motor" were built by Marsh-Metz.

Arrow (1909–1916)
Chicago, Illinois
The Arrow was a rebadged Marsh-Metz. (See page 22.)

Atco (1912)
Pittsburgh, Pennsylvania

ATK (1987–)
Centreville, Utah
ATK offers a ten-model roster of off-road/dual-sport motorcycles with Rotax engines. (See page 24.)

Below: The ATK dirt machines, four- and two-stroke models, are built for off-road racing and recreation.

Aurora (1910–1911)
Aurora, Illinois (?)

Auto-Bi (1900–1912)
Buffalo, New York
One of America's earliest mass-production motorcycles, by E.R. Thomas of Buffalo, New York. (See pages 26-29.)

Auto-bike (1915–1916)
Chicago, Illinois

Auto Car (1899–1904)
Pittsburgh, Pennsylvania
Auto Car built cars and trucks, and also a three-wheeler incorporating the engine and rear axle.

Autocyclette (1921)
New York, New York

Autoette (1911)
Detroit, Michigan

Auto Four (1971–1972)
Chicago, Illinois

Autoped (1915–1921)
New York, New York
One of the original motorscooters; a front-wheel drive, semi-folding scooter ridden standing up. (See page 30.)

Avenger (1994–) American Dirt Bike, Inc.,
Commerce, California
These are craft-built off-road/dual-sport machines running 350 and 600cc Rotax engines. Optional electric start.

B

Badger (1919–1921)
Milwaukee, Wisconsin
A small machine fitted with a 160cc engine.

Above: The Autoped was something new and stylishly romantic.

The Autoped for Outdoor Sports

FOR THE BEACH

FOR GOLFING

The Autoped, in addition to being a practical and economical form of transportation, is an exhilarating form of exercise. For the beach, for going to and from the links, for the country club, etc., it establishes a new ideal in out-of-doors enjoyment. DEMONSTRATION UPON REQUEST

Above: Autopeds as golf scooters; an idea whose time never came.

Barber (1900)
Brooklyn, New York

Baysdorfer-Dumbleton (1903)
Omaha, Nebraska
Catchy name.

Bailey Flyer (1913–1917)
Chicago, Illinois
Originally built in Portland, Oregon,
the Bailey Flyer was purchased by a
Chicago firm. The inline opposed
twin was shaft drive.

Bean (1903)
Boston, Massachusetts

Beard & Abel (1903)
Boston, Massachusetts

Bi-Auto-Go (1908–1912)
Detroit, Michigan
Only one prototype of this machine
was built. It was a type of two-
wheeled car with stabilizers, enclosed
bodywork and a 5.5-liter V8 engine.

Bi-car (1911)
Detroit, Michigan
Another car/motorcycle hybrid that
used a four-cyclinder engine and
shaft drive.

Big Dog (1996–)
Wichita, Kansas
Custom V-twins in the Harley FX-
style. (See pages 32.)

Black Diamond (1904–1905)
Philadelphia, Pennsylvania
A loop-frame single built by Reeser
and MacKenzie. The throttle
mechanism included an intake-valve
release, in contrast to the standard
exhaust valve compression release.

Black Hawk (1911–1914)
Rock Island, Illinois
Hard by the Rock Island Line (a
mighty good road), Black Hawk
built a 500cc single with chain or
belt drive. A complete model hasn't
been seen for decades. Iowan Bob
McClean has an engine.

Bobcat (1956–1960)
Wheeling, Illinois
A cute little golf scooter.

Above: "The sterling worth of the Black
Hawk design and equipment places it in
a class far above the $235 asked for it."

Above: The Big Dog is built in Wichita,
Kansas, home to some of the original big
dogs driven out of Texas.

BLACK HAWK   BLACK HAWK

MODEL G 1. SINGLE CYLINDER, BELT DRIVE

Above: The Black Hawk had a spring fork and seat post, and a rear hub clutch.

Boland (1903)
Rahway, New Jersey

Bonanza (1967–1969)
San Jose, California
This builder of two-stroke minibikes came and went in the late 1960s.

Bowman (1905)
New York, New York

Bown (1902)
Youngstown, Ohio
Clifford E. Bown constructed a reinforced bicycle frame with a Thomas engine. Throttle and spark were both controlled by the right-hand grip. The drive belt was laced rawhide.

Bradford (1907)
Bradford, Pennsylvania

Below: George Wayman rode, mostly, a California across the United States in 1903, in 50 days.

Bradley (1905–1912)
Philadelphia, Pennsylvania
In 1911, Bradley built a 500cc overhead-valve boardtrack racer. The machine was direct-drive from the crankshaft but had a hub clutch. The motorcycle had a short wheelbase and high fear factor.

Breed (1912)
Bay City, Michigan

Buckeye (1905)
Columbus, Ohio
The short-lived single was built by the Lear Automobile Company of Ohio.

Buell (1988–)
East Troy, Wisconsin
Former Harley engineer Erik Buell began with Harley-powered sportbikes. The company was recently acquired by Harley-Davidson. (See pages 34-37.)

Buffalo (1984)
Buffalo, New York

C

California (1901–1903)
San Francisco, California
Another of the moto-pioneers, Roy C. Marks built the California and later sold the rights to Consolidated Manufacturing, which built the Yale-California. The Marks model was the first motor vehicle to cross the United States in 1903. (See page 38.)

Callie (1933–1937)
Detroit, Michigan

Camden (1906–1908)
Camden, New Jersey

Canda (1900)
New York, New York
The Canda Auto-Tricycle and Quadricycle had a 1.75-horsepower engine and 46-inch (117cm) wheelbase. The quad's forward passenger seat could be replaced by a delivery box, making it the Auto-Quadricycle Van. With both components, the price was $560.

Cannondale (1999–)
This New England bicycle company developed a 400cc four-stroke, aluminum-framed motocross bike for release in 1999.

Centaur (1961)
New York, New York

Century (1916–1917)
Chicago, Illinois
The Century Auto Cycle Company produced a lightweight, two-stroke single. "100 miles in 3 Hours on a Gallon of Gas - 100 pounds -Sells for $100."

Champion (1911–1913)
St. Louis, Missouri
Champion was licensed by the Militaire Autocycle Company to build the four-cylinder runabout. The name later gained fame in the spark plug business.

Chicago (1904–1905)
Chicago, Illinois
The Hoffman Motor Works sold belt-drive singles under its own name and the Chicago 400 label.

Clark (1903)
Torrington, Connecticut

Classic Motorcycles (1996–)
Murray, Utah
Classic builds six Harley-style customs with numerous options. Prices run from $19,000-30,000.

Clemens (1901–1903)
Springfield, Massachusetts
The diamond-frame single was designed by Chester Clemens, and featured twistgrip controls. The left grip controlled both compression release and spark advance; the right grip was the throttle.

Clement (1903–1909)
New York, New York
The Clement Motor Equipment company sold the French engine as a bicycle attachment, and also marketed complete machines.

Cleveland (1902–1905)
Hartford, Connecticut
(1915–1929)
Cleveland, Ohio

The early Clevelands were built by the American Cycle Company of New England. The same machine was sold under numerous bicycle brand names. The Ohio Clevelands spanned a range of two-stroke and four-stroke singles, and eventually four-cylinder machines. (See pages 42-49.)

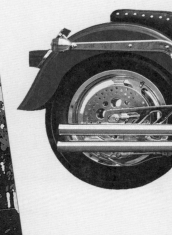

Left: The sporting gentleman of 1920 was at home on a Cleveland.

Below: And the Cleveland also appealed to the smartest of young ladies.

Above: The California Motorcycle Company of today is located in Gilroy, California, the garlic capital.

CMC (1995–)
Gilroy, California
The California Motor Company builds 24 models of Harley-style V-twins. The company was recently named to build the latest revival of the Indian marque. (See page 40.)

Coleman (1903)
Boston, Massachusetts
The 300cc belt-drive F-head single was built by H.P. Coleman. It weighed 118 pounds (53.5kg).

Columbia (1902–1905)
Hartford, Connecticut
The Columbia was one of many bicycle brand names brought to motorcycling by Colonel Alfred Pope. The 1902 model had the engine mounted aft of the seatpost in a loop frame. (See page 50.)

Comet (1911)
Elwood, Illinois
Drawings of the Comet show a direct-drive V-twin in a loop frame with an arched center tube over the cylinders. Low handlebars and seat indicate a racing model.

Commando (1950)
Minneapolis, Minnesota

Confederate (1996–)
Abita Springs, Louisiana
Contemporary Harley-style V-twin in a road warrior chassis. (See page 50.)

Crawford (1913–1914)
Saginaw, Michigan
The Crawford was marketed by the Mid-Land Manufacturing Company of Michigan. The motorcycle was built in Illinois with the DeLuxe engine, and was identical to the Sears and Eagle.

Crescent (1902–1905)
Hartford, Connecticut
This was another of the many marques that originated with the American Cycle Manufacturing Company.

Crocker (1934–1941)
Los Angeles, California
Al Crocker built speedway machines and high-performance V-twins for the road. The former Indian dealer built about 100 of the advanced road bikes in the late 1930s. (See pages 52-59.)

Crosley (1939–1952)
Marion, Indiana
Crosley manufactured refrigerators, radios and eventually cars. In the late 1930s they built a few prototype motorcycles for military testing. (See page 60.)

Crouch (1905–1908)
Stoneham, Massachusetts
The Crouch belt-drive single established a good reputation for reliability. (See page 62.)

Crown (1910)
La Porte, Indiana
A belt-drive single built by the same company that manufactured the America marque.

Culp (1903)
Columbus, Ohio

Curtiss (1901–1913)
Hammondsport, New York
Glenn Curtiss was a tinker, bicycle and motorcycle racer before becoming one of America's seminal aviation pioneers. Early on he established the credo of minimum weight and maximum horsepower, and rode his own V-8 machine to 136mph (219kph) in 1907, Jim. (See pages 64–73.)

3 H. P. SINGLE CYLINDER   **PRICE $200.00**

Below: The Curtiss V-8 was designed as an aircraft engine, and tested by Glenn H. at 136mph (219kph) on the beach in Florida.

Above: The Curtiss three-cylinder made considerable power and vibration. Very few were built.

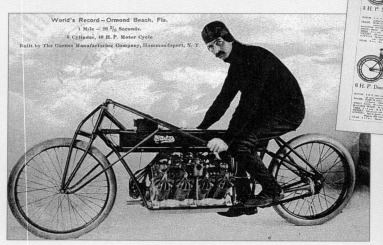

440

Above: Shown on the left are Tank Waters and his wife. Glenn and Lena Curtiss are on the right. Waters was a racing buddy of Glenn Curtiss.

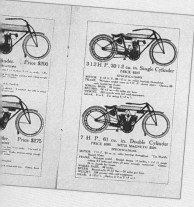

Above: Curtiss offered two each of the singles and twins, perfect for your personal horsepower needs.

Cushman (1936–1965)
Lincoln, Nebraska
The Cushman Auto-Glide, designed by Charles Ammon, appeared in 1936. Following World War II, the Nebraska company grew to be the country's largest scooter manufacturer. (See pages 74-79.)

CVS (1911–1917)
Philadelphia, Pennsylvania
The C.V. Stahl Motor Works built a 500cc and 1000cc V-twin.

Cyclomobile (1917)
Toledo, Ohio

Cyclemotor (1916–1924)
Rochester, New York
The Cyclemotor Corporation sold an engine attachment for bicycles, and later expanded with a complete machine under the Evans name. (See page 92.)

Cycle-scoot (1953–1955)
Indianapolis, Indiana
Small scooters using proprietary engines.

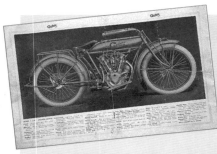

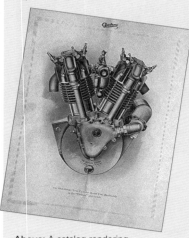

Above: The Cyclone Model 7 was one of the fastest production motorcycles of its day.

Above: A catalog rendering of the 1915 V-twin engine that powered the Cyclone to the front of the pack.

Above: The Dayton was presented as stately transport for the stylish fellow.

Cyclone (1913–1916)
St Paul, Minnesota
The Cyclone effectively created the horsepower race among American motorcycle manufacturers. In addition to Indian's racing models, these were the original factory hot rods. (See pages 80-83.)

D

Day (1903)
Lake View, New York

Dayton (1911–1917)
Dayton, Ohio
The Davis Sewing Machine Company produced an front-drive engine attachment for bicycles. The company later adopted the DeLuxe V-twin under the Dayton banner. (See page 84.)

Delaware (1908)
Delaware, Ohio

De Long (1902)
Phoenix, New York
The Industrial Machine Company produced a seatpost-single designed by bicycle dealer G. Erwin De Long. The two-inch (5cm) tube frame carried the gasoline at the top and the batteries and coil in the front downtube.

Below: The production cafe racer concept began with the Cyclone as long ago as 1914.

DeLuxe (1912–1915)
Chicago, Illinois
The DeLuxe was offered by the Excelsior Cycle Company of Chicago, which was unrelated to the Schwinn-owned Excelsior Motor Manufacturing and Supply company of the same city. The De Luxe engine was supplied to numerous manufacturers.

Below: Soon to become the capital of automobile production, Detroit, Michigan produced few motorcycles.

Detroit (1910)
Detroit, Michigan
A four horse-power single; chain and belt drive. "Simplicity. Durability. Strength. Power. Speed. Comfort."

Doodle Bug (1946–1950)
Webster City, Iowa
The mini-scooter was marketed by the Gamble Hardware Company. (See page 84.)

Left: Doodle Bugs were usually powered by Briggs & Statton engines, and briefly by the Clinton.

Dorsey (1902)

Winchester, Massachusetts

The Dorsey had a horizontal parallel twin mounted behind the seat. The cylinder was supported by trunnions pivoted at the top of two vertical tubes, the lower ends of which attached to the axle. The rider used a hand lever to tilt the engine forward, which brought the leather-covered flywheel into contact with the rear tire.

Driver (1902)

Philadelphia, Pennsylvania

Walter Driver and Sons built an attachment engine for bicycles, and a seatpost-single with both 1.75 horsepower and V-belt drive. The company also produced a racing model that reportedly made seven horsepower.

Duck (1903–1906)

Stockton, California

The Duck was a rebadged California.

Dusenberg (1903)

Rockford, Iowa

Dukelow (1913)

Chicago, Illinois

Dyke (1903–1906)

St. Louis, Missouri

Dynacycle (1949-53)

St. Louis, Missouri

Manufacturer of an engine that clipped on to a bicycle frame.

E

Eagle (1909–1915)

Brockton, Massachusetts

The Eagle was another product of the American Motor Company, and used the DeLuxe singles and V-twins built by the Spacke Company in Indiana. (See page 86.)

Economy (1908)

Detroit, Michigan

Edmond (1902)

Matteawan, New York

E.J. Edmond built a three-wheeler with a De Dion engine mounted at the lower rear frame junction. The passenger seat was between the two front wheels. The front axle could be removed and the machine converted to two-wheeler.

Electra (1912)

An ill-fated attempt at an electrically powered motorcycle.

Elk (1911)

Elkhart, Indiana

Emblem (1907–1925)

Angola, New York

The Emblem was a popular marque in New York, Pennsylvania and the northeast. In 1913 the company introduced a 1255cc V-twin, and the machine was built for strength. (See pages 86-91.)

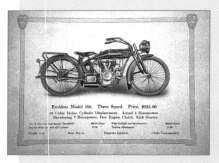

Above: The Emblem Model 106 used a 820cc engine and three-speed transmission. The price was $225.

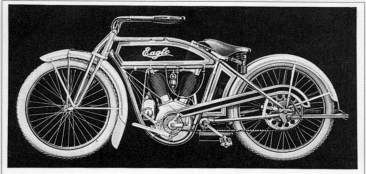

Latest 1914 Eagle 9-12 Direct Drive showing auxiliary brake, foot board and ⅞″ chain, price $265.
Ride the best and beat the rest

Above and left: In 1914 the Eagle V-twin was available for $265, for which you could "ride the best and beat the rest."

Below: The Evans was one of several popular lightweight machines made in New York state.

Erie (1906–1911)
Hammondsport, New York
A product of the Motorcycle Equipment and Supply Company, the Erie was offered in both belt-drive and friction-drive models. Either drive system was available in kit form for bicycle attachment.

Eshelman (1954)
Baltimore, Maryland

Evans (1916–1924)
Rochester, New York
The Cyclemotor Corporation began with attachment engines for bicycles. In 1918 it produced a complete machine as the Evans, powered by a two-stroke single. (See page 92.)

Left: The Erie two-stroke was an economical lightweight at $150.

Above: Excelsior quickly emerged at the primary competitor of both Indian and Harley-Davidson in the 1910s and 1920s.

Below: With experienced riders and a 1000cc V-twin, Excelsior had early success on the racetrack.

Excelsior (1908–1931)
Chicago, Illinois
Excelsior entered the industry five years after Harley-Davidson's debut, but was a contender within a few short years. Its V-twin appeared in 1910, and the following year the company was acquired by Ignaz Schwinn, the bicycle builder. For the next two decades Excelsior was a major player in the market. To distinguish it from the British Excelsior, the Chicago brand was known in Europe as the American X. (See pages 92-101.)

Excelsior-Henderson (1998–)
Belle Plain, Minnesota
The revival of Excelsior-Henderson has generated considerable interest. (See page 102.)

F

Fairchild (unknown)
Pasadena, California

Feilbach (1912–1915)
Milwaukee, Wisconsin
The Feilbach Motor Company built a five-horse Long Stroke single and an 110cc twin. The horizontal seat spring in the center frame tube was a unique touch. (See page 104.)

Flanders (1911–1914)
Detroit, Michigan
The Motor Products Company offered a belt-drive four-horsepower single and a side-valve V-twin. (See page 106.)

Above: The Flanders was the "Packard of Motorcycle Value."

Fleming (1900–1902)
New York, New York
The Fleming Motor Bicycle had a 1.25-horsepower motor fitted to the front of the steering head, driving the front wheel via leather belt. Front fork/engine assembly was $150; the complete bike cost $200.

F&M (1902–1907)
Columbus, Ohio

Fowler (1905)
Chicago, Illinois
The Fowler-Manson-Sherman Cycle Manufacturing Company built the Manson motorcycle. (See Manson below.)

Francke-Johannemyer (1905)
Milwaukee, Wisconsin

Franklin (1899–1900)
Mt. Vernon, Washington

Freyer & Miller (1901–1907)
Cleveland, Ohio
The Freyer & Miller had a steel crankcase brazed rigidly to the frame aft of the seat post. The company was joined with Oscar Lear's outfit also to manufacture Buckeye motorcycles.

Above: The Gibson Mon-Auto of 1915 was among the first efforts to build a simple motorscooter.

G

Geer (1905–1909)
St. Louis, Missouri
Harry R. Geer was an early motorcycle entrepreneur in the wilds of Missouri. His company had an extensive catalog of engines and components, in addition to complete machines. (See page 108.)

Gere (1901–1904)
Grand Rapids, Michigan
The Gere Launch and Engine Works offered four sizes of single-cylinder engines for bicycles. Customers could also buy the castings and assemble their own engines.

Geneva (1900)
Geneva, Ohio

Gerhart (1915)
Harrisburg, Pennsylvania
Inline fours that were based on the Belgian FN machines.

Gibson Mon-auto (1915)
New York, New York
A rudimentary scooter-type of motorcycle with an inclined engine mounted below the saddle.

Above "Speed, Quality and Comfort" were combined in the Feilbach Limited.

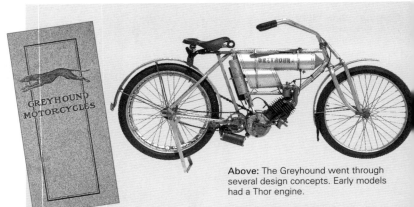

Above: The Greyhound went through several design concepts. Early models had a Thor engine.

Above: Greyhound cultivated a fleet-of-foot image.

Globestar (1946–1949)
Joliet, Illinois

Greyhound (1907–1914)
Aurora, Illinois
The Greyhound was associated with both the Aurora Automatic Machinery Company and E. R. Thomas of Buffalo, New York. (See pages 108-111.)

H

H&H (1902–1903)
San Diego, California

Hafelfinger (1901)
New York, New York
The engine designed by Emil Hafelfinger was apparently the foundation for a handful of early powerplants, including Indian. The Hafelfinger Motor Bicycle carried a 1.5 horsepower single fitted between the seat post and crank hanger.

Hampden (1901–1903)
Springfield, Massachusetts
The Hampden Manufacturing Company built a machine to "stand the strains which such a machine is subjected, and every detail has been carried to the highest point of mechanical perfection." Twist grip controls, 25mph. $200.

Harley-Davidson (1903–)
Milwaukee, Wisconsin
Harley-Davidson reaches its 100th anniversary in 2003, and by 2005 will have been building motorcycles twice as long as its closest competitor. Harley has built more American motorcycles, by a considerable margin, than any other manufacturer. While their roster of competitors continues to grow, there is as yet no indication that Milwaukee is likely to relinquish that position. (See pages 112-227.)

Hausmann (1918)
Milwaukee, Wisconsin

Hasty (unknown)

Haverford (1909–1914)
Philadelphia, Pennsylvania
The Haverford Cycle Company sold Marsh-Metz motorcycles under its own name.

Below: The Haverford Big 4 was fitted with a Bosch magneto and Schebler carburetor.

Above: Harley-Davidson was one of the first companies to spend a lot of money on advertising.

Hawthorne (1911–1912)
Chicago, Illinois
The Hawthorne was another marketing label for the Armac, similar to the AMC. The Hawthorne was sold mail order by the Montgomery Ward company of Chicago. (See page 228.)

Hemingway (1905)
Glenwood, Illinois
Apparently just an earnest effort.

Henderson (1912–1931)
Detroit, Michigan
The legendary fours of William Henderson, eventually built under the auspices of Excelsior, evolving to the Ace and finally the Indian Four. (See pages 228-239.)

Above and below: Henderson became the dominant builder of four-cylinder machines in the 1910s, and it was later acquired by Excelsior.

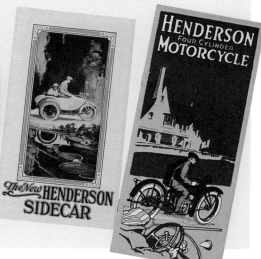

Hercules (1902–1903)
Hammondsport, New York
The Hercules was the first motorcycle built by aviation pioneer Glenn Curtiss. (See page 240.)

Below: The 1903 Hercules showed the early interest of Curtiss in lightness and handling.

Left: Brochure extolling the virtues of Hercules roller bearing motors.

Herring (1900)
St. Joseph, Michigan
Herring built a 2.75-horsepower tandem and a 2.25-horse solo with double frame tubes.

Hilaman (1906–1912)
Moorestown, New Jersey
Hilaman had a seven-horsepower twin and 3.5hp single on the market in 1907. Optional V- or flat-belt drive. The twin was $285, the single $210.

Hoffman (1903–1904)
Chicago, Illinois
The Hoffman Motor Works made singles, twins and fours and components for most of the motorized trades. The Chicago 400 was one of its motorcycles.

Holley (1902–1911)
Bradford, Pennsylvania
The Holley brothers began building attachment engines before the turn of the century. In 1901 they began manufacturing complete motorcycles, and later switched, at the request of Henry Ford, to carburetors. (See pages 240-243.)

Horten (1911)
Detroit, Michigan
Manufacturer of the Autoette.

Hudson (1910–1911)
Middletown, Ohio

I

Imperial (1902–1905)
Hartford, Connecticut
The Imperial was another of the numerous bicycle brand names to appear on machines built by the American Cycle Manufacturing Company. It was identical to the early Cleveland. (See page 42.)

Below: The Holley of Pennsylvania was among the first production motorcycles.

Indian (1901–1953)
Springfield, Massachusetts
The Hendee Manufacturing Company built "America's Pioneer Motorcycle," and was at one time the largest manufacturer in the world. The rivalry between Indian and Harley-Davidson was a half-century campaign. (See pages 244-325.)

Above: The Indian Service Car was touted as the best means of light delivery.

Below: Weekend fun was only minutes away on a 1916 Indian.

Above: Indian was first to acknowledge, and exploit, the relationship between power and performance.

Below: The latest Indian, built by CMC in California, appeared in 1999.

Above: The Iver-Johnson was built by the noted firearms manufacturer.

Industrial (1903)
Syracuse, New York

Iver Johnson (1907–1916)
Fitchburg, Massachusetts
Iver-Johnson was a well-known manufacturer of firearms long before it entered the motorcycle business. The twins and singles featured a number of engineering innovations. (See pages 326-329.)

J

Jack & Heintz (1949–1955)
Cleveland, Ohio

Jeepette (1943)
Los Angeles, California

Jefferson-Waverly (1910–1914)
Jefferson, Wisconsin
The Jefferson, Waverly, Jefferson-Waverly and occasional Kenzler-Waverly and P.E.M began with the designs of Perry E. Mack. The convoluted corporate history is interesting, as were the overhead-valve V-twins and vertical leaf-spring front fork.

Joerns (1910–1916)
St. Paul, Minnesota
The Joerns Motorcycle Manufacturing Company produced the Cyclone machines. (See pages 80-83.)

Johnson (1918–1922)
Another manufacturer of clip-on engines for bicycles, in this case a 155cc two-stroke twin.

Jonas (1902)
Milwaukee, Wisconsin
The Jonas Motor Bicycle had its single mounted to the front of the seatpost, with direct chain drive. The rig weighed 85 pounds (39kg), and the two-horse engine was good for 25mph (40kph). Riders could choose 23- or 24-inch (58.5 or 61cm) frame.

Above: Minnesota's Joerns Manufacturing Company hoped to establish the Cyclone both as practical transportation and championship racer.

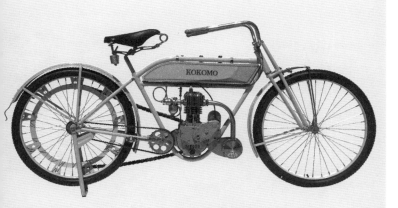

K

Above: Kokomo had a brief life in Indiana, then came under control of the Shaw Company in Kansas.

Kaestner (1903)
Chicago, Illinois

Kaye-Pennington (1896)
Racine, Wisconsin

Keating (1901–1902)
Middletown, Connecticut
The Keating single was configured like the early Cleveland, with the engine behind the seatpost. "The crankshaft is a combined clutch and coaster brake, controlled by means of the pedals... but in case of accident or lack of gasoline can be disconnected by a thumb screw and the wheel ridden with a perfectly free wheel, same as an ordinary bicycle."

Kenzler-Waverly
(See Jefferson-Waverly)

Keystone (1902)
Philadelphia, Pennsylvania
This was a re-branded Orient, the early version with the DeDion engine.

Keifer (1909–1911)
Buffalo, New York

Kimball (1902)
Lynn, Massachusetts
H.L. Kimball built a 320cc F-head single in a modified bicycle frame with a very short wheelbase. It sold for $200.

Kokomo (1909–1911)
Kokomo, Indiana
The Kokomo single appeared only shortly under its native name, and was soon absorbed by the Shaw Company of Kansas. (See page 330).

Kulture (1909)
Rochester, New York

L

Lamson (1902–1903)
Abington, Massachusets
Lamson offered an A and B single; the former was 1.5 horsepower in a 100-pound (45kg) package with round-belt drive for $150. The B model made 2.25 horsepower at 1800rpm. This had three inches (7.62cm) more wheelbase (49in/124.5cm) and was 12 pounds (5.4kg) heavier. The price was $200.

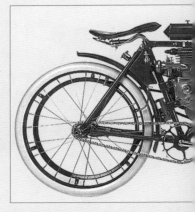

Landgraf (1906)
Chicago, Illinois

Langford (1917–1921)
Denver, Colorado

La Ray (1946–1948)
Milwaukee, Wisconsin
Powered by a Clinton engine.

Leflem (1901)
Philadelphia, Pennsylvania
The Leflem had a Fleming single fitted to the seat post, and a combined coaster brake and friction clutch in the rear hub.

Leo (1905)
Oakland, California

Lewis (1901)
Brooklyn, New York

Liberty (1918)
A military prototype developed jointly between Excelsior, Harley-Davidson and Indian. The effort ended with the war.

Light (1901–1911)
Pottstown, Pennsylvania
Originally powered by the Thor engine, the firm later acquired the Merkel company and used the name Merkel-Light. (See page 332.)

M

Mack (1909–1913)
Milwaukee, Wisconsin
Percy Mack designed engines that were used in the P.E.M., Waverly, Jefferson, Jefferson-Waverly and Kenzler-Waverly.

Below: The Light Manufacturing & Foundry Company of Pennsylvania built the Light, also called the Thor-bred.

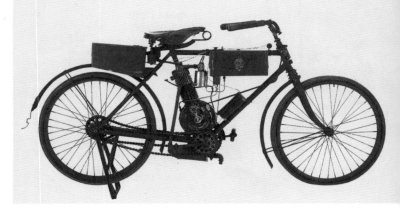

Majestic (1912–1913)

Maltby (1902–1903)
Brooklyn, New York
Frank D. Maltby built singles with the engine mounted low in a keystone frame. The Maltby Motor Bicycle had 54-inch (137cm) wheelbase and sold for $250.

Manson (1905–1908)
Chicago, Illinois
The early Manson had the same configuration as the Indian, including the Thor engine. The machine, with twistgrip controls and a tool set, sold for $210. A later model had the Thor engine mounted vertically in a larger frame with a long tank with containers for fuel, oil and batteries. They also offered a five-horsepower V-twin for $275.

Left: The tiny Lilliputian, built by Abner B. Lilliput of Missouri in 1913, was designed for his 4-foot 7-inch body. Owner – Jeff Slobodian, Ojai, California.

Marathon (1910)
Hartford, Connecticut

Marman (1948)
Inglewood, California

Marks (1898–1902)
San Francisco, California
Roy Marks designed the California, which became the Yale. His design was also sold under the Duck brand in the West.

Marsh, Marsh & Metz, M.M. (1900–1913)
Brockton, Massachusetts
The Marsh brothers were among the earliest pioneers in motorcycle design, performance and manufacture. (See pages 334-337.)

Marvel (1910–1913)
Hammondsport, New York
These were Curtiss motorcycles sold in the closing years, when Glenn Curtiss was fully occupied with aircraft development. Marvel was headed by his old riding pal Tank Waters.(See pages 338-341.)

Below: The Marsh brothers of Massachusetts built a six-horsepower racing model in 1901, and logged a speed of 57mph (92kph).

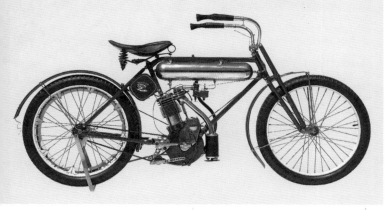

Maxim (1893)
Hartford, Connecticut

Mayo (1905–1908)
Pottstown, Pennsylvania
The Mayo Damper Company built a single and twin, 2.75 and five horsepower respectively; the prices were $175 and $275 in 1907.

MB (1916–1920)
Buffalo, New York

McDonald (1905)
Chicago, Illinois

Meadowbrook (1905)
Hempstead, New York
The Meadowbrook Cycle Company produced a 185cc single-cylinder diamond-frame machine.

Mears (1903)
Brooklyn, New York

Mecky (1903)
Philadelphia, Pennsylvania

Menns-Van Horn (1903)
Boston, Massachussetts

Merkel (1902–1915)
Milwaukee, Wisconsin;
Pottstown, Pennsylvania;
Middletown, Ohio
Early Merkels were built in Wisconsin. A merger with the Light Motorcycle Company of Pennsylvania moved them east three years later. In another three years the company was sold to the Miami Cycle Manufacturing Company of Ohio. A number of interesting machines were produced along the way.
(See pages 342-349.)

Mesco (1905)
Buffalo, New York
This was a brand name of the Motorcycle Equipment Supply Company. The single-cylinder bicycle attachment engine drove a friction wheel against the rear wheel.

Above and right: Middletown, Ohio become more well known for the Flying Merkel, including the "prize-winning" Yellow Jacket.

Above: Official factory racing ended in 1911, but Maldwyn Jones continued Merkel's winning ways for several more years.

Miami (1905–1916)
Middletown, Ohio
In addition to the Flying
Merkel, Miami offered a
lightweight Motor Bicycle.
(See page 350.)

Right: With its 236cc single,
and weight of only 125
pounds (57kg), the Miami
was reportedly good for 100
miles on 10 cents worth of
fuel.

Above: The Miami Power Bicycle was
an Ohio lightweight incorporating
chassis elements from the Merkel, then
built by the same firm.

Michaelson (1908–1915)
Minneapolis, Minnesota
The Michaelson and Minneapolis
were produced by the same
company. (See Minneapolis.)

Michigan (1911)
Detroit, Michigan

Midget Bi-car (1908–1909)
Lynnbrook, New York
The British Midget Bi-car was built under licence by the Walton Motor Company of New York.

Militaire, Militor (1911–1919)
Cleveland, Ohio; Buffalo, New York
The Militaire was a grand experiment in automotive-style motorcycles, for which a broad demand was less than certain. (See pages 350-355.)

Millet (unknown)

Minneapolis (1908–1914)
Minneapolis, Minnesota
The Minneapolis, and Michaelson, were built by the same Minnesota company. Early Minneapolis singles and twins were Thor engines. A side-valve engine was introduced in 1911, and swingarm suspension in 1912. (See pages 356-359.)

Above: The Militaire Autocycle attempted to combine motorcycle and automobile elements.

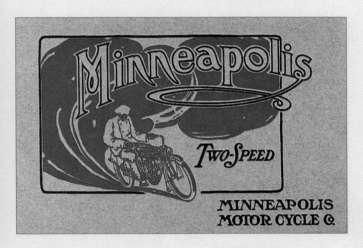

Above: The Minneapolis and Michaelson were built by the same Minnesota company.

Mitchell (1901–1906)
Racine Junction, Wisconsin
The Mitchell Motor Bicycle was built by the Wisconsin Wheel Works. The company advertised a stout frame with a 1.5-horsepower engine mounted high on the front downtube. Choice of wood or steel rims; belt drive, $200.

M.M. (See Marsh, Marsh & Metz)

Monarch (1902–1904)
Hartford, Connecticut
Yet another product of the American
Cycle Company. Mostly
interchangeable with Cleveland,
Columbia, Imperial, etc.

Monarch (1912–1915)
Owego, New York
The New York Monarch was a
separate firm that built singles and
twins. (See page 358.)

Below: The Big 5 in Monarch's title
referred to horsepower. The Road King
Supreme came from Owego, New York.

Monnot (1903)
Canton, Ohio

Moore-car (1917)
Indianapolis, Indiana

Morgan (1901–1902)
Brooklyn, New York
The Morgan Motor Company single
was similar in design to the
Mitchell. The company sold engine
kits in 1-, 1.5- and 2.25-horsepower
ratings. The smallest engine
weighed 23 pounds (10kg).

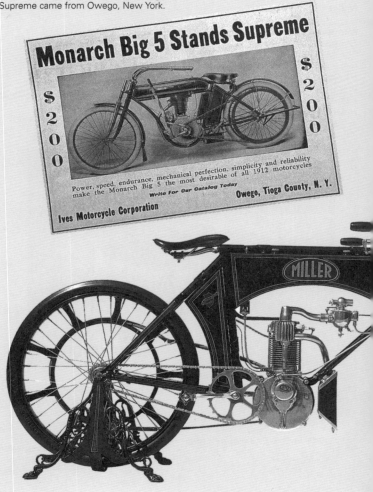

460

Morris-Corkhill (1903)
Rochester, New York

Morse-Beauregard (1912–1917)
Detroit, Michigan
This company built a 500cc vertical twin with two-speed transmission, and optional chain or shaft drive.

Moto-pede (1921)
Rutherford, New York

Moto-Racycle (1905)
Middletown, Ohio (See Racycle.)

Motormaster (1938–1939)
Cleveland, Ohio
Roadmaster bicycles were among the most popular brands of the 1930s. The revival of lightweight, motorized bikes persuaded the Ohio company to adapt an Evinrude two-stroke for such use, and offer the machine as a complete package. But the Motormaster didn't catch on and was abandoned after a short production run.

Above: The Motormaster was a short-lived Ohio motorbike. Owner – Mort Wood, Marathon, Florida.

Moto-Scoot (1936–1949)
Chicago, Illinois
Designed by Norman Siegal, the Moto-Scoot was also licensed to the Mead bicycle Company and sold as the Mead Ranger. The streamlined 1938 Moto-Scoot, with wicker-pattern engine cover, was cute as a bug.

Mustang (1946–1977)
Glendale, California
The Mustang was the first American high-performance motor scooter, and the first two-wheeler with a telescopic fork. (See pages 360-365.)

Left: Ostensibly built by car legend Harry Miller, this machine's authenticity is unverified. Owner – Jim Lattin, Encinitas, California.

Below: The Nelk was well ahead of its time, with an overhead-cam, liquid-cooled and rubber-mounted engine. It was built in Palo Alto, California.

N

Nelk (1905–1912)
Palo Alto, California
A motorcycle that featured numerous advanced features for its day. The overhead-cam single was rubber-mounted, liquid-cooled and had a rear wheel clutch. (See page 366.)

Neracar (1920–1927)
Syracuse, New York
The Neracar was created by Carl Neracher of Syracuse. The low-slung, two-stroke motorbike featured hub steering. The 210cc engine transfered power to the rear wheel by friction wheel. (See page 368.)

Below: The Neracar was not deterred by a bit of snowfall in Syracuse.

Above: Carl Neracher's two-stroke conveyance was an easy rider.

New Era (1909–1913)
Dayton, Ohio
The New Era Autocycle company built an interesting hybrid that may qualify as one of the first cruisers in the motorcycle market. (See pages 370-373.)

New London (1896)
New London, Ohio

Nioga (1903)
Whitney Point, New York

Nyberg (1913)
Chicago, Illinois

Above: The New Era was another approach to refined two-wheel motoring.

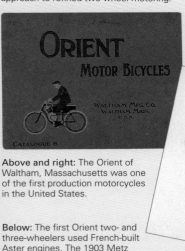

Above and right: The Orient of Waltham, Massachusetts was one of the first production motorcycles in the United States.

Below: The first Orient two- and three-wheelers used French-built Aster engines. The 1903 Metz engine improved the design.

O

Oakes (1916)
Johnstown, Pennsylvania

OK (1916)
Brooklyn, New York

Orient (1900–1905)
Waltham, Massachusetts
The Waltham Manufacturing Company was, with Thomas and Steffy, one of the first American manufacturers of motorcycles. Early three-wheelers were called Orient-Aster for the French engine. Designer Charles Metz left to build his own machines, and subsequently entered into partnership with the Marsh brothers to form Marsh-Metz. (See page 374.)

Overman (unknown)

P

Pam (1921–1922)
New York, New York

Pansy (1905)

Panzer (1997–)
Canon City, Colorado
The Panzer is a retro-1950s
Panhead-style V-twin.
(See page 374.)

Paramount (1917)
Columbus, Ohio

Patee (1901)
Indianapolis, Indiana
Patee built a solo and tandem single,
with the Morris Sager engine
mounted behind and below the
pedal crank. "Will run over any roads
and grades," boasted the ads. The
price was $200.

Parkin-Leflem (1903)
*Philadelphia, Pennsylvania (See
Leflem)*

Peerless (1912–1916)
Boston, Massachusetts
The Peerless was another marketing
label for the Marsh & Metz machine.

PEM (1905–1912)
Jefferson, Wisconsin
The initials stand for Perry E. Mack,
who designed the original Waverly.

Pennington (1894)
Trenton, New Jersey
This early example had the engine
mounted aft of the rear wheel.

Phaeton (unknown)

Pierce (1909–1913)
Buffalo, New York
The Pierce singles and fours
employed oversized frame tubes to
carry gas and oil. Perry Pierce, whose
father George owned the Pierce
Arrow car company, founded the
motorcycle division. The four became
both the first American four-cylinder
machine and the first successful shaft
drive system on a domestic machine.
(See pages 376-379.)

Above: A magazine piece on the history
of the motorcycle. Shown is a small
machine manufactured by the Standard
Oil Company that resembles an 1894
Pennington.

Pioneer (1903)
Jersey City, New Jersey

Pioneer (1908–1910)
Worcester, Massachusetts
The final versions of the Royal were
labeled Royal Pioneer, distinguished
by its horizontal overhead valves.
The free engine clutch preceded
the Eclipse unit that became
standard equipment on numerous
motorcycles. The work of engineer
William McGrath, it also lead to
development of the Bendix
automobile starter.

Pirate (1912–1915)
Milwaukee, Wisconsin
The Milwaukee
Motorcycle
Company built a six-
horsepower single
and an 1130cc V-twin
rated at ten
horsepower. They
used an Eclipse
clutch, Corbin brake
and Schebler or Siro
carburetor. The
wheelbase was 58 inches
(147cm); price was $275 in 1914.

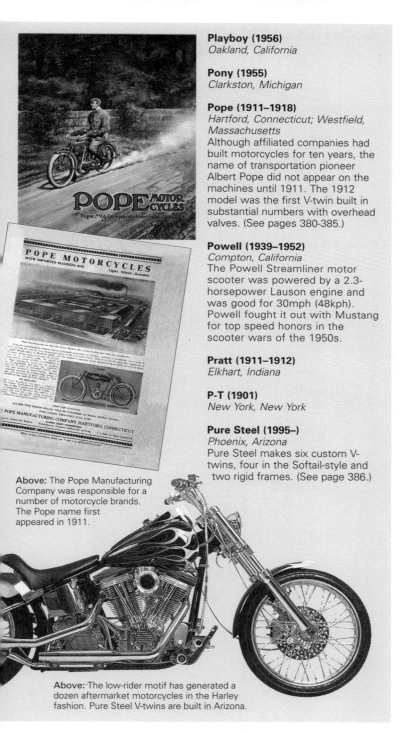

Playboy (1956)
Oakland, California

Pony (1955)
Clarkston, Michigan

Pope (1911–1918)
Hartford, Connecticut; Westfield, Massachusetts
Although affiliated companies had built motorcycles for ten years, the name of transportation pioneer Albert Pope did not appear on the machines until 1911. The 1912 model was the first V-twin built in substantial numbers with overhead valves. (See pages 380-385.)

Powell (1939–1952)
Compton, California
The Powell Streamliner motor scooter was powered by a 2.3-horsepower Lauson engine and was good for 30mph (48kph). Powell fought it out with Mustang for top speed honors in the scooter wars of the 1950s.

Pratt (1911–1912)
Elkhart, Indiana

P-T (1901)
New York, New York

Pure Steel (1995–)
Phoenix, Arizona
Pure Steel makes six custom V-twins, four in the Softail-style and two rigid frames. (See page 386.)

Above: The Pope Manufacturing Company was responsible for a number of motorcycle brands. The Pope name first appeared in 1911.

Above: The low-rider motif has generated a dozen aftermarket motorcycles in the Harley fashion. Pure Steel V-twins are built in Arizona.

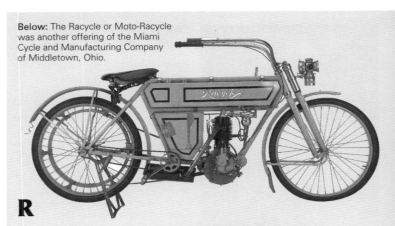
Below: The Racycle or Moto-Racycle was another offering of the Miami Cycle and Manufacturing Company of Middletown, Ohio.

R

Racine (unknown)

Racycle (1905–1911)
Middletown, Ohio
Early Racycles were duplicates of the Indian motorcycle. The Miami Cycle & Manufacturing Company acquired Merkel-Light in 1911, and discontinued the Racycle line. (See pages 386-389.)

Rambler (1903–1914)
Hartford, Connecticut
Still another American Cycle Company product. Early models were fitted with Thor engines.

Ranger (1938)
Chicago, Illinois

Razoux (1903)
Boston, Massachussetts

Reading-Standard (1903–1922)
Reading, Pennsylvania
The early Thoroughbred was based on the Thor engine and Indian design. R-S, as the marque was also known, produced the first side-valve engine for American motorcycles. In 1908 it released an F-head twin. (See pages 390-393.)

Above: Reading-Standard, in a 1912 ad, was suitable for "Profit or Pleasure."

Right: "Built and Tested in the Mountains" was the proclamation of Pennsylvania's Reading-Standard.

Above: The Reliance single was not widely known beyond the northeastern United States.

Red Arrow (unknown)

Redman (1902–1909)
This was apparently an Indian copy.

Regas (1900–1902)
Rochester, New York
The Regas Motor Bicycle, with 22- or 24-inch (56cm or 61cm) frame used a 1.5-horsepower Thomas engine.

Below: In 1909, Reliance offered V-twins in 446cc and 848cc configurations, as well as a 424cc side-valve single.

Reliance (1906–1915)
Addison, New York; Owego, New York; Elmira, New York
The Reliance company moved around a bit. In 1908 it was in Owego, New York, and built a two- and three-horsepower single in a loop frame. The smaller model sold for $125. (See page 392.)

R&H (1905)
Brockton, Massachusetts

Riotte (1895)
New York, New York

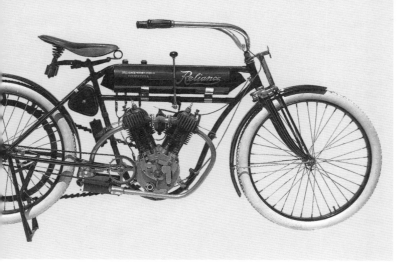

Rocket (1962)
Columbus, Nebraska

Rock-ola (1938–1940)
Chicago, Illinois
A cute scooter using a side-valve engine built by jukebox entrepreneur David Rockola. "America's Newest Mode of Transportation! It's Fun to Scoot!"

Roper (1869)
Roxbury, Massachusetts
An early steam-powered machine.

Rokon (1962–)
Keene, New Hampshire
The New England firm began with a unique two-wheel-drive machine called the Trailbreaker. Later it expanded to include enduro and motocross machines. (See page 394.)

Rollaway (1919–1925)
Toledo, Ohio
The Rollaway Motor Company offered a motorbike with a 115cc two-stroke single that produced one horsepower, transmitted to the rear wheel by belt drive.

Royal (1901–1910)
Worcester, Massachusetts
The Royal was designed by Emil Hafelfinger in 1900. Taken off the market in 1903, it was back in 1907 with belt drive and a larger engine. In 1909 the name changed to Royal Pioneer. (See page 396.)

Royal Pioneer (1909–1910)
Worcester, Massachusets
Evolution of the Royal incorporating more advanced engineering and suspension. The factory was destroyed by fire.

Ruggles (1903)
Brooklyn, New York

Rupp (1960–1974)
Mansfield, Ohio
Manufacturer of snowmobiles and several mini-bike models powered by Tecumseh engines, including the Black Widow.

S

Safti-cycle (1946–1950)
La Crosse, Wisconsin
A bicycle/scooter hybrid. (See page 396.)

Salsbury (1936–1951)
Oakland, California
E. Foster Salsbury, inspired by seeing Amelia Earhart on a Motoped, created the American scooter movement in 1935. Cushman and others quickly followed.

Schickel (1912–1924)
Stamford, Connecticut
One of the two-stroke pioneers, Schickel offered a 500cc and 700cc lightweight single with either chain or belt drive. The final 300cc model had a two-speed transmission, gear-driven countershaft and chain drive only. (See page 398.)

Scout (1911)
Detroit, Michigan
The belt-drive 500cc single was built by the Michigan Motorcycle Company.

SDM (1910-11)
Brooklyn, New York

Below: Shaw progressed from bicycle attachment engines to finished bikes, and later acquired the Kokomo brand.

Sears (1912–1916)
Chicago, Illinois
The first Sears, Roebuck mail order motorcycles were made by Thor. The second generation was produced by the Excelsior Cycle Company. The latter models employed the DeLuxe engine. (See page 400.)

Shaw (1903–1914)
Galesburg, Kansas
Stanley Shaw was among the first large-scale manufacturers of attachment engines for bicycles. The company later offered complete assembled machines. (See page 402.)

Above: The mail order giant Sears, Roebuck offered singles and twins with the DeLuxe engines.

Above: The Shaw Motor Attachment could transform a bicycle for an investment of $90.

Above: The Smith Motor Wheel was the quick way to motorcycling for the entire family.

Above: The Spiral was built by immigrant machinist Herman Jehle, who updated the machine as technology progressed.

Below: Jim Kersting's Simpletag. Simplex chassis, Maytag motor.

Skootmobile (1938)
Chicago, Illinois

Simplex (1935–1960)
New Orleans, Louisiana
The pride of New Orleans. Created by designer Joseph Treen, the simple two-stroke motorbike was in production for more than 20 years. (See page 404.)

Sinclair-Militor *(See Militaire)*

Singer (unknown)

Slattery (1903)
Brooklyn, New York

Smart (unknown)

Smith Motor Wheel (1914–1924)
Milwaukee, Wisconsin
The motor-and-wheel attachment was fitted to bicycles as a powered third wheel.

Snell (1905)
Toledo, Ohio
The Snell Cycle Fittings Company and Kirk Manufacturing firm combined to become the Consolidated Manufacturing Company. Their first products were the Snell-California and Yale-California motorcycle, which later became the Yale. (See page 424.)

Spiegel (1948)
Chicago, Illinois

Spiral (1896–1902)
New York, New York
The one-off toolroom special was begun by German immigrant Herman Jehle in 1896. (See page 406.)

Springcycle (1938–1942)
Los Angeles, California

Stahl's (1902–1907)
Philadelphia, Pennsylvania
The Home Motor Manufacturing
Company sold engine kits and
complete machines. The Stahl's
Motorcycle was offered with 1.5- and
two-horsepower engine, at $150 and
$200. The engine was fitted in a loop
at the bottom of a standard bicycle
downtube. Belt drive.

Starlin (1903)
Yonawanda, New York

Stearns (1901–1902)
The Stearns, powered by a DeDion
engine, was built as a bicycle pacer
for velodromes. Patterned on French
designs, this and other pacers were
used as windbreaks for drafting
bicycle racers.

Steen (1962–1975)
California
A minibike manufacturer that
entered the market in the 1960s.
Later models were more
sophisticated – the Allsport model of
the early 1970s used a 100cc
Hodaka two-stroke engine.

Steffey (1900–1905)
Philadelphia, Pennsylvania
The Steffey Manufacturing
Company claimed to be the first
American manufacturer of
motorcycle engines. In addition
to standard air-cooled singles,
Steffey built a water-cooled
engine in 1901. It offered a range
of engine sizes, all with one-
piece steel crankshaft and
aluminum crankcase, all
equipped with the Steffey
Perfect Silencer.

Sterling (unknown)

Stormer (1907)
Hartford, Connecticut

Stratton (1901)
New York, New York
Produced a belt-drive bicycle-like
machine powered by small F-
head engine.

Suddard (1905)
Providence, Rhode Island

Surgical-Steeds (1989–)
Scottsdale, Arizona
Six Softail-style custom V-twins are
offered with upscale aftermarket
components. A Monoglide frame kit
is also sold separately. (See page
406.)

Sylvester & Jones (1902)
East Weymouth, Massachusetts
The Sylvester & Jones F-head
single was sold under the S&J
brand. This was a belt-drive design
in a loop frame.

T

Thiem (1900–1913)
St. Paul, Minnesota
Thiem built proprietary engines and
motorcycles in addition to its own
marque. The 500cc side-valve
single, with gear-drive magneto, was
nicely turned out. The Joerns-Thiem
Motor Company achieved lasting
fame as builders of the Cyclone
motorcycle. (See pages 80-83.)

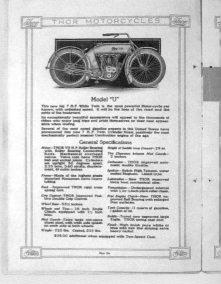

Thomas Auto-bi (1900–1912)
Buffalo, New York
E.R. Thomas was one of America's motorcycle pioneers, and sold engine kits to many of the early builders.

Thompson (1909)
Beverly Farms, Massachusetts

Thor (1902–1917)
Aurora, Illinois
Thor began as an engine supplier for Indian motorcycles. The company went on to supply other manufacturers and built its own complete machines. It competed in competition racing against the likes of Indian and Harley, with mixed success. Early Thors were singles, but in 1910 the company introduced its own V-twin. (See pages 408-412.)

Right: Thor, god of thunder, son of Odin in Norse mythology, and Chicago, Illinois in moto genealogy.

Below: The handsomely illustrated Thor five-horsepower single.

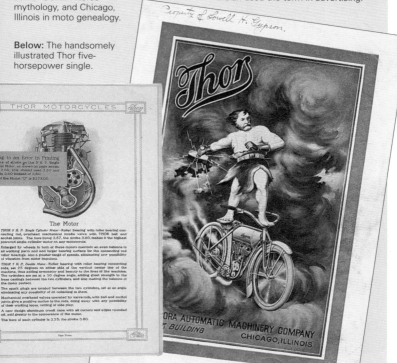

Above: Both E.R. Thomas and Steffey claimed to be *the* pioneer builder, and Indian used the term in advertising.

473

Thoroughbred (1904–1905)
Reading, Pennsylvania
Built by Reading-Standard. (See pages 390-392.)

Tiger (1906–1909)
New York, New York

Tiger Autobike (1915–1916)
Chicago, Illinois
The Tiger Autobike was similar to the Simplex, but two decades earlier. Designed by C.E. Frederickson, the 240cc two-stroke was mounted low in a keystone frame. The engine included a "combined intake and decompressing valve." The V-belt drive machine had a 47-inch (119cm) wheelbase and weighed only 100 pounds (45kg). Despite a $300,000 investment, the Tiger lasted only two years.

Tinkham (1898–1899)
New Haven, Connecticut

Below: The Titan Gecko, a V-twin custom cruiser produced in Phoenix, Arizona.

Titan (1993–)
Phoenix, Arizona
Titan makes eight rubber-mount V-twin customs with selected appointments. The price range is $26,000-40,000. (See page 412.)

Below: The 1916 Traub was probably the most well-developed and engineered home-built ever made.

Torpedo (1907–1910)
Whiting, Indiana; Geneseo, Illinois
Mainly loop frame singles built by the Hornecker Manufacturing Company of Geneseo, Illinois, although the Model F was a V-twin using a Thor engine. Suspension was by telescopic front forks and seatpost saddle suspension.

Torque (1943–1945)
Plainfield, New Jersey
A company formed by the Belgian Stockvis brothers to build lightweight American motorcycles. The vertical singles and twins came to market under the Indian imprint.

Tourist (1905–1907)
Newark, New Jersey
The Breeze Motor Manufacturing Company offered a 500cc belt-drive single, the engine inline with the front downtube of a loop frame. A mixing valve was fitted in lieu of a carburetor, and overall weight was 160 pounds (73kg). The Tourist had rubber-covered footpeg attached to the the engine. "This rubber acts as a buffer in case of an accidental fall, and prevents damage to the machine."

Traub (1916)
Chicago, Illinois
Two Traubs, a twin and a single, were produced by a Chicagoan of the same name. The twin was discovered many years later under a porch. (See page 414.)

Tribune (1903–1914)
Hartford, Connecticut
Yet another product of the American Cycle Manufacturing Company, sold with bicycles of the same name.

Trimoto (1900)
Hartford, Connecticut

Triumph (1908–1912)
Chicago, Illinois; Detroit, Michigan
In 1908 Triumph (not connected with the British firm) used a 2.25-horsepower Thor engine in a keystone frame. Twistgrip controls, 53-inch (135cm) wheelbase, 150 pounds (68kg). The price was $185.

Twombly (1895)
Portland, Maine

Ultra (1995–)
Riverside, California
The eight models in the Quality Custom series V-twins are distributed by Bikers Dream Superstores and selected dealers. (See page 414.)

v

Valiant (1964–1965)
A version of the Simplex two-stroke powered by a Villiers engine.

Below: The Victory cruiser from Polaris is the latest challenger to Milwaukee.

Vard (1944)
Pasadena, California
A 350cc side-valve single, it is thought that only a prototype was made.

Victor (1911)
Cleveland, Ohio

Victory (1998–)
Minneapolis, Minnesota
Recreational vehicle specialist
Polaris Industries joins the Harley-
style queue with a 1500cc V-twin
cruiser. (See page 416.)

W

Wagner (1901–1914)
St. Paul Minnesota
Wagner was one of the first to
mount the engine quite low in a
loop frame, a technique adopted
for racing machines. The Wagner
combined elements of the loop
and diamond frame. (See pages
416-419.)

Below: The Ultra Avenger is one of several models built by Bikers Dream in Riverside, California.

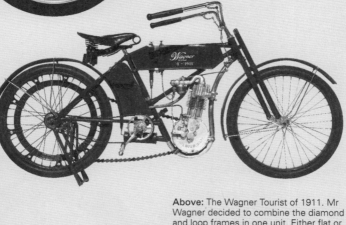

Above: The Wagner Tourist of 1911. Mr Wagner decided to combine the diamond and loop frames in one unit. Either flat or V-belt drive was available.

Waltham (c.1900)
Waltham, Massachusetts

Warwick (1903)
Springfield, Massachusets

Wasson (1903)
Haverhill, Massachusetts

Waverley (1905–1912)
Jefferson, Wisconsin
Also known as the Jefferson, Jefferson-Waverley and Kenzler-Waverley. The PEM badge was also used briefly. The company built ohv singles and twins of 500cc and 1000cc capacity.

Westfield (1916–1918)
Westfield, Massachusets

Westover (1912–1913)
Denver, Colorado

Whipple (1903–1905)
Chicago, Illinois
The Whipple single was fitted to the seatpost. This was probably a Thor engine. Belt-drive and two-speed.

Whizzer (1939–1962)
Los Angeles, California
The Whizzer engine, a 140cc side-valve, was sold as a bicycle attachment kit and as a complete motorbike on a Schwinn chassis. Postwar the company offered a handy little three-horsepower motorbike called the Pacemaker. (See page 420.)

Widmayer (1907)
New York, New York

Williams (1912–1916)
New York, New York
An interesting experiment in radial engine-within-rear-wheel motivation. The motorcycle never reached production and only a handful were built, one of which is pictured in this book. (See page 422.)

Williamson (1902–1903)
Philadelphia, Pennsylvania
The Williamson Motor Cycle "weighs about 90 pounds ready for use, has a 1-inch flat belt transmission, is furnished with the Little Giant Vaporizer and will speed from eight to thirty-five miles per hour."

Willis (1903)
New York, New York

Above and right: Waverley went through several management shifts in its relatively brief career.

Below: The Zort is a retro creation with a Triumph Terrier engine. By Don Huebert, Re-Cycle Motor Works, Henderson, Nebraska.

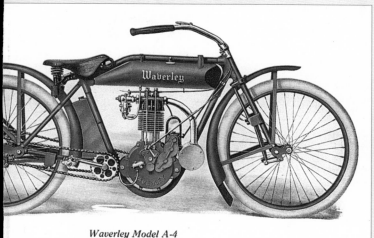

Waverley Model A-4

Wilson (1910)
Wichita, Kansas

Wisconsin (1903)
Racine, Wisconsin

Woods (1914)
Denver, Colorado

Woods-Meagher (1896)
Richmond, Virginia

Wysecycle (1947–1950)
Dayton, Ohio
A small motorcycle with partially enclosed bodywork and 322cc engine aimed at the youth market.

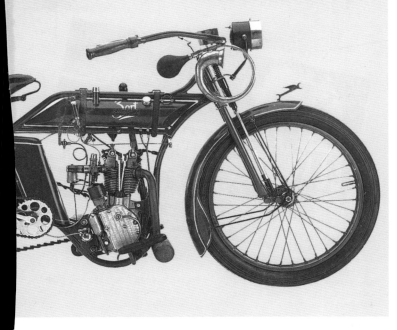

Y

Yale-California
(See Yale)

Yale (1902–1915)
Toledo, Ohio
The midwestern bicycle
company acquired the
California motorcycle marque
in 1903, the first motor
vehicle to cross the United
States. In 1909 the
hyphenation was dropped and
the Yale name adopted. The
singles and twins were well
built and featured a number of
engineering innovations. The
company shifted to munitions
work with the advent of World
War I. (See pages 424-427.)

Above: Yale made a
mid-year change in
1910 to solve frame-
cracking problems.
The new single sold
for $200 and the
twin at $300.

Above: The Ohio-built Yale
Motorcycle achieved considerable
popularity in the midwest.

Yankee (1922–1923)
Chicago, Illinois
Lightweight two-strokes built by
The Illinois Motor Company of
Chicago.